The Purpose Driven Disciple

The Purpose Driven Disciple

Implementing Wisdom Pearls for Spiritual Growth

JOHNNY TURNER
Foreword by D. Z. Cofield

WIPF & STOCK · Eugene, Oregon

THE PURPOSE DRIVEN DISCIPLE
Implementing Wisdom Pearls for Spiritual Growth

Copyright © 2025 Johnny Turner. All rights reserved. Except for brief quotations in critical publications or reviews, no part of this book may be reproduced in any manner without prior written permission from the publisher. Write: Permissions, Wipf and Stock Publishers, 199 W. 8th Ave., Suite 3, Eugene, OR 97401.

Wipf & Stock
An Imprint of Wipf and Stock Publishers
199 W. 8th Ave., Suite 3
Eugene, OR 97401

www.wipfandstock.com

PAPERBACK ISBN: 979-8-3852-5811-6
HARDCOVER ISBN: 979-8-3852-5812-3
EBOOK ISBN: 979-8-3852-5813-0
VERSION NUMBER 12/17/25

PERMISSIONS

All Scripture quotations, unless otherwise indicated, are taken from The Holy Bible, New International Version®, NIV®. Copyright © 2011 by Biblica, Inc. Used with permission of Zondervan. All rights reserved worldwide. www.zondervan.com.

Scripture quotations marked (ESV) are from The ESV® Bible (The Holy Bible, English Standard Version®), © 2001 by Crossway, a publishing ministry of Good News Publishers. Used by permission. All rights reserved.

Scripture quotations taken from the King James Version (KJV) are in the public domain.

Scripture quotations marked (NASB) are taken from the New American Standard Bible®, copyright © 2020 by The Lockman Foundation. Used by permission. All rights reserved. lockman.org.

Scripture quotations marked (NKJV) are taken from the New King James Version®. Copyright © 1982 by Thomas Nelson. Used by permission. All rights reserved.

Scripture quotations marked (NLT) are taken from the Holy Bible, New Living Translation, copyright © 2015 by Tyndale House Foundation. Used by permission of Tyndale House Publishers, Carol Stream, Illinois 60188. All rights reserved.

Scripture quotations marked (RSV) are from Revised Standard Version of the Bible, copyright © 1971 National Council of the Churches of Christ in the United States of America. Used by permission. All rights reserved worldwide.

I dedicate this book to the faithful believers who press through oppositions and challenges to become better witnesses for Christ. To those who desire a closer walk with Christ through prayer and the study of the holy word. I dedicate this book to pastors who need encouragement to lead their congregations in these challenging times, as well as to future generations. Additionally, I dedicate this book to other leaders in the church, encouraging all to cultivate a desire to grow in the knowledge of our Lord and Savior, Jesus Christ. I also dedicate this book to the Mt. Sinai Baptist Church, Orlando, Florida, where I serve as a teacher. Finally, I dedicate this book to my lovely wife, Doris Bourgeois Turner, who encouraged me to persevere in writing this book. I pray that this book will provoke disciples of Christ to engage in meaningful ministry.

Contents

Foreword by D. Z. Cofield	xiii
Preface	xvii
Acknowledgments	xix
Introduction: Spiritual Growth Matters	xxi

PART ONE: WISDOM PEARLS FOR SPIRITUAL GROWTH — 1

DAY 1	The Pearl of Love Is Key	3
DAY 2	The Pearl of Prayer Is the Pathway to God	11
DAY 3	The Pearl of Forgiveness Is Vital	19
DAY 4	The Pearl of Faith Pleases God	25
DAY 5	The Pearl of Commitment Shows Spiritual Progress	30
DAY 6	The Pearl of Mercy Reveals Kindness	35
DAY 7	The Pearl of Patience Shows Calmness	41
DAY 8	The Pearl of Hope Prevents Despair	46

PART TWO: WISDOM PEARLS OF HONEST LIVING — 51

DAY 9	The Pearl of Justice Affirms Truth	53
DAY 10	The Pearl of Peace Comforts the Mind	58
DAY 11	The Pearl of Obedience Reflects Love	64
DAY 12	The Pearl of Contentment Revitalizes Your Outlook	69
DAY 13	The Pearl of Humility Builds Character	74
DAY 14	The Pearl of Honesty Is Pure Religion	80
DAY 15	The Pearl of Dedication Is a Sacred Promise	85

PART THREE: WISDOM PEARLS THAT HONOR GOD — 93

DAY 16	The Pearl of Trustworthiness Breeds a Positive Reputation	95
DAY 17	The Pearl of Perseverance Is a Strong Anchor	101
DAY 18	The Pearl of Sanctification Is a Genuine Identity	106
DAY 19	The Pearl of Confession Renews the Soul	112
DAY 20	The Pearl of Grace Is Sufficient	117
DAY 21	The Pearl of Friendship Matters	123
DAY 22	The Pearl of Wisdom Is an Insightful Treasure	128
DAY 23	The Pearl of Hospitality Is a Comforting Presence	133

PART FOUR: WISDOM PEARLS THAT GLORIFY GOD — 139

DAY 24	The Pearl of Fruit Is a Relationship Factor	141
DAY 25	The Pearl of Spirituality Is Enlightenment	146
DAY 26	The Pearl of a Gentle Tongue Is a Discipline Factor	152
DAY 27	The Pearl of Compassion Is a Touch of the Heart	158
DAY 28	The Pearl of Servanthood Is a Five-Star Ministry	163
DAY 29	The Pearl of Silence Is Listening to God	168
DAY 30	The Pearl of Conviction Is a Positive Reality	174

PART FIVE: WISDOM PEARLS THAT PLEASE GOD — 179

DAY 31	The Pearl of Worship Shows Adoration	181
DAY 32	The Pearl of Discipleship Is the Apple of God's Eye	187
DAY 33	The Pearl of Stewardship Is Accountability	192
DAY 34	The Pearl of Evangelism Is a Passionate Endeavor	197
DAY 35	The Pearl of Missions Cares About the Unredeemed	202
DAY 36	The Pearl of Praise Touches God	207
DAY 37	The Pearl of Respect Creates a Loving Environment	213
DAY 38	The Pearl of Sacrifice Is the Excellent Way	218
DAY 39	The Pearl of Resilience: Trials, Testing, and Tribulation	224
DAY 40	The Pearl of Meekness Embraces Serenity	231

Epilogue	237
Appendix 1: Wisdom Pearls Evaluation	239
Appendix 2: The Purpose Driven Disciple Life Pledge	243
Bibliography	245

Subject Index 249
Scripture Index 265

Foreword

It is a rare and precious gift when a book not only inspires its readers but also provides them with a clear road map for spiritual maturity. Rev. Dr. Johnny Turner's *The Purpose Driven Disciple: Implementing Wisdom Pearls for Spiritual Growth* is such a book—a timely, Spirit-led resource designed to guide disciples of Jesus Christ into a deeper, more intentional walk with God. With wisdom drawn directly from Scripture, pastoral insight forged from years of ministry, and a heart that longs to see every believer grow in grace, Dr. Turner has written a work that is both deeply theological and profoundly practical.

The imagery of a pearl is central to the message of this book, and for good reason. Pearls, as Dr. Turner explains, are unique among gems because they are not formed in the earth but in the depths of the sea, the result of a natural yet transformative process. An oyster takes what begins as an irritant—a piece of grit, a small intruder—and through a process of covering and refinement, turns it into a thing of great value. Likewise, God takes the irritants of life, the pain of sin, and the struggles of spiritual growth, and through his grace transforms us into disciples of beauty and worth. Each "Wisdom Pearl" in this book is a spiritual principle designed to shape us into people who reflect the glory of God.

The heartbeat of this book is spiritual growth. In an age where spiritual shortcuts and shallow discipleship often dominate the conversation, Dr. Turner calls us back to the essence of following Jesus: growing daily in Christlikeness. As the introduction declares, *spiritual growth matters because it is at the core of your faith's development*. This is not a casual suggestion; it is an urgent invitation to go deeper with God. Dr. Turner reminds us that spiritual maturity is not achieved through occasional inspiration but through daily, disciplined devotion. This book provides a structure for consistent reflection, prayer, and application—a spiritual growth plan that every believer can use to strengthen their walk with Christ.

What makes *The Purpose Driven Disciple* stand out is its balance between theological depth and practical application. Each chapter is built around a Wisdom Pearl—timeless biblical truths that, when understood and applied, lead to transformation. These pearls are not abstract ideas; they are practical tools for living out the Christian faith. They challenge readers to examine their relationship with God, their character, and their calling as disciples. They also emphasize that spiritual maturity is not optional; it is the expectation of every follower of Jesus.

The book's structure reflects Dr. Turner's pastoral heart and teaching gift. At the end of each chapter, he provides essentials to guide the reader: opportunities for self-reflection, memory verses for meditation, evaluation questions for honest self-assessment, and practical steps for application. These elements turn the book from a simple devotional into a discipleship training manual. Churches, small groups, and individual readers alike will find that this structure encourages accountability and consistency—two things every disciple needs to grow.

Another unique feature of this book is its biblical imagery. Dr. Turner reminds us that pearls are a recurring symbol in Scripture. Jesus used pearls to describe the kingdom of God in Matt 13:45–46: "Again, the kingdom of heaven is like a merchant looking for fine pearls. When he found one of great value, he went away and sold everything he had and bought it." Pearls represent something worth sacrificing everything to possess. Similarly, the believer's walk with Christ is of such value that it should inspire wholehearted devotion. By drawing on this symbolism, Dr. Turner elevates the reader's vision of discipleship from duty to delight—from a burden to a treasure.

This book is deeply rooted in Scripture. Each Wisdom Pearl is supported by passages from both the Old and New Testaments, demonstrating that spiritual growth has always been central to God's plan for his people. The inclusion of biblical characters, principles, and exhortations provides readers with a firm foundation for faith. Yet,

Dr. Turner's writing is never academic for its own sake; instead, it is pastoral and practical, calling readers to live out the word they study.

The Purpose Driven Disciple also addresses a critical need in today's church: intentional discipleship. Too often, believers settle for inspiration without transformation. We attend services, hear sermons, and even participate in Bible studies, yet we frequently fail to implement what we learn. This book challenges that pattern. It emphasizes that wisdom is not simply knowing biblical truths but applying them daily. As Jas 1:22 reminds us, "But be doers of the word, and not hearers only, deceiving yourselves." These Wisdom Pearls are meant to be implemented, not merely admired.

Rev. Dr. Johnny Turner writes as a seasoned pastor, teacher, and disciple-maker. His decades of ministry experience give this book a unique richness; it is filled with pastoral insight, biblical wisdom, and a deep understanding of human nature. But even more than that, it reflects his love for God and his desire to see believers grow into maturity. This book is not simply a devotional resource; it is a mentor in written form, guiding readers step by step into a deeper, more meaningful walk with Christ.

I encourage you to read this book slowly and prayerfully. Take the time to meditate on each Wisdom Pearl, memorize the Scriptures, and engage with the reflection questions. If you do, this journey will not only strengthen your personal walk with Christ but also equip you to impact others. Discipleship is not merely about personal growth; it is about reproducing that growth in others. As you grow in Christ, you will naturally become a source of encouragement and wisdom to those around you.

In a world that often feels chaotic, confusing, and spiritually dry, *The Purpose Driven Disciple* is a refreshing call to depth, authenticity, and intentional growth. These pages invite you to trade superficial religion for a life deeply rooted in Christ's love, grace, and truth. They challenge you to examine your spiritual foundations, grow in your character, and walk daily with the Savior. They remind you that discipleship is not a one-time decision but a lifelong journey.

If you are ready to grow, to be transformed, and to live as a true disciple of Jesus Christ, then accept the invitation of this book. Let these pearls of wisdom shape your heart, strengthen your faith, and draw you closer to the One who is your greatest treasure. The next forty days can be a turning point in your spiritual life. As you journey through this book, may your heart be captivated by Christ, your life be anchored in his word, and your soul be filled with his Spirit.

This document is more than a book. It is a discipleship tool, a devotional guide, and a mentor for your walk with God. Receive it with an open heart, and you will discover that the Wisdom Pearls within these pages can truly lead to spiritual maturity and lasting transformation.

Rev. Dr. D. Z. Cofield

Senior Pastor, Good Hope Missionary Baptist Church, Houston, Texas

Principal Teacher and Senior Consultant, Church Training Institute

Preface

This book serves as a guide that revitalizes the spiritual journey of disciples. I am not the only author who has written to encourage disciples to evaluate their lives to become better disciples of Christ. Therefore, I offer a significant caveat: to examine the Wisdom Pearls that will guide one to focus on redeeming the time, because the days are evil (Eph 5:16). The aim is to make every moment count. I present biblical and theological themes, encouraging believers to study, reflect, and do personal introspection for spiritual growth. Present-day disciples must strive to be assertive in the church and community, serving as a greater witness for Christ. This book also serves as a spiritual pilot, providing a positive liftoff that helps bridge the gap between the church and the academy. It is an essential tool for a forty-day study and reflection designed to revitalize the church's work. Every believer is endowed with spiritual gifts to do ministry. However, the desire must be to cherish and go deeper into the spiritual root.

Specifically speaking, this book encourages readers to become passionate about the chapter headings, providing fresh ideas that invigorate the mind and heart, and blaze the path for others to follow. Its goal is to ask what drives you to do ministry. The Holy Spirit drives the purpose driven believer to effectuate change and seek to become closer to God. However, the believer must avoid being driven by personal agendas that have no merit. The intention is to become excited about serving Jesus and fulfilling the assigned ministry, such as preaching, teaching, evangelism, and witnessing. You must be able to visualize the big picture of serving for the glory of God. Some examples of themes in this book are love, grace, hope, humility, faith, and prayer. All the themes help revitalize your life for a better, stronger, and meaningful life. The church in Sardis had lost its spiritual life and was stagnant, lacking prayer, power, and purpose. It needed revitalization (Rev 2:22–23). They needed a revival, restoration, and a significant retransformation. Tom Rainer is right when he says, "When a church ceases to have a heart and ministry for the community, it is on the path toward death."[1] That statement holds that all churches have a purpose: to rise above stagnation and elevate to stimulation.

Furthermore, this book emphasizes the importance of spiritual growth as the foundation for a positive ministry. I am passionate about helping pastors, leaders, and all parishioners catch the vision of revitalization, which involves being a purpose driven disciple and developing into a viable, dedicated one. It is not just what you do, but about who you are and what you feel about yourself. At the end of each chapter, a summarization, point of emphasis, relevant question, and prayer are provided to capture the chapter's significance. These methods reveal the theological and biblical essence that should be applied in your life. I pray for individuals and the body of Christ to integrate the principles of *The Purpose Driven Disciple* as a relevant guide. Consequently, I trust that this book will have an impact on you as a follower of Christ, encouraging and energizing you for a fruitful life.

Johnny Turner

---

1. Rainer, *Autopsy of a Deceased Church*, 28.

Acknowledgments

It takes quality time for prayer, reflection, and meditation to write a book that has positive significance and encourages the body of Christ. It takes patience to develop thoughts that help others see the broader context of the writing. The core thoughts of this book began while I was pastoring in New York. Due to my busy schedule, I was unable to bring my thoughts to fruition. I know that other writers experience a similar process of staying the course to complete the arduous task. I have been preaching for well over fifty years, and new thoughts merit penmanship for encouragement.

I acknowledge the guidance of the Holy Spirit for inspiration, direction, and tenacity never to give up, but listen to the voice of thunder. I thank the late Bishop James Evans Jr., one of my former teachers and a former president of Colgate Rochester Divinity School in Rochester, New York, and founder and pastor of St. Luke Tabernacle Community Church in Rochester, New York, who said after reading my last book that I should get busy with the next. Special appreciation to my endorsers, especially Rev. Linda Hickmon Evans, pastor of St. Luke Tabernacle Community Church in Rochester, New York, for her valuable suggestions. Thanks for the blessings from Pastor Jim Cymbala's office, Brooklyn Tabernacle, Brooklyn, New York, and the blessings from the office of Fred Maxwell. The editorial staff of Wipf and Stock is greatly appreciated for their assistance in clarifying the manuscript. I extend my gratitude to my partner in ministry, Doris Bourgeois Turner, for her interaction, encouragement, and patience as I completed this work.

Introduction

Spiritual Growth Matters

MAKING EVERY MOMENT COUNT

Making every moment count means treasuring your time with God for spiritual growth and benefit. The use of pearls for this reading journey refers to Wisdom Pearls. Making every moment count is to cherish God's Pearls, which symbolize wisdom and insight. The road to the sacred life is under the divine Pearl of God's presence and providence, and each day is a blessed gift from God. The Bible is full of pearls of wisdom. Wisdom Pearls guide and advise one to make wise decisions about spiritual living. They are valuable symbols of God's imagery in addition to the Wisdom Pearls mentioned in Proverbs (3:13–20; 4:5–9; 8:11–13).

Pearls have an insatiable effect among believers, so that a songbook titled *Gospel Pearls* was published in 1921 by the Sunday School Publishing Board of the National Baptist Convention of America, eight years before the Great Depression of 1929.[1] The lyrics of the songs in that book, from that era and presently, express a connection to God's presence through singing hymns, gospels, and spirituals. Spiritual growth and spiritual living were impactful as individuals and families worshiped God. Moreover, "gospel pearls" significantly relate to the title of this book, *The Purpose Driven Disciple: Implementing Wisdom Pearls for Spiritual Growth*. You are gearing up for a fruitful and meaningful forty-day journey for spiritual blessings in heavenly places in Christ (Eph 1:3–14; 2 Pet 1:3–4; see also Matt 5:3–11; Phil 4:19).

---

1. Townsend, *Gospel Pearls*.

The Value of Wisdom Pearls

True believers value Wisdom Pearls because they serve as spiritual building blocks that foster a godly character. For a believer, the word *value* is about being an authentic and genuine follower of Christ. The *Purpose Driven Disciple* challenges believers to be serious learners and followers of Christ. When this happens, one action and commitment reveal faithful and fruitful living. It is therefore wise to implement Wisdom Pearls and pursue spiritual growth. The Pearls serve as spiritual ingredients that build character through purity and wisdom. I'm not suggesting that Pearls make one perfect, but they encourage maturity and obedience, because maturity is rooted in being grounded in faith. Wisdom Pearls are an exemplar of spiritual introspection to improve intimacy with God. The purpose driven disciple is a life of passion, discipline, and spiritual growth. Spiritual growth matters because it is at the core of your faith's development.

This book is a *forty-day spiritual growth journey and a guide, serving as a benchmark* for a deeper dive into the spiritual depths of Wisdom Pearls, while helping readers make the best choices to live a more prosperous life as they prepare for eternity. *Prosperous* here is not a reference to secular and material wealth, but the spiritual prosperity of the fruit of the Spirit (Gal 5:22–23). Spiritual prosperity is about having a growing relationship with God through the conviction of the Holy Spirit. It fosters the richness of walking in the Spirit (Rom 8:3–4; Gal 5:16, 25). Spiritual prosperity helps one focus on the last days; it is *a theology of eschatology*, and a personal reflection of making every moment count. A theology of eschatology involves understanding, cherishing, and studying the end times, with an emphasis on death, heaven, and hell. The purpose is to spend quality time with God to maximize your time wisely because the days are evil (Eph 5:16). Each Pearl has a theological relevance, emphasizing truthful and faithful moments with God (Ps 145:18). This book, with all types of Wisdom Pearls, is spiritually driven for God's glory and your edification, and presents challenges for your life to direct you to make every moment count for spiritual maturity. Wisdom Pearls emphasize the importance of using wisdom during spiritual implementation.

IMPLEMENTING THE SPIRITUAL JOURNEY

A Theology of Spiritual Growth

While on this journey, there is a need to ignite the torch for a passionate *theology of spiritual growth* to survive life's rugged road. Amid life's challenging confrontations and distractions, make the best of your relationship with Jesus, the Son of Man. Unequivocally, you will experience a more affluent life knowing that Jesus will comfort your walk. Reflect on your spiritual foundation as you grow and mature in the faith. Hold on to your theology and aspiration. Your journey will always be blessed and fruitful because you believe in God. The psalmist's testimony is "Your Word is a lamp to guide my feet and a light for my path" (Ps 119:105 NLT). You are a disciple who must "look carefully then how you walk, not as unwise but as wise, making the best use of the time, because the days are evil" (Eph 5:15–16 ESV). The above Scriptures serve as a reminder of God's power and protection as you confront all issues. Keep your focus on pleasing God. Through it all, pledge to God. The objective to make every moment count is a commitment to God for the next forty days of your life to understand the significance of Wisdom Pearls. I remind each reader to continually reflect on the words of the apostle Paul above, because "the days are evil." This will help shape the next forty-day journey of spiritual refreshment—a positive motto to move forward in faith for a fruitful future.

The Purpose of Implementing Pearls

Engaging with and implementing each Pearl is about connecting to its central message while growing and making the most of life. This spiritual growth journey emphasizes the implementation of the Pearls because they are valuable for preparing for the pearly gates (Rev 21:21). Therefore, each Pearl embodies the element of wisdom, as each Pearl is from God. Wisdom is the necessary factor to grow and implement the Pearls in this book. A starting question for discussion is, What do pearls symbolize in the Bible? It is a vital question because it will answer the purpose of every Pearl in this book. Pearls represent purity and perfection of God's kingdom. This spiritual growth guide emphasizes the significance of each Pearl in developing spiritual character for ministry. It is wise to implement each Pearl for the glory of

God. Believers should never assume that they will be perfect, but it is wise to persevere in spiritual excellence and grow in the knowledge of our Lord and Savior Jesus Christ (2 Pet 3:18). The aim is to strive to do our best to please God. Therefore, we must have a more profound conviction for genuine living, because there is no alternative to achieving spiritual maturity. What God expects of us is not difficult, but it involves embracing the crucial Pearls, spending time with God, and developing a credible character.

The Significance of the Spiritual Life

The Purpose Driven Disciple is a book in which we are encouraged to live closer to God and identify with each Pearl. It urges believers to discover the significance of the spiritual life, how to appreciate Wisdom Pearls, and how to know what they are. The Bible describes and teaches that pearls symbolize the significance of Jesus' parabolic lessons to his disciples and the emphasis on the value of a hidden treasure (Matt 13:44). These hidden treasures are referred to as the "Pearls of Wisdom." He expands the small discourse contextually to a different level by saying, "Again, the kingdom of heaven is like a merchant looking for fine pearls. When he found one of great value, he went away and sold everything he had and bought it" (Matt 13:45–46). Pearls hold valuable spiritual significance, conveying credibility and authenticity.

Pearls are uniquely different from other gems in that they were not created on earth but from the sea. Earthly pearls are created from the oyster shell and must undergo an intensive process called secretion from natural irritants. These irritants are smooth white surfaces created in place of dirt and grit. Heavenly Pearls come from God's bosom to remind us of his gifts to humanity. It is wise to value Pearls as having a heavenly meaning for an earthly purpose. Disciples of Christ must experience the process of spiritual secretion from the natural irritants of sinful acts. This secretion is through the power of Jesus' blood, and it is vicarious for our redemption. Therefore, it behooves us to cherish these Pearls and their divine sanctity because they represent God's grace, mercy, and love. Theoretically, believers must desire to develop a deeper relationship with God after separation from sin. These Pearls are untapped, divine, hidden blessings of radiance that enrich the lives of believers and are costly, beneficial, and valuable to their Christian journey. Pearls connect to Christ when he shed his blood on Calvary for our redemption. The Pearl of Christ's blood was the only gift from God that could pay for our sins. Pearls are pure and remind us daily that Christ died for the church to make her unblemished and holy, applying them for authentic servanthood. Eventually, the church would become the Pearl of great price (Matt 13:45–46). A day spent with God is a day that God appreciates from each of us, and it is the Pearl of great price of being with God. Each day is valuable in his eyes, and you should value every moment.

The enthusiasm and richness of the content of this book highlight the fruit of the Spirit. These nine qualities form a bridge of spiritual connection with other attributes, validating the continuity of thought. Valuable thoughts highlight a meaningful relationship with Christ. Paul says, "But the Holy Spirit produces this kind of fruit in our lives: love, joy, peace, patience, kindness, goodness, faithfulness, gentleness, and self-control. There is no law against these things!" (Gal 5:22–23 NLT). Each day, we can gain spiritual refreshment and reflection for a stronger intimacy with God through engaging thoughts that inspire believers to continue the journey. We live in the most challenging and perilous times, facing numerous threats and attacks. The apostle Paul further says, "So be careful how you live. Don't live like fools, but like those who are wise. Make the most of every opportunity in these evil days" (Eph 5:15–17 NLT). Everyone should ask, "Do I value the life that God has given me?" Am I wasting it on things that are meaningless and unfruitful? We can be fruitful only through living and showing Wisdom Pearls in our lives.

Every chapter in this book speaks to theology and the integrity of the believer's life to know that you are on board the heavenly train, and for the unbeliever to get on board. The following forty days are designed to transform your life significantly. It is vital to reflect on theology and what it means to embrace the Holy One. The results of this study will elevate your spirituality to a new level as you experience God. Therefore, the rest of your life will be a blessing as you grow and develop spiritually. Believers will grow with passion, spiritual intuition, and integrity. This book inspires and encourages you to make the most of your life before transitioning to eternal glory. It is essential to value this journey while reflecting on the symbolism of pearls. Pearls symbolize strength, purity, sacredness, and transformation.

It is an encouragement to seek to understand what it means to value the pearls God requires for spiritual nourishment and implementation. First, define and explain the word *pearl* in the biblical context. The term "pearl" is derived from the Greek word *margarités*,[2] meaning Pearls are consistently portrayed as treasures of the highest worth. The Bible says we should let nothing hold us back from seeking after God and all that God has for our lives (Prov 4:12–14; Heb 12:1). Every day is priceless and has been adorned by God's presence for our purpose. Each day is a precious gem. It sparkles, glows, illuminates, and has a purpose. As you complete each day of meditation on the value of living life as a spiritual *gem for God*, you will never be the same again. Examining each Pearl will encourage motivation to strive for the best that God expects. This experience will foster an appreciation for the fact that Godly living is about living each day to shine for God in a chaotic, sadistic, and cantankerous world. While focusing on understanding each Pearl, we will feel better about life and be excited about what it truly means to live on this earth, making every moment count.

It is a blessing for every believer to make each day count by focusing on God and praising him for life. Believers must live a life of honor before God as a moment of pure sacredness. It is pure sacredness because there is no better way to start each day than by pursuing a Pearl to recognize God and to glorify his name, *Elohim*, for he is the strong one. While reading, praying, and reflecting, focus on the following: as you finish each day, *pray and thank God* for giving you the strength to read, reflect, and recapture the meaning of walking with God and understanding and passionately applying each Pearl for discipleship development. The goal is to cherish each day. This vital forty-day journey will transform your life to do the following:

SEVEN ESSENTIALS TO GUIDE YOU

1. **Shaping your life.** This reading is a personal encounter with God that can help expand your ideas for making a difference in your daily life. It is with much hope that your life has been reshaped for effective spiritual growth. The apostle Paul says, "Therefore, I urge you, brothers, in view of God's mercy, to offer your bodies as

---

2. Bible Hub, "Margarités."

living sacrifices, holy and pleasing to God—this is your spiritual act of worship. Do not conform any longer to the pattern of this world but be transformed by the renewing of your mind. Then you will be able to test and approve what God's will is—his good, pleasing, and perfect will" (Rom 12:1–2). These verses attract inward holiness to expand your spiritual horizon.

2. **Memory verse.** What verse of the Bible struck you as you engaged in reading each chapter? When you focus on remembering Bible verses, they become indelible marks in your mind and spirit for further use in your Christian walk. Therefore, your daily conversation will have significant meaning because memorizing Bible verses is another way of *keeping in touch with God when challenged by the evil forces of this world*.

3. **Evaluate your spiritual growth.** You must consider evaluating your discipleship maturity as a genuine steward for God's glory. This action entails honestly evaluating your spiritual walk and relationship with the Creator. For example, consider your spiritual growth on a scale of one to ten, one being the lowest and ten the highest. Suggestion: don't evaluate what you want it to be, but what it is.

4. **Reflective summary and responses to action.** The reflective summary of each chapter is crucial for your moments with God. It is designed to prompt you to reflect on what you have read and how your responses motivate you to act and become a better believer. The summarization at the end of each chapter guides you to think deeply about what you have read. The goal is to determine what action you will take going forward.

5. **Point of emphasis.** This essential idea is a small idea that highlights a truth that captures the focus of your reflection for the day. If you want to discover what drives and inspires you, the point of emphasis brings everything full circle.

6. **The relevant question.** The relevant question will prompt you to consider each Pearl and its significance for your spiritual growth. This question stands out from any questions that apply to your situation and personal relationship with God. I encourage you to reflect on the question and honestly express your feelings as you prepare for this reflection.

7. **Prayer and personal application.** I recommend that you take a serious look at yourself and apply what you have read for personal growth. A prayer that each Pearl will be used in your life. A life of obedience pleases Jehovah. It pleases him because you have taken the time to express yourself and strive to live a sacred life for the Creator. Additionally, it can facilitate group discussions on prayer and personal application. Individuals can share how each day allows them to apply their learning through study, reflection, prayer, and application of Biblical truth for personal growth and development. At the end of each day, I have chosen four essentials of the seven to maximize the big picture of spiritual maturity.

PART ONE

Wisdom Pearls for Spiritual Growth

The Pearls' purpose in this section is to illuminate spiritual maturity as the fundamental pattern for spiritual discipline. This part of the book identifies the proper foundation for spiritual maturity. Maturity is why you can abide under the anointing of the Holy Spirit. The proper foundation is the true foundation for becoming a purpose driven disciple. It is foundational because humanity cannot experience growth without the basics. You stand on the shores of opposition and are sustained by the Holy Spirit during turbulent moments. Make the best of every moment as you walk and talk with God, but most importantly, listen for jewels of divine thoughts initiated by the Holy Spirit. The foundation for daily living equips every believer to be prepared to communicate with God and develop a lifelong relationship of faith, hope, and direction. Simple possession with the proper focus and purpose prepares you for eternity. It is based on what you do, connected to your ministry and spiritual gift or gifts, while cherishing every Pearl mentioned in this book. Your spiritual gifts are essential for ministry and kingdom building. When they are correctly used, they move the heart of God to bless you for your spiritual sincerity and commitment. Daily living is authentic, with the heartbeat of God breathing into your soul for a closer and more intimate walk with the Creator. Each Wisdom Pearl in this section is connected because of its subject matter, foundation, and purpose.

DAY 1

The Pearl of Love Is Key

For God loved the world so much that he gave his one and only Son, so that everyone who believes in him will not perish but have eternal life.
—John 3:16 NLT

Darkness cannot drive out Darkness: only light can do that.
Hate cannot drive out hate: only Love can do that.
—Martin Luther King Jr.

The Pearl of Love serves as a symbol for expressing heartfelt devotion, nurturing genuine affection, and forging a meaningful connection that deeply resonates within the soul.

Without it, you dangle in a dark tunnel of hopelessness in search of belonging. At the heart of every spiritual journey lies a longing—a yearning for something more profound than mere affection, something that endures beyond fleeting moments and superficial gestures. This longing is for the Pearl of Love, the essence that transcends circumstance and transforms the ordinary into the extraordinary. It is the light that shines through the cracks of our brokenness, guiding us toward wholeness and purpose. True love is not a passing sentiment; it is an intentional choice, a divine invitation to participate in the sacred flow of mercy and grace. In seeking authentic love, we awaken to a reality greater than ourselves, one that binds us to both the divine and the human, reminding us that every soul is worthy of compassion, connection, and comfort. Therefore, God's love fills the gap between deception and deficits, failures and frustrations. The promise is that you will experience the expression of his grace and mercy amid triumphs and tragedies. God looked through eternity and knew you needed a fresh start on life. Love is the key that unlocks the dark tunnels of distractions to see the traveling light of peace for comfort. All believers inherit the loving nature of the Creator, enabling them to interact and experience interrelatedness. Paul is a comforting confirmation about light: "For you were once darkness, but now you are light in the Lord. Live as children of light" (Eph 5:8). Strange love is a camouflaging effect in the church, and it becomes your dark path. Even worse, peculiar love is not the Pearl of Love but a stone of slyness; it puts on a good front, covers up the true essence, and leaves a stark pretension. Strange love is another form of being untruthful, and it blocks the action of genuine love.

The theological message of the Pearl of Love is the implementation of genuine love at the core of God's heart: "agape love." The love that never ends is saturated with grace that empowers us to overcome sin and temptation. Real love is the anatomy of the soul that massages the spirit of humans and gives sincere thoughts of righteousness. Righteousness that pleases the Creator. Regardless of your lifestyle, nothing can ever honestly replace love, because authentic love forms an enduring and ineffaceable bond, the love that links us to the divine and others. Oswald Chambers beautifully observes, "When the Holy Spirit has begun its gracious work in your soul and heart, you see a new light on the cross—and the 'martyr' becomes the Savior of the world."[1] His boundless love changed the course of life, from ruin to redemption, and deception to deliverance.

---

1. Chambers, *Love of God*, 15.

LOVE NOURISHES THE SOUL

The divine conduit nourishes the soul, fostering a continuous relationship and communication. Authentic love is a continuing bond and the reason for being a purpose driven disciple.

Further, love is the symbol of all of life's encounters. It will gratify your life to excel abundantly above reproach while encountering oppositions. Without love, you dangle in a dark tunnel of hopelessness. Love is the first of the nine qualities of the fruit of the Spirit in Gal 5:22–23. When real love is understood and appreciated, it brings joy to you from all walks of life. The strangeness of love is that it stands alone to embrace the most unusual circumstances and oppositions in life, regardless of harsh attacks (1 Cor 13:4). The world will be much more peaceful, happy, and encouraging if people learn to love. It is essential to note that love originates from God because God is love. It began with Jesus, the Son of God. Jesus demonstrated love while he was on earth. He did many things to touch people through compassion and healing. Love is an action verb that connects the dots in life and bridges the gap between people who have perhaps met for the first time and those who have bonded previously. To live a purposeful and happy life, you must begin with God.

Have you interacted with many people and wondered how they view and understand love, given that many treat others harshly? God's profound love impacts the heart and makes it hard to share with others genuinely. Every believer must decide about love and practice it daily in their life. Love does not love until it is shared with others. It must have purpose and meaning. Love is nothing to take lightly. The Scriptures say, "But the eyes of the LORD are on those who fear him, on those whose hope is in his unfailing love" (Ps 33:18). Life is not successful without God's love. Moreover, it is the epitome of all our affairs and encounters in life. Regardless of what others say about love, one cannot truly love without God as the focal point of love. If God is not the key point, then we are pointing effortlessly. Focusing on God's agape love will foster a stronger relationship that glorifies God. Jehovah has the world at heart and expects the world to reciprocate and extend compassion to others amicably.

THE DEMONSTRATION OF LOVE

Some only desire to receive love and are unwilling to practice reciprocity, which is the opposite of the nature of God. God created us to love and not hate. Every day we wake, love should be on our minds to leave a positive, indelible mark on others. Leaving an indelible imprint on others is a genuine act of demonstrating love. *God's love demonstrates compassion for sinners to experience the union of his Son's blood shed on the cross.* The apostle Paul passionately says, "But God demonstrates his love for us in this: While we were still sinners, Christ died for us. Since his blood has justified us, how much more shall we be saved from God's wrath through him?" (Rom 5:8–9). The goal is to leave others craving the experience of love and share it. It is impossible to forget how much God and Jesus love us.

There's no substitute for the supreme love of God, because its theology is woven into the divinity of God's presence. The significance of God's love reveals that "God's love means that God eternally gives himself to others."[2] We must eagerly accept God's love as a significant part of life. When we do this, we thank God for creating us to love God's way. Many books, plays, stories, and magazine articles attempt to describe love. We can't genuinely express love because it is too deep, spiritual, and theological. It must be lived. However, you can glean ideas from books, plays, stories, and other sources. There is nothing wrong with looking at other avenues; they can encourage us to take a deeper look at ourselves and look forward to living the actual life of God's love. The Pearl of Love refines and elevates our spiritual journey, inviting reflection on how genuine affection shapes those who, even in the face of injustice, continue to embody love. This book guides believers through a contemplation of spiritual living, exploring metaphorical Pearls that illuminate the divine qualities manifest in everyday life. Rather than claiming to hold every answer, its pages encourage thoughtful attention to the essence of leading a life marked by spiritual pride and meaningful purpose. It is a gentle call for each believer to honor the sacredness woven into every day. God fashioned us for a divine purpose, elevating us to please him. The aim is to live a purpose driven life and show it by loving others. The goal is never to let others cheat you out of your blessings of showing compassion. The Bible

---

2. Grudem, *Bible Doctrine*, 103.

declares, "Above all, keep loving one another earnestly, since love covers a multitude of sins" (1 Pet 4:8). Many are living today who have no idea what it means to love. They only understand love when they are in dire need of help from God. After God rescues them, many return to their normal lives. If anything, this book can help and encourage you to set sail on the ocean of God's love. Knowing the difference between God's agape love and how we love each other is paramount to developing a passionate Christian life. To set sail on the ocean of God's love is to experience the waves of God's power and presence as he anoints you for the journey.

For this reason, it is essential to yearn for God's presence to be at work within you. When God's love does not resonate in your heart, spiritual vitality and abundant compassion are absent. Possessing material wealth yet refusing to assist those in need is a clear sign that God's love is missing from your life (1 John 3:17).

Søren Kierkegaard, a renowned nineteenth-century philosopher, says this concerning love: "To cheat oneself out of love is the most terrible deception; it is an eternal loss for which there is no reparation, either in time or in eternity."[3] He clarified that true love is no joke, and one must seriously connect love to God's time and eternity. There is much to be said about love and the meaning of life, because the reality of love is authentic. It is impossible to live a peaceful life without the love of God. To not love disturbs and tarnishes the path we tread, rips the seed of comfort, and leaves one's life unfulfilled; the best way to impress God is to walk in his ways and utilize spiritual Pearls for his glory. God has not created us to live without love. You must discover the genuine love of God to live a productive and purposeful life. The Bible teaches love from Genesis to Revelation. There is no way you can overlook it, because its unforgettable atmosphere attracts the most negative nature of people who do not engage in love as a life's priority.

The Gospel of Matthew demonstrates compassion through testing; it says, "One of the teachers of the law came and heard them debating. Noticing that Jesus had given them a good answer, he asked, 'Of all the commandments, which is the most important?' 'The most important one,' answered Jesus, 'is this: "Hear, O Israel, the Lord our God, the Lord is one. Love the Lord your God with all your heart and with all your soul and with all your mind and with all your strength."

---

3. Kierkegaard, *Works of Love*, 23.

The second is this: "Love your neighbor as yourself." There is no commandment greater than these'" (Mark 12:28–31). How have you demonstrated love when interacting with others, whether family, friends, coworkers, or strangers you meet? Your response determines the depth of your love. It takes a strong, willing mind to love with all your heart. You will also benefit from pondering the following Scripture: "But I tell you, love your enemies and pray for those who persecute you, that you may be children of your Father in heaven" (Matt 5:44–45). As believers, we are called to extend agape love to everyone. Praying for those seeking to destroy our name, character, and reputation is necessary. Howard Thurman's encouraging words sum up the integrity of love; he says, "The religion of Jesus says to the disinherited: love your enemy. Take the initiative in seeking ways by which you can have the experience of a common sharing of mutual worth and value."[4] Convincing people to love is another form of evangelism and conversion. Evangelism is when your life is moving in the context of love. You have a permanent new walk and talk when you have been transformed into love. This new direction pleases Jehovah God, which convinces people that love is another form of evangelism and conversion.

CHERISHED LOVE

When you cherish the Pearl of Love, your life will be honored by God due to your spiritual focus and sincerity. Cherished love goes beyond, and it touches people in so many ways: through unemployment, sickness, death, loss, and homelessness. Moreover, the church must reach out to people from all walks of life and support them with kindness that will spark interest in their lives. People generally crave agape and *philos* love, which is godly and brotherly love. God requires that you love everyone regardless of differences, egos, concepts, ideas, opinions, and perspectives. The message of love binds us because of God's will. Pleasing God is showing genuine love for all. Our lifestyle must be embedded in positive actions that compel us to please God and keep the pathway of charity open to sharing with all. As believers, we must embrace all with the Spirit of comfort to encourage them with the wisdom Pearl of Love so that all can and will appreciate and adopt the exact nature and behavior. The good news confirms that we are commanded

---

4. Thurman, *Jesus and the Disinherited*, 90.

to love (1 John 4:21). It is impossible to love God and hate or despise others, which makes one a liar (1 John 4:20). When believers implement duty and responsibility central to their walk and interaction with others, they will fulfill their contributing mission on earth for the glory of God. A Christian can't live in anger, bitterness, fury, and disrespect. The reason for living on the other side of hatred is the connectedness of the Holy Spirit that empowers you to keep love alive and express its powerful impact on society and the world.

The Pearl of Love must be cherished, respected, and taken seriously. You must be conscious of exhibiting truth and obedience in the presence of God. It charts the spiritual course to fulfill the commandment given by Jesus to express and walk with high energy for God's glory. Cherished love cannot be kept secret and remain quiet because of its impact on others.

REFLECTIVE SUMMARIZATION AND RESPONSES TO ACTION

The summary response to action is a response to the inspiration and information provided by the Pearl of Love, which engages the mind and heart in pursuit of spiritual maturity. The extent of your impact dictates the urge to act. If you are aware of a need, act accordingly. Don't let your ego and pride cheat you out of implementing God's gracious love for humanity. It is comforting to know that you are in alignment with the Creator and fellowship with one another.

The Point of Emphasis

Real love is the anatomy of the soul that connects to the spirit of humans and gives sincere thoughts of righteousness.

The Relevant Question

How eager are you to live a life of love?

A Prayer of Love

Jesus, thank you for your abiding love, which led you to die on the cross for my sins. Thank you for the opportunity to praise your holy name. Direct my footsteps, heart, and soul on this heartfelt journey. Help me appreciate the Pearl of Love while sharing love with others in your name. Amen.

DAY 2

The Pearl of Prayer Is the Pathway to God

"Have faith in God," Jesus answered. "I tell you the truth. If anyone says to this mountain, 'Go, throw yourself into the sea,' and does not doubt in his heart but believes that what he says will happen, it will be done for him. Therefore, I tell you, whatever you ask for in prayer, believe that you have received it, and it will be yours. And when you stand praying, if you hold anything against anyone, forgive him, so that your Father in heaven may forgive you your sins."

—MARK 11:22–25

The Pearl of Prayer is an essential and valuable conduit for daily living. It is crucial because it tests your willingness to communicate with God regarding all circumstances and encounters. The conduit of prayer is the pathway to God's heart and is the power that builds strength for life's most challenging encounters. What confidence it is to rely on Jesus' words of encouragement that whatever you need, just ask in prayer and believe, and it will be done (Mark 11:24). Prayer is the doctrine of a believer's belief and lifestyle of eternal connectedness with significant meaning. The doctrine of prayer gives credence to one's witness. It provides reason to trust and connect with God for total spiritual growth amid all opposition, challenges, and tests during personal journeys. It means that faithful praying is always dependent on God, while on the island of loneliness, while confronting anxiety and the unknown.

It is striking when prayer is the go-to when you are in serious trouble, tragedy, or severe circumstances, and it is when one buckles down with faith to overcome the imminent trials of painful pressure. The above Scripture confirms that one must practice praying through faith. If one does not believe in the power and promise of prayer, then praying without believing is only a formality in God's sight. Jesus challenged his disciples to include faith in their lives so that prayer could work. He taught them a simple *theology of prayer*. It is the humbleness of bowing down before the throne of grace, asking for mercy for a wounded soul.

Here is a striking request from Jesus' disciples as they are about to pray: "One day, Jesus was praying in a particular place. When he finished, one of his disciples said to him, 'Lord, teach us to pray, just as John taught his disciples'" (Luke 11:1). From that request, Jesus shaped the disciples' discipline wholeheartedly and their theology without using the term. His words were profound and powerful. This moment was a graceful and intimate moment when a disciple asked for instruction. "They had learned to believe in him as a Master in the art of Prayer. No one could pray like Him."[1] Emphasis is on the school of prayer with Jesus. The theological relevance of prayer is *consecration*. Consecration is vital to our prayer life because the example was made plain during Moses' leadership. God told Moses to "speak to the entire assembly of Israel and say to them: 'Be holy because I, the Lord your God, am holy'" (Lev 19:2). Holiness connects to consecration through the anointing presence of God. It is giving complete attention to the Almighty. Therefore, one must live in holiness while striving to live amicably with others. The Bible further states, "Make every effort to live in peace with everyone and to be holy; without holiness no one will see the Lord" (Heb 12:14).

Believers in the church in Rome were encouraged to present their bodies as a holy living sacrifice to God. Paul declared it reasonable to do so (Rom 12:1–2). The power and authenticity of believers lie in the power and the hiddenness of prayer. True prayer is praying in secret, with the hiddenness of God working on our behalf. God knows our

---

1. Murray. *With Christ in the School of Prayer*, 9.

thoughts during prayer, but we don't know God's thoughts and plan. The bosom of God seals the hiddenness of prayer and the blessings of God. These blessings are inherent because of his power and presence. Prayer is a private form of communication, enabling believers to cultivate and maintain a pure and authentic relationship with God. The power of prayer is that the enemy is not aware of the work of God. It is the conduit of communication for strength, hope, and assurance. It is a privilege because prayer historically embodies the African American tradition. African Americans experienced hope and assurance during slavery, the Jim Crow years, the Civil Rights movement, and modern-day times. When believers pray, it is more of a duty than a privilege. It is a duty because praying is an honor in a Christian's life when they are in the school of prayer with Jesus. It takes an in-depth passion to pray and pray with a purpose, because God grants us the grace to pray. Jesus' disciples were in his school, and he taught his disciples to pray. Prayer is by no means an apparent or natural activity.

Jesus intercedes on behalf of all Christian prayers to God. Most people pray spontaneously, and others read prayers. If any form is from the heart, God hears it. Solemn prayer captures God's attention, focusing on the praying believer and waiting for an answer. Without prayer, the believer is useless and will have difficulty communicating with God. Prayer is the robust spiritual anchor for the believer. The more sincere the believer is in their prayers, the more God blesses them. There is no substitute for praying. The Bible says, "Therefore confess your sins to each other and pray for each other so that you may be healed. The prayer of a righteous person is powerful and effective" (Jas 5:16). God desires pure passion from praying saints.

Fervent prayer keeps one connected to God. E. M. Bounds authentically says, "God wants warmhearted servants. The Holy Spirit comes as a fire to dwell in us; we are to be baptized with the Holy Spirit and with fire. Fervency is the warmth of the soul."[2] How wonderful it is to start the day off with fervent prayer, prayer that heats the path for hope. A day without prayer is a day without communication with God. This study examines the doctrine of prayer and explores people's thoughts on prayer and its significance. God and prayer are inseparable. There can never be a relationship with God without prayer because prayer is the lifeline for spiritual growth. You must strive to

---

2. Bounds, *Complete Works*, 35.

cultivate a profound relationship with the Creator within the broader community. A strong relationship with Jehovah builds confidence, credibility, and certainty. Besides Jesus, many Old and New Testament servants lived a prayer life and prayed with faith, such as David, Solomon, and Paul. Jesus led by example by stressing belief. "Faith needs a life of prayer for its full growth."[3] Faith is the moving conduit through which prayer reaches its goal and purpose. The purpose is to maintain a connection with God. Therefore, genuine prayer shines through the soul, mind, and heart. The Pearl of Prayer keeps the correct agenda before God through the brushfires of temptation. Divine communication and inspiration keep one spiritually afloat with the proper plan to present to God through the Savior. It keeps God's heavenly door ajar for direct contact, even in the face of the most challenging opposition from the enemy. Prayer is the antidote for life's complexities and profound problems. It focuses on God's direction and experiences an intimate and meaningful relationship.

The Pearl of Prayer sets the stage for spiritual illumination that sparks peace, love, and joy. There is no way to live in peace without a life of prayer. There is no substitute for prayer because the Pearl of Prayer shines brightly in our consciousness, heart, mind, and soul. The connection with God is a robust embellishment of spiritual passion for growth in all areas of life. Therefore, we must communicate with God and Christ through the right thoughts and moments of waiting on God for explicit directions. When the mountains of opposition and trials surround us, prayer is a guaranteed guide from the Holy Spirit that keeps us close to the heartbeat of God. Loyal believers live with a passionate heart to walk humbly before God in a world where chaos is a complexity of ruined thoughts and actions. Consequently, prayer is the ointment that heals all burdens and beliefs, allowing us to reach out to God during dark moments. Prayer shines a light on our thoughts, ideas, passions, and actions. We are never to hold grudges against others. The Pearl of Prayer guides one to have faith and practice genuine forgiveness as we seek God's forgiveness for our sins. Genuine prayer does not allow one to live a life of spiritual imbalance and give up on waiting on God. God's presence in prayer is embedded in the Holy Spirit to guide our destiny in trying and lonely times. When we pray,

---

[3] Murray, *With Christ in the School of Prayer*, 98.

we are in the channel of God's leading while gaining strength from the chamber of God's bosom.

PRAYER IS THE IMMANENT FACTOR

Daily communication with God is evidence of an ongoing, genuine relationship. Prayer is not exclusive to tragedies, catastrophes, and personal mishaps; it aims to maintain a connection with the Creator. The title of a famous song by Dr. Charles G. Hayes & The Cosmopolitan Church of Prayer is "Every Day Is a Day of Thanksgiving." The song reminds believers that in all moments of life, we must remain objective with hope, trust, and faith for spiritual travel through the mountains of despair. The Old Testament character Jabez experienced a mountain of despair. He called upon God because of his situation and asked to enlarge his border and protect him from harm and pain (1 Chr 4:10). When you are pressed and delirious, remember, the inherent factor of prayer is keeping you keen and implementing personal spirituality. You must make time for God and pray daily, rather than waiting for a tragedy to happen. The renowned Richard J. Foster, in his book *Celebration of Discipline: The Path to Spiritual Growth*, says, "To pray is to change. Prayer is the central avenue through which God transforms us. If we are unwilling to change, we will abandon prayer as a noticeable characteristic of our lives."[4] Prayer is a significant part of our journey that needs shaping so you can have the proper foundation to grow. There are familiar prayer lifters that can make a difference in one's prayer life; they are:

1. Confessing Sins: Confessing sins allows one to move forward and do God's will.
2. Walking by Faith: Walking by faith is trusting God.
3. Following God's Will: Following God's will depends on Jehovah for all encounters for direction on every life's path.
4. Forgiving Others: Forgiving others affirms the desire to pray authentic prayers, regardless of the situation or circumstances.
5. Living by Obedience: Living by obedience affirms and validates one's prayer life.

---

4. Foster, *Celebration of Discipline*, 33.

SOME TYPES OF PRAYERS

The source for these types of prayers is the Holy Scripture. There are many prayers, and different descriptions to identify them. For example, 1 Tim 2:1 says, "First of all, then, I urge that supplications, prayers, intercessions, and thanksgivings be made for all people." For this forty-day journey, I share the following prayers for thought and consolation.

The Prayer of Adoration

This type of prayer gives God respect in worship and praise, praying during the celebration of the bread and wine during the Eucharist or Lord's Supper, baptism, or baby dedication. Be diligent and passionate about this prayer in your quest for intimacy. This type of prayer focus on the efficacious action of humbleness.

The Prayer of Intercession

Intercessory prayer involves praying for others and asking God to help them. One may be heavily burdened and need others in the body of Christ to intercede. "First of all, then, I urge that supplications, prayers, intercessions, and thanksgivings be made for all people" (1 Tim 2:1 ESV). Be thankful for Christ's intercession as you intercede on behalf of others.

The Prayer of Faith

The prayer of faith identifies your position and relationship with the Trinitarian Godhead: God the Father, the Son, and the Holy Spirit. No matter the danger you may face, you must step out on faith and completely trust in the power of God to deliver you and answer you during your risks and dilemmas. The prayer of faith is a tower prayer because the focus is on faith alone for God's answer. "Therefore I tell you, whatever you ask in prayer, believe that you have received it, and it will be yours" (Mark 11:24 ESV). This type of prayer embodies confidence and conviction. When we ask God by faith for favoring grace, he responds favorably.

The Prayer of Thanksgiving

The prayer of thanksgiving is a prayer that shows divine appreciation for what the Creator has done. It is wise to thank Jehovah for waking you up from your rest last night. It's good to pause during the day and thank God for protection, comfort, and provision. We could never thank him enough for all that has been. The psalmist says, "This is the day that the Lord has made; let us rejoice and be glad in it" (Ps 118:24 ESV).

The Prayer of Consecration

Believers must take the time and focus on setting themselves apart for service. Jesus prayed a prayer of consecration before his crucifixion: "Going a little farther, he fell with his face to the ground and prayed, 'My Father, if it is possible, may this cup be taken from me. Yet not as I will, but as you will'" (Matt 26:39). As you start each day, seek a closer walk with God to keep you spiritually fit for kingdom service.

REFLECTIVE SUMMARIZATION AND RESPONSES TO ACTION

An authentic prayer life is the epitome of peace with self and God. It is a disciplined effort to prioritize prayer for a vibrant and spiritual walk with God. Adequate time with God affirms quality communication that pleases him. No one should live without prayer because it should be an ongoing enterprise that keeps us in touch with the Almighty.

The Point of Emphasis

Prayer is the antidote for life's complexities and profound problems.

The Relevant Question

Are you willing to prioritize prayer to validate your relationship with God?

A Prayer of Anointing

Eternal God, I seek your anointing for spiritual growth and to walk in the pathway of righteousness. I thank you for the desire to keep prayer alive in my heart so that I can be a genuine witness to your glory. Thank you for your gracious anointing, which allows me to experience your presence. Allow me to walk with you and obey your instructions forever. In your holy name. Amen.

DAY 3

The Pearl of Forgiveness Is Vital

For if you forgive other people when they sin against you, your heavenly Father will also forgive you. But if you do not forgive others their sins, your Father will not forgive your sins.

—MATTHEW 6:14–15

Forgiveness allows us to learn from the past instead of being haunted by it. Forgiveness allows us to prepare for the future instead of trying to control it.

—BRAD HAMBRICK

Forgiveness is the road of the spiritual life because it represents the genuine nature of God and the vital responsibility of action. When you earnestly forgive others, it is a kind act of compassion. Jesus emphasizes the truth that we should follow, and he said we must be willing to forgive others as the Father forgives us our sins. Moreover, it is God's mandate for our manners to practice forgiveness. The path of forgiveness is a prodigious requirement for you and a mandate for authentic spiritual relationships. It is like a breath of fresh air that authenticates the meaning and essence of experiencing God. You cannot be a genuine believer and deeply knowledgeable about God while shunning forgiveness of others. Therefore, living the life of forgiveness is the Magna Carta of your spiritual relationship, testimony, and belief in the Creator and compassion for others. The Pearl of Forgiveness glitters in the core of your soul and prepares your heart for the foundation of spiritual living and to sincerely worship God. Forgiveness is paramount to your faith and spiritual walk. It encompasses a genuine relationship with Christ through the practice of sound theological principles. There is an old saying, "I will forgive but will never forget." That is not what Jesus taught his disciples in the Gospel. That is not living by the Scripture in Matt 6:15–16. When we grow in maturity, forgiveness has it hold and we will abide by these words: "Do not take revenge, my dear friends, but leave room for God's wrath, for it is written: 'It is mine to avenge; I will repay,' says the Lord" (Rom 12:19). These readings focus on the heart of the believer. You must be willing to forgive because God forgave you of your sins. It must be clear that forgiving others for their sins, meaning their vindictive treatment of you, reflects the nature of God's loving grace. When God forgives us, it is a clear-cut action, no strings attached, because our forgiveness connects to salvation, and our forgiveness toward others connects to our relationship.

The purpose of forgiveness is a testimony about the nature of God's work through grace because of guilt and sin. Forgiveness has the power to change anyone's situation amid moral disgrace. It is not just the work that God has done for us, but how we use forgiveness in our lives toward each other. We must learn the magnitude of overlooking frivolous talk, and implement this wisdom: "Forbearing one another and, if one has a complaint against another, forgiving each other; as the Lord has forgiven you, so you also must forgive" (Col 3:13 RSV). When we examine our faults, wrongdoings, and mistakes, we should consider how we can demonstrate forgiveness to those who mistreat us.

A prime example of true humanitarian forgiveness is found in the story of Joseph and his brothers. Joseph was one of Jacob's twelve sons. He was dedicated and loving. His devious brothers were jealous and schemed to kill him. To make matters worse, they sold him into slavery. His brothers had to look up to him when the famine arose in Egypt (Gen 37:18–20, 21–36; 45:4–7; 47:13–27). There is a lesson in this saga to encourage believers to demonstrate genuine forgiveness. The New Testament records a powerful story of forgiveness by Stephen. He was an example of Jesus and forgave those who murdered him: before he was sentenced to death, he prayed for his attackers (Acts 7:54—8:2).

When we forgive others, it is related to Christ's genuine demonstration of salvation. It was at the cross where we all shared commonality. There are three Greek words for forgiveness. Forgiveness in Matt 6:14 is the verb *aphiémi*, which means to properly send away, release.[1] There should be no limitation on forgiveness to others. The following passage uses forgiveness in a different context. Here, the Greek word is the verb *charizomai*, which means to bestow a favor unconditionally (Eph 4:32; Col 2:13; 3:13; Luke 7:42–43; see also 2 Cor 2:7, 10).[2] The third Greek word is *aphesis*, which refers to the dismissal or release of our sins. Through grace and mercy, God has accepted us and disregarded our sins.[3]

Forgiveness is integral to your relationship with the Divine Creator, which gives credence to your witness and life as believers. There is no fellowship with Jehovah if there is no forgiveness for others. Many believers and nonbelievers need to know and learn the value of authentic forgiveness. The Pearl of Forgiveness is associated with God's presence. Therefore, forgiveness must become an indelible mark of the theology of emptying your heart of hurt, shame, and pride and accepting others' pardons. In this context, forgiveness is the theology of receiving when you are mistreated or abused. The real test of forgiveness will challenge you to reevaluate your walk with God and Christ. The Pearl of Forgiveness reminds you of your responsibilities as a genuine believer. Witness and testimony will never be authentic without extending forgiveness because God granted it. Therefore, you must be willing to do the same for others. Forgiveness can sometimes be challenging, but it is an act of humility and compassion, expressed in the character God has given us. Forgiveness repairs broken hearts and restores fragile and broken relationships. When one lets go of ill feelings, one practices a theology of forgiveness and living as authentic and genuine disciples.

The Markan account of forgiveness leans more toward the power of forgiveness (Mark 2:1–17). Regardless of race, creed, or color, everyone shares a common denominator: we all need cleanness of sins.

---

1. Bible Hub, "Aphiémi."
2. Vine, *Expository Dictionary*, 123.
3. Vine, *Expository Dictionary*, 123.

Before cleanness of sins, we all were living in frustration and guilt. "The bondage of guilt stifles their ability to give and receive love."[4] Freedom comes through the presence of God and the power of Jesus' blood. Jesus not only forgave us of our sins, but he also forgave those who crucified him. He said, "Father, forgive them for they know not what they are doing" (Luke 23:24). Jesus pleaded in his prayer that his Father would forgive those at the foot of the cross. Individuals must desire total independence from the bondage and shackles of sin and join a new life of peace. Live the life demonstrating the move of God and never allow the spirit of unforgiveness to take residence. Some people refuse to forgive others, instead holding grudges. Unforgiveness will produce bitterness and anger. Pride is the culprit that causes unforgiveness to fester; that is a sin.

Let us acknowledge the unforgiveness of others as a serious sin in the eyes of God. It is serious because of three factors:

1. *It is an offense to God.* The God of eternity does not want to see us perplexed, in dismay, or bewildered. You can make spiritual restitution and live a life that is well-pleasing to him. If you are out of fellowship with God because unforgiveness is embedded in your heart, ask God for *koinonia* renewal, which is the Greek word for "fellowship" and means "communion, fellowship, sharing in common."[5] Unforgiveness causes bitterness to block your spiritual blessing.

2. *It is the cause of a spiritual decline.* The state of unforgiveness is a sign of unfruitful living. When there is a lack of spiritual power and anointing of the Holy Spirit, it is because your life is declining. It lacks spiritual strength and credibility. Spiritual decline is a deficit that affects one's ability to communicate with God. Christ died because he was the forgiving factor on the cross. The power of God through Christ has favor and grace for your next move, the move from decline to deliverance.

3. *It is causing the church to suffer because of unforgiveness.* When the church fails to continue practicing not holding grudges through teaching, it stifles its power, witness, and authenticity. The church serves as a spiritual anchor in the community and globally,

---

4. Stanley, *Experiencing Forgiveness*, 8.
5. Vine, *Expository Dictionary*, 90.

providing change and hope for believers. Too many believers can easily fall prey to the unforgiving influence of evil, allowing it to distract them from the path of righteousness. Wisdom speaks loudly: "Don't let unforgiveness allow Satan to distract you so that your Father in heaven may forgive you your sins." May God lay the burden of forgiveness on your heart to implement the above principle.

GOD'S RESPONSE TO SIN

The former life was a life of sin and unrest. That life was miserable because sin and unforgiveness worked together to block and bleed a life of peace and joy. God's response to sin is that God calls us to repentance through his divine acts of grace. God understands how hurtful evil is to us. He desires that we be cleared of the guilt of sin. God's response to sin started with Adam and Eve in the garden. Shame settled in their conscious (Gen 3:6–7). God's response to sin is also shown in the life of David when he says, "Wash me clean from my guilt, purify me from my sin" (Ps 51:2). However, it is seen with David. Only God's grace removed the deepest stain of the sin of unforgiveness in exchange for forgiveness. We must recognize the goodness of God (Rom 11:21–22). God will not allow us to be tempted beyond what we can do (1 Cor 10:13). Romans 4:7 says, "Blessed are those whose transgressions are forgiven, whose sins are covered." God declares us righteous based on our faith. Individuals must thank God for forgiveness because sin needs attention in the body of Christ and the world. We are all guilty of sin and in need of a covering.

God is offended by sin for many reasons, such as it leads to more evil actions; they are: (1) sin dominates, (2) sin is devious, (3) sin separates, (4) sin destroys, and (5) sin is deceptive. Thank God for looking through his divine lens and seeing our catastrophic condition. He sends Jesus to eradicate the monster of evil, to the merciful ministry of salvation. How blessed we are to experience the cleansing power and presence of God's anointing in our lives. This intimate salvific experience compels us to be faithful to God because "*Jesus emptied Himself!* He set aside the prerogatives and powers of the Godhood to identify fully with us."[6] The main lesson in this chapter is to urge us to be devoted to God and God alone; this authenticates our humbleness for his holiness. The Pearl of Forgiveness shines in the souls of believers, coupled with God's earnest guidance for resolution. Believers must be encouraged about the favor of God and strive to be waiting for the response of connecting to the divine presence of the Almighty for eminent, faithful, fruitful, and forgiving followers of Christ.

REFLECTIVE SUMMARIZATION AND RESPONSES TO ACTION

Forgiveness is a profound spiritual responsibility that requires forgiving others. It is a humble act that repairs broken consciences and prepares us to worship God genuinely. A forgiving spirit is a healthy spirit as you access and evaluate your relationship and walk with the Creator. Most importantly, forgiveness challenges you to think about theology in perspective and live the way God is pleased.

The Point of Emphasis

There is no fellowship with Jehovah if there is no forgiveness for others.

The Relevant Question

Have you pondered over the significance of genuine forgiveness?

A Prayer of Forgiveness

Jesus, thank you for forgiving me of my sins. Now that I'm forgiven give me the compassion to forgive others who may have mistreated me, abused me, or even scandalized my name. Keep me well-disciplined with the Holy Spirit's guidance, and help me to overlook their mistakes. In your name. Amen.

---

6. Stedman, *Authentic Christianity*, 19–20.

DAY 4

The Pearl of Faith Pleases God

And it is impossible to please God without faith. Anyone who wants to come to him must believe that God exists and that he rewards those who sincerely seek him.

—Hebrews 11:6 NLT

Now to Him who is able to do exceedingly abundantly above all that we ask or think, according to the power that works in us, to Him be glory in the church by Christ Jesus to all generations, forever and ever. Amen.

—Ephesians 3:20–21 NKJV

As you delve into this day of spiritual discipline, exploring your allegiance to God, I would like to propose a brief *theology of faith* to help jump-start your thinking about trust and confidence. A theology of faith is that you believe all you can about confidence in God, and God is able to come through on his promise of present and future acts. Having a theology of faith is the kind of faith that ultimately pleases God. Here is the reason for such trust. The emphasis of Mark's Gospel on faith is the claim that whatever you ask in prayer with a believing heart and attitude, you will receive (Mark 11:14). Believers are required to implement living faith that pleases God.

When pressing circumstances arise, faith is the anchor that reaches the depth of your soul, providing spiritual fervor. God is expecting a plan of action as you implement your faith. The above verses establish the relevance and context for understanding the term *faith*. The believer's life is incomplete without faith. The book of Ephesians guides the church and explicitly states that salvation is achieved through faith alone (Eph 2:8–9). It is impossible to be saved without this wisdom Pearl. This Pearl challenges you to contemplate an intimate walk in the darkness of stress, frustration, anxiety, and depression. Pressing through those terms is a positive sign of pleasing God. Faith is the favor of God in your life, and it is impossible to survive without it. God gave this Pearl the spiritual stamina needed on this journey. Therefore, faith is the catalyst of hope. It is the catalyst that enables believers to experience the Almighty's presence amid life's perils and terrors. The apostle Paul reminds the body of Christ about the importance of trust: "So faith comes from hearing and hearing through the word of Christ" (Rom 10:17 ESV). In a more profound realm, faith is the citadel of strength, zeal, and spiritual tenacity, enabling one to navigate life's erratic tides amid spiritual warfare designed to destroy spiritual strength and perseverance. Many believers claim to have faith, but often, when faced with a crisis, their faith is dormant. Therefore, the authentic disciple must measure their walk with their talk. "Faith" comes from the Greek word *pistis*, including "trust and firm persuasion,"[1] which is the dominant word for faith in the New Testament. It is a noun in Eph 2:8–9 and Heb 11:6, and many other passages. Pistis is translated to mean a variety of things, including trust and firm persuasion. Strong translates it to mean "belief, confidence, fidelity," and Thayer says, "When it relates to God, [pistis] is 'the conviction that God exists and is the Creator and ruler of all things, the provider and bestower of eternal salvation through Christ': Hebrews 11:6; Hebrews 12:2."[2] What a powerful term to provide hope for a long journey building a fond relationship with God. The Almighty is faithful to the end of the age. The road we travel is a road of challenges, tests, and accomplishments through rugged pressures. While in seminary, my classmates and I struggled to understand the

---

1. Vine, *Expository Dictionary*, 71.
2. Bible Hub, "Pistis."

book *The Dynamics of Faith* by Paul Tillich, which expresses profound principles of faith that can be difficult to decipher. He describes faith as "the most centered act of the human mind. It is not a movement of a special section or a special function of man's total being. They are all united in the act of faith."[3] The purpose of this Pearl is to strengthen one's spiritual foothold, to cling relentlessly to Jehovah, regardless of the mesmerizing antics that agitate our paths. Faith is a testimony that you know God. Consequently, the writer of Hebrews says, "Now faith is the assurance of things hoped for, the conviction of things not seen" (Heb 11:1 ESV). To maintain the connection of your faith, you must walk by faith, act with conviction, talk confidently, and be assured of the outcome. Walking by faith is the immediate assurance of the work of the Holy Spirit, and the regenerate heart bears witness to knowing God. The truth is that through the Holy Spirit, God helps us to know him better (Eph 1:17). Through this experience, it solidifies stronger relationships with Jehovah.

THE MOOD OF FAITH

Many individuals are on life's roller coaster; their minds are up and down, and they struggle to discern the true essence of faith. Individuals must realize that faith is a test of our faith in the God who created faith and is faithful to humanity. Therefore, you must utilize faith as best you can. People struggle to use faith because of their moods. One may be in a good mood and have deep faith in God or not be in a good mood at all. God provides faith in response to the constant attacks by the evil one. The apostle Paul says, "So I find this law at work: Although I want to do good, evil is right there with me" (Rom 7:21). Evilness attacks our emotional character to divert our attention from our faith in God and focus on the current condition. Faith must become the epitome of life because it impacts your intellect in pursuing the totality of specific answers. It is beyond the infinite mind as you grapple for the comfort of the mind and heart. Your faith will be strengthened by accepting the present frame of mind, focusing on every moment of thinking, and trusting God. The apostle Paul said it best: "Not that I am speaking of being in need, for I have learned in whatever situation I am to be content. I know how to be brought low, and I know how to abound. In

---

3. Tillich, *Dynamics of Faith*, 4.

any and every circumstance, I have learned the secret of facing plenty and hunger, abundance and need. I can do all things through him who strengthens me" (Phil 4:11–13 ESV). In a meaningful manner, trusting and depending on God. That is his theology of faith in a nutshell.

Furthermore, individuals must emerge from being entrapped in thoughts and hopelessness and keep their eyes on the Creator. The Bible says, "Trust in the Lord with all your heart and lean not on your understanding; in all your ways submit to him, and he will make your paths straight" (Prov 3:5–6). Believers must cultivate a passion for maintaining constant contact and a deep trust in God for everything. God is the path director, protector, and provider. Trusting in God is enough to inspire our intellect, emotions, and spiritual walk in his presence and comfort.

FAITH AND GRACE

The presence of faith is connected to grace; they merge to reveal the love of God. Without grace, faith has no final merit or purpose for survival. It is all from God—every thought of our consciousness clings to God's gift of focus. Grace is the main factor by which we have been saved, and since we have been reserved for eternity with the Creator, it gives us a reason to trust in God. Trusting in the Creator is genuine faith that remains unwavering. We are declared righteous because of the grace of God and, therefore, are saved by grace and our faith (Eph 2:8–9). Grace integrates with all the Pearls in this book to make a statement and show the love of God in every aspect of life. Every day is a day of faith for a new journey and challenges. Here is a question for reflection: What is your understanding of faith? Since Jehovah has provided and blessed us with confidence, we should appreciate this Pearl with divine honor and walk by faith every moment, because it keeps us focused on achieving positive outcomes and victory.

REFLECTIVE SUMMARIZATION AND RESPONSES TO ACTION

Just thinking about the power of faith encourages trust and confidence. God is waiting to see how you utilize your faith daily. Every day should be a day of thanksgiving. The goal of the believer should be to please

God. The only way to build trust is to have confidence in oneself, which in turn fosters confidence in the Creator. It is crucial to demonstrate faith and reflect on your theology of faith for a closer walk with God. Most importantly, faith is the guiding factor for answers from God.

The Point of Emphasis

Faith is the anchor that is the depth of your soul, that provides spiritual fervor.

The Relevant Question

What is your understanding of faith?

A Prayer of Faith

Everlasting God, thank you for the Pearl of Faith. Help me continue walking in faith, so that I may please you in all that I do. I strive to focus on you and live a life of faith, trust, and determination. Teach me, oh God, to know the steps of faith I need to take to embrace your presence. Teach me to adore your glorious majesty. Amen.

DAY 5

The Pearl of Commitment Shows Spiritual Progress

And may your hearts be fully committed to the Lord our God, to live by his decrees and obey his commands, as at this time.

—1 KINGS 8:61

Trust in the Lord with all your heart and lean not on your understanding; in all your ways acknowledge Him, and He shall direct your paths. Do not be wise in your own eyes; fear the Lord and depart from evil. It will be health to your flesh, and strength to your bones.

—PROVERBS 3:5–8

Living a life of commitment and trust is a spiritual progression that honors God. My fifty-six years of preaching are an example of what Bill Hull emphasizes: "Healthy Christianity is based on truth and is lived by committed Christians."[1] I concur with his idea that being a believing disciple and preacher is paramount, regardless of the ministry, multiple church services, Zoom meetings, pastoral schedules, and

---

1. Hull, *Building High Commitment*, 64.

other leaders being challenged to maintain healthy Christianity. God is seeking a life of committed honor. Regardless of schedules, you are required to commit to the Eternal Redeemer. The Pearl of Commitment is one of the essential cores of Wisdom Pearls, which is the centrality of this book. It seeks to show believers how to appreciate the purpose driven life. All the Pearls are incredibly critical for *spiritual edification* in a world that is increasingly engrossed with strife, anger, and bitterness. Consequently, ministry and spirituality are not authentic without exemplifying commitment.

Solomon penned Proverbs to remind believers of the significance of a committed life. The above Scripture is a testimony to the writer's emphasis on the importance of a tenacious attitude, which is a divine asset for a Spirit-filled life. The Spirit-filled life never leans on your understanding, but on the Creator. It is prudent to fear the Lord and focus on the present and the future for greater spiritual awakening. However, you must fear the Lord and detach from the clutches of evil. Your path may have hiccups and bumps but strive to start each day with a purpose and a fresh start, with a personal devotion to respect Jehovah's sovereignty.

Both individuals and churches must be committed to cultivating a deepening relationship with the Lord. Committed individuals aspire to associate with dedicated and committed churches. Essentially, God expects genuine commitment as we pray for guidance under the Holy Spirit. Commitment is the validity and authenticity of being a true disciple of Christ. Being a genuine disciple represents an authentic believer, which includes a consecrated lifestyle. How do you know that you have total commitment? The answer to that question is my estimation of knowing that you are walking in the Spirit and are "sealed by the Holy Spirit" (Eph 1:13). If you are not committed to being a genuine servant of God, then all of what appears real is worthless to God. The above verse challenges you to deeply introspect what it means to walk worthy of being a faithful witness. What does it mean to trust in the Lord with all your heart? That question is the sum of the Pearl of Commitment. Chapter 3 of Proverbs is the core meaning of the book of Proverbs because it emphasizes the commitment, communion, and confidence of relying on the Creator for guidance, understanding, and wisdom. Solomon was committed to building the temple in Jerusalem (1 Kgs 6). He stayed with the task until the first temple was built. It is paramount for believers to have the Spirit of commitment in serving the Lord God. There must be effort, resiliency, and tenacity to please God with a committed life. Without effort, the church and believers do not show commitment.

COMMITMENT AND DISCIPLINE

Nelson Mandela was a great example of a committed servant. He was disciplined and worked tirelessly to accomplish his goal. Each day, we have been blessed to experience ministry, and we must show dedication to the Creator; this dedication is linked to our spiritual rejuvenation. Commitment is the scope of being valid in thoughts, actions, and state of mind. It rests in the core of our consciousness and keeps us in tune with faithful actions as we interact with humanity and the divine. It is a significant aspect of your character as you discipline your actions and reach your desired goals. God is the reason for your existence; we adhere to his knowledge, wisdom, and guidance.

Regarding the validity of commitment, God is the object of our commitment. Therefore, our commitment has no merit without God's blessings. The Bible says, "Commit to the LORD whatever you do, and he will establish your plans" (Prov 16:3). When you trust God, accept Christ, and follow the Holy Spirit, your commitment is genuine because commitment is the flip side of faith; both work for the same purpose. Jehovah works out every detail of our plans for his glory. Jehovah is watching and waiting for our commitment through prayer, discipleship, ministry, and servanthood. A commitment must be to things that matter for servanthood.

Bill Hull states, "Many commit themselves to the unimportant by default. They may be highly committed, but they are committed to the wrong thing, the unimportant thing."[2] It is a sad commentary when some individuals, regardless of race, culture, or religion, are committed to things detrimental to their lives. Commitment to worldly affairs and not Jesus is futile. It is essential to redirect our discipline of commitment, balance our playing field, and set higher standards for the committed life. Believers may cling to important things, and dedication should be an indelible mark on our consciousness and character. Therefore, whatever task or project, the same energy and focus must

---

2. Hull, *Building High Commitment*, 83.

be applied for positive results. Stay the course and never give up, but seek the guidance of the Holy Spirit for the outcome, even when challenges and oppositions arise. I remember the gospel song "Lord Help Me to Hold Out."[3] The lyrics of this song emphasize the determination to persevere until the end. Therefore, staying close to the Trinity—God the Father, God the Son, and God the Holy Spirit—is a faith move that requires relentless commitment. Help is needed where and when there are so many distractions that deter us from our intended goals and objectives; the apostle Paul says, "In the same way, the Spirit helps us in our weakness. We do not know what we ought to pray for, but the Spirit himself intercedes for us through wordless groans" (Rom 8:26). When we feel the walls caving in on us, we have the Holy Spirit to guide our minds and affirm our direction in accomplishing our humble tasks.

The Pearl of Commitment is the assurance that there is hope during your frustrations and rugged challenges in the world in which you live. Genuine devotion is challenged by the troubles of this world amid racial inequality, segregation, and racism. Believers must remain loyal to the Creator. Dedicating time to Jehovah means to divorce from the world's tasks while worshipping God sincerely and passionately. When commitment impacts the soul of humanity, it speaks the truth of honesty, never surrendering to the world's foes. Time spent with God is devoted, valuable, serene, and admirable. A. W. Tozer says, "The average Christian today does not make much spiritual progress at all."[4] I concur with Tozer; limited spiritual commitment impedes spiritual progress. It is valuable to be with God and grow in the grace and knowledge of our Lord and Savior Jesus Christ (2 Pet 3:18).

The purpose of commitment is to challenge you to start your journey of walking with God. Your dedication must be unwavering and relentless as you struggle to accomplish personal tasks and goals. One must be passionate to stay the course and push until the end. A clear example of love, dedication, and commitment is related to Jacob wrestling with the angel, a theophany, or God in a different form (Gen 32:22–32). Other characters in the Bible exemplified the message of faithfulness including Ruth, Moses, David, Joshua, and the apostle Paul. Today's church must show spiritual energy and devotion to keep the commitment light burning with passion.

3. Cleveland, "Lord Help Me."
4. Tozer, *Crucified Life*, 84.

REFLECTIVE SUMMARIZATION AND RESPONSES TO ACTION

The essence of time encourages you to reflect on the incredible moments that hold significance and demonstrate commitment. Commitment is never sitting and wondering. It is an action in progress. You cannot give up when it seems like life is collapsing around you. Spend quality time with God and move forward with a positive action plan.

The Point of Emphasis

Your character is the essence of your spiritual survival.

The Relevant Question

Has your commitment kept you on the right road?

A Prayer of Commitment

Lord, thank you for the strength and fortitude to follow you. I plead with you to give me the faith to be committed to riding the storms of life and continue to be devoted to the work of the kingdom. Amen.

DAY 6

The Pearl of Mercy Reveals Kindness

He has shown you, O mortal, what is good. And what does the Lord require of you? To act justly and to love mercy and to walk humbly with your God.
—Micah 6:8

Teach me to feel another's woe, to hide the fault I see, that mercy I to others show, that mercy show to me.
—Alexander Pope

It is human nature to desire mercy. God says we must show mercy. To love mercy is kindness, and to value it no matter the circumstance. Implementing mercy as disciples is prudent, as it involves showing kindness. You must reflect on the meaning of the essence of mercy when you are at the end of your road; the only resolve is mercy. You look to God for help. Remember, God's mandate is that you show mercy to others regardless of how people treat you. Kindness is a matter that can't be overlooked. As you meditate today, consider the concept of mercy and its significance in God's eyes. Disciples are responsible for showing kindness and mercy in the most daring times. Jesus sets the example of true mercy for anyone in need. If you are bogged down in the pit of hopelessness, reach out to God. If others are in despair, reach out to offer them help. Reaching out is mercy in action.

Mercy is one of God's attributes, and its theology is a profound statement of God's compassion. This Pearl describes the truth of God's mercy because it is the ultimate resort for help in times of dire need or distress. Mercy is a Pearl that you must pursue because it is from God. It is essential for your spiritual DNA. A profound statement by A. W. Tozer says, "The mercy of God will never be any less than it is now, because the infinite cannot cease to be infinite, and the perfect cannot admit an imperfection."[1] The above passage sets the stage for mercy.

God is the originator and giver of mercy. Knowing that God's mercy is endless inspires the weary to see illumination. Therefore, mercy is in God's bosom, mind, and heart as it gives hope in the most delicate and difficult circumstances. The prophet Micah, a minor prophet, prophesied during the eighth century BC with a significant message. Micah was a contemporary of Isaiah, and Isaiah encouraged him. The above passage encourages Israel and the present-day church to treat people with dignity, love, and mercy. Justice was needed because Israel exploited people experiencing poverty, and judgment was on them, but Micah had hope.

MERCY IS THE CENTRAL FACTOR

God directs the prophet Micah to make mercy the central factor for spiritual development, to be fair with acts of justice, and to love mercy. Just as God gave Micah the divine directive to implement justice and mercy, the same applies to the modern-day church. "In the Bible, *hesed* often describes the mercy and compassion of God."[2] The intense action is that we are to love mercy. Mercy tests our true spirituality and obedience. Compassion, pity, and love remind us to stay focused and be genuine in our beliefs.

God, in his wise providence, knew that people would cry out for mercy. There are many instances and stories about pleading for mercy. We are expected to do three things, according to the above verse: to act justly, to love mercy, and to walk humbly. Those three actions

---

1. Tozer, *Into the Father's Heart*, 82.
2. Got Questions, "Hesed," para. 4.

authenticate the validity and veracity of your spiritual walk. However, a prime example is the case of the Israelites, who were in bondage in Egypt under the bitter rule of Pharaoh for over four hundred years (Exod 1:11–14; 12:40). It took resilience, grit, and obedience for the Israelites to endure the pain of Pharaoh's camp. They continued to hope for release and deliverance. God is a God of mercy and justice. As you read this chapter, it should remind you of when you received freedom and redemption. Thinking about God's love and compassion makes you want to say hallelujah when deliverance emerges on your path. Your challenge is to emulate mercy, which must be done with a warm, passionate heart that melts the anxiety of those who are passionately reaching out for help. Jesus urged the teachers of the law and the Pharisees who brought in a woman caught in adultery to have mercy on her (John 8:1–9).

MERCY CRIES FOR COMPASSION

A lesson well taught about mercy, Jesus said to the woman, "Then neither do I condemn you. . . . Go now and leave your life of sin" (v. 11b). Therefore, the voice of mercy is still speaking and asking for compassion. African Americans were subjected to racist actions during slavery without mercy. Hundreds of thousands were lynched, abused, and dehumanized. They cried and pleaded for mercy during the Jim Crow era and the degrading symbol of the lynching tree, but still no mercy from the white masters. Enslaved people were embittered by many unmerciful acts, even as Christians. Riggins Earl Jr. states that the master's ideal intent was that "Christianity would transform the enslaved person into a servile temperament."[3] The goal was that the enslaved person would succumb to the master's unmerciful treatment to keep them under subjection. That is injustice of the highest order. Inequality was the prevailing order of the day back then and remains so now. Implementing the purpose driven disciple challenges you to walk humbly before God. Harriet Tubman had the spirit of understanding. She was kind, compassionate, and humble. Her personality touched people's lives remarkably. She lived Mic 6:8 during her ministry. The world asked God for mercy during the COVID-19 pandemic. Many pandemics were encountered, including racism, injustice, gun violence, murder, theft,

---

3. Earl, *Dark Symbols and Obscure Signs*, 126.

etc. Living a life without justice and mercy is empty and without meaning. Living without mercy is like living in hell. God is the liberator who brings mercy and justice for all, regardless of circumstances.

This passage aims to speak to individuals to practice justice and mercy. The Lord God continually embodies and advocates for compassion. We are living in an unmerciful world, a world of sadistic sensationalism amid inflamed egos, and you must have a heart to live compassionately. In essence, uncompassionate individuals don't care about those who need mercy. Unmerciful acts are represented from every culture, race, religion, and political identity. Many are prone to respond without compassion and concern for others. During the pandemic, people were, for the most part, far more merciful because the focus was on the dying, and the problem was about being safe. However, there were incidents, acts of violence, and murders that occurred. For example, George Floyd suffered the knee of police officer Derek Chauvin on his neck for nine minutes and twenty-nine seconds. However, as the pandemic ended, the uprisings began to regain momentum. Some lessons were learned from the pandemic, while others acted as if it had not occurred. The first responders, medical staff, and others showed extreme mercy to the sick.

PRACTICING MERCY PLEASES GOD

Regardless of how we are treated, we must practice mercy to the highest level. Avoid retaliation against the unmerciful acts of the adversary, because God's rewards are more substantial than the sadistic acts of the enemy. Jesus Christ was the anchor and advocate of liberation from degradation and oppression. James Cone put it this way: "The grounding liberation in God's act in Jesus Christ is the logical consequence of any Christian theology that takes scripture seriously as an important source for the doing of theology."[4] The Creator sent Jesus to advocate for mercy because sin had marred and snatched justice and mercy from humanity. Jesus visited the synagogue and read the passage as quoted in Isa 61. He advocated healing the brokenhearted and freeing the captives (Luke 4:16, 18–19). The brokenhearted applies to all people who have been mistreated.

---

4. Cone, *God of the Oppressed*, 139.

Jehovah God spoke to Micah and urged him to practice walking humbly. We are God's creation and have been granted mercy from the God of Abraham, Isaac, and Jacob. Believers must know God to effectuate the power of compassion. Another passage that declares God's mercy is Deut 4:31, which says, "The Lord your God is a God of mercy." The Hebrew word here is *rachum*, which describes God's consistent character of tenderness and love for his people, Israel. This verse demonstrates that God goes above and beyond, showing love. Since the Creator goes beyond and offers love, we too must know God, and practice and implement Mic 6:8. A. W. Tozer says, "The more perfectly we know God the more we will feel the desire to translate the new-found knowledge into deeds of mercy toward suffering humanity."[5] There is no doubt that believers must implement justice, love, and compassion. This action must be implemented in the ministry of the church and by individuals. Jehovah is always watching and keeping a record of your stewardship. You must show more than speak and be more than do.

REFLECTIVE SUMMARIZATION AND RESPONSES TO ACTION

The Wisdom Pearl of Mercy recounts the joy of thanking God for his extended compassion. It is imperative as a disciple to remember God's mandate to show mercy to others amid ruthless treatment. The story of African Americans' degrading experience is the story of the lack of mercy under Jim Crow Laws in the South. Regardless of the past and the present, you must extend mercy to others and act justly. This Pearl describes the truth of compassion, emulating God's action of justice.

The Point of Emphasis

A life that is without justice and mercy is empty and without meaning. Mercy tests our true spirituality and obedience.

The Relevant Question

Have you pondered the significance of mercy and justice?

---

5. Tozer, *Knowledge of the Holy*, 116.

A Prayer of Humble Mercy

Lord God, I need the anointing of the Holy Spirit to prepare and keep me focused on having a heart of justice, love, and mercy. Help me practice this needed word to show compassion and humility. Thank you for creating this gem and for sharing love with others. Amen.

DAY 7

The Pearl of Patience Shows Calmness

Be still in the presence of the Lord, and wait patiently for him to act. Don't worry about evil people who prosper or fret about their wicked schemes.
—Psalm 37:7 NLT

When you sit still and wait for God, it is the first act of faith. You learn how to implement and apply it with calmness. Pastors, ministers, and Christian educators must be examples of patience in their use and implementation. The Pearl of Patience relates to the previous Pearl, mercy, because God is patient and merciful. It also connects to the Pearl of Faith. The theological relevance is *waiting*. God is our refuge and strength when we are in trouble. Strength is a reality of resiliency (Ps 46:1). It is impossible to speak about patience without mercy and faith because they are biblically intertwined.

The worst mistake for you as a believer is to lack participatory patience, and the relationship with the Creator can be weakened due to the absence of patience. Patience is the test of spiritual resilience in the most daunting and challenging moments, particularly when faced with social and emotional interactions. It takes resiliency to sustain your focus while waiting. As a disciple, you must demonstrate resilience, as you are aware of the responsibilities that come with a purpose driven life. The purpose of this chapter on patience is to encourage believers to develop better patience skills and maintain a positive focus from day to day. Don't worry about the evils of the world, especially those in the communities where we live. As you experience evil interactions and oppositions, develop your theology of patience. Here is an example: *My theology of patience is to walk by faith in humility with God, focusing on the upward journey with the fortitude to see what the end will be.* Stay on track despite all odds against you and wait until things happen. Job talked to his friends but did not feel they were listening, so he decided to transition and speak directly to God: "But I desire to speak to the Almighty" (Job 13:3). You will know when to talk with God for a merciful response. Job's anxiety was changed for comfort because he said he would have to wait until his change came (Job 14:14). This change was the hope of the future resurrection before Christ was born, who brought all mercy with him as he went to the cross. Patience is the jewel of life and the Pearl of Hope. The strength of waiting is a benefit to experience. Those who are in leadership know the value of patience.

THE WILL TO WAIT ON GOD

We must have the spirit of waiting on God. You must have a strong constitution and the faith to wait on God no matter the circumstance. The prophet Isaiah wrote to the Jews in exile under the Babylonian captivity. If anyone needed mercy, they did. His message to them was vital for those who would wait on God to receive the benefits of renewing their strength and soaring like eagles without getting tired (Isa 40:31). Waiting on God is an honor. "It is an honor because there is happiness because God has a stalwart blessing for those who wait patiently for him."[1] Patience is the strength of survival, the source of hope, and the state of one's faith. David stresses the significance of being still in the presence of God; utilizing trust until there is an answer from God is the answer for the spiritual journey. The main thing is keeping the focus on God's direction and guidance. The present-day church must be resurrected from the clutches of impatience and acknowledge the robust arm of patience. We must know God to practice the virtue of patience. Job was the epitome of a servant who had a clinch on true patience and

1. Turner, *God Is a Strong Shelter*, 80.

had the resilience to withstand suffering. He was a personal witness to the significance of true patience through perseverance. He says, "I know that my redeemer lives, and that in the end he will stand on the earth" (Job 19:25). When one can wait like Job, the rewards are greater than stress and anxiety. Jehovah will provide strength day by day to experience the presence and power of God. The Creator remains with us in our willingness to witness the move of God during our survival. There are enduring tests among evil and sadistic confrontations. Don't become unfocused or distracted by the cunningness of the wicked. The Wisdom Pearl of Patience tells everything required for a closer and deeper walk with God. Patience is a spiritual jewel for development as a genuine servant.

PATIENCE IS A TEST AND A TESTIMONY

There are times when all of us are tested to the max regarding patience. In the long run, God has the answer and a plan to bring you through. The goal is to have the deep drive to persevere and face your challenges. Many people are always in a rush during the hustle and bustle of life. When I lived in New York, I used the subway many times. I noticed people were always moving fast. Waiting for the next train on the ramp was a tense experience. Many would walk over you. If you were in their way, you might get pushed onto the track of the oncoming train. That's just a snippet of impatience seen in action. Patience is a robust virtue in social, religious, and spiritual contexts. Impatience often drives us to make rash decisions. There are times when necessity dictates that we make decisions quickly. Therefore, patience can be both short-term and long-term in nature. It depends on the circumstances. Patience is not valued by time but by the quality of waiting. You must refrain from being anxious during the waiting period. If unable to withstand the rigor of anticipation, you can lose your footing and fall short of your goal. God gives the fortitude to keep pushing until something happens. No matter the task, stay the course. Patience is the most challenging action for you to adapt to amid distractions. Regardless of the slippery slopes of nature, God provides the energy and eagerness for you to trust God and walk by faith. During the moments of waiting, there will be some mental highs and lows. You must take the time to wait because "waiting is the core of faith for spiritual strength."[2] Have faith in God for guidance to conquer, hoping the highs outweigh the lows.

EFFECTIVE PATIENCE IS A BRIGHT GEM

Adequate patience is a spiritual gem that shines in your darkest moments. It charts the course of action in your life. One must be willing to wait and follow the strength of patience. For patience to be sufficient, you must be determined to persevere in any situation or circumstance. Joseph was another example in the Old Testament who displayed effective patience in delicate situations. God elevated him from servant to ruler. He had experienced harshness from his brothers and was sold into slavery (Gen 37:12–13). After being sold, he ended up being the prince of Egypt (Gen 42:6–8). The result of his patience was effective through God's protection and preserving grace. Adequate patience is the key to the longevity of resiliency, grit, and courage in facing challenging issues. It is built with the spiritual tools of relentlessness for all life challenges. The answer to waiting lies in God, his lead and answer. All one must do is wait patiently for the Lord.

REFLECTIVE SUMMARIZATION AND RESPONSES TO ACTION

The level of patience as a believer is a level of respect. This spiritual growth journey teaches the significance of waiting on God's lead and answer. It takes guts to maintain the formula for patience when all odds are against you. The Almighty has the answer for all your encounters, but you must hunker down and focus on preserving resiliency until the end. Some highs and lows will challenge your journey. Prayer, meditation, and living by the word are the formula for maintaining and implementing patience.

The Point of Emphasis

Utilizing trust is the answer for the spiritual journey.

2. Turner, *God Is a Strong Shelter*, 88.

The Relevant Question

What is the reason for your waiting?

A Prayer of Waiting

Oh, Lord God, grant us the strength to appreciate and practice patience, for it is the virtue of longevity. It is needed to combat the winding and wretched paths of life. Grant me peace to sit peacefully in my tent until the sunrise of hope and deliverance shines on my heart and confirms my answers. Amen.

DAY 8

The Pearl of Hope Prevents Despair

But those who hope in the Lord will renew their strength. They will soar on wings like eagles; they will run and not grow weary, they will walk and not be faint.

—Isaiah 40:31

There is always a bright future when hope is alive. The path of hope is an assurance from God to keep you alert in the face of challenges. You face opposition, challenges, tests, and trials on every occasion. All these reasons lead you to become a candidate for despair. Every time you think positively, Satan steps up to throw a monkey wrench in your path to cause you to stumble in despair. The theological relevance of the Pearl of Hope is *living faith*. Faith is the thread that keeps hope alive. You must constantly focus on your future goal to maintain hope. Isaiah prophesied that the compassion of God brought hope to the Israelites when they were in Egypt. The Egyptians were mean, harsh, and ruthless toward the Israelites. They pressed and pushed them to the max to break their spirit (Exod 1:13–14). Isaiah gave them hope that when they experience times of weakness and feel like they can't push through their pain and plight, "God will renew their strength" (Isa

40:31). It is well assured that the Israelites did not have to be weary and lose hope. The key to your hope is waiting patiently in God's direction, no matter the circumstance. Never give up, pursue and push to the end. One of the most assuring descriptions of hope is from the writer of Hebrews, who says, "Looking unto Jesus, the author and finisher of our faith, who for the joy that was set before Him endured the cross, despising the shame, and has sat down at the right hand of the throne of God" (Heb 12:2 NKJV).

You must have the endurance that Jesus had when he faced the cross. Endurance prepares you to conquer your crosses. The good news is that your hope is embedded in the reality of the power of the cross. I reflect on this line from the chorus of an old church hymn: "On Christ, the solid rock, I stand."[1] Just this one line from that hymn is a strong foundation for building your hope. It is a theological statement of exclusive dependability on Christ. The pain of your cross connects to the cross of Jesus because he suffered for your redemption. Jürgen Moltmann says, "The death of Jesus on the cross is the *centre* of all Christian theology."[2] His sufferings were those of grace at work on the cross. The grace of God is hope for our frailties. When you know what is essential, you live close to hope for your total dependence on the Almighty.

The strength and significance of hope is the essence of your theology. The above verse tells the story of Christ's determination to press forward, clinging to hope with joy. The longer you cling to hope, the stronger your courage ripens to keep anticipating God's movement. God provides hope to allow you to excel in faith. No matter the difficulty, you have the stamina to continue and will be assured that joy is on the way. The biblical meaning of hope is vast. However, the Hebrew word for "hope" in Isa 40:31 is *qavah*, which means "to wait, to look for, to hope, to expect."[3] It also means waiting with a twist. The longer you wait, the stronger you become. Hope in God is experiencing faith to the fullest. Hope is a resounding call to depend on God for the things we cannot see. It is a strong, binding, profound statement of depending on God for all your needs and never giving up. You must wait with an urgent expectation. The apostle Paul affirms, "And my God will

---

1. Mote, "My Hope Is Built."
2. Moltmann, *Crucified God*, 204.
3. Bible Hub, "Qavah."

supply every need of yours according to his riches in glory in Christ Jesus" (Phil 4:19 ESV). This verse solidifies how hope is genuine in Paul's ministry. He speaks from experience about how God delivered him through extenuating situations. You can be well assured that hope works because deep-seated faith prevents all weariness. Hope alone is a theology that brightens your path from dark moments of despair.

HOW HOPE BEGINS

The genesis of hope begins for many reasons and situations. Hope may start with you through frustration, unemployment, grief, obstacles, disappointments, or adverse medical reports, among other challenges. Whatever the reason, you must decide what fuels your hope. You may be thinking of a situation now where you are at your wits' end. Whatever causes you to have hope, at least you are heading in the right direction. It must be noted that Satan seeks to interrupt your hopeful moment, causing despair. It is not the end when and how hope begins, but how it ends with victory or God's answer for your endurance. Rest assured, there is a plan because you are not alone in your dilemma. No matter the size of your dilemma, hope is much broader and goes deeper.

WHY IS HOPE SO CRUCIAL?

Hope is crucial because it teaches us the importance of seeing God at work in challenging and awkward circumstances. Hope is the passport for your next journey, no matter the turbulence you experience. There will always be bumps, but God has blessings for your burdens. The profound story of hope is about Israel, who was under Pharaoh's servitude for 430 years. It was a bumpy ride. Pharaoh enslaved the Israelites and took advantage of their mandated service (Exod 1:11–14; 12:40–41). They were experiencing brutality, which gave them the eagerness to hope for deliverance. God called and assigned Moses to the burning bush to deliver them (Exod 3:1–5). The Israelites were hopeless until Moses appeared. Moses had the leaders in the camp sacrifice a lamb and put the blood over the doorpost, which was a sign of hope. They were spared when the firstborn of Egypt died; the blood saved them (Exod 12:13–28). What God did for Israel is a testimony of his miraculous power, grace, and favor. After Pharaoh's mandate to release them, hope settled in with excitement. They left, but blamed Moses for bringing them to die in the wilderness (Exod 14:11). That was a test for them, but God revived their hope when Moses said, "Stand still and see the salvation of the Lord" (Exod 14:13–14 NKJV). Regardless of the lack of faith, God kept favor alive so they could keep hope alive. Hope came alive again when the Egyptians pursued them into the Red Sea.

Moses continued to lead them, and they witnessed God leading them by a pillar of fire by night and a pillar of cloud by day (Exod 13:21). This experience is like a theology of deliverance through hope. Hope in the church is evident in God's guidance, as revealed through an individual's knowledge of the Red Sea. Hope is crucial because waiting includes patience. The Pearl of Patience is featured in the previous chapter but is particularly well-suited for this section. When Israel worked long hours for 430 years, they had to wait until God was ready to release them. What God did for Israel through Moses holds for you as well. Don't turn loose; keep waiting until Jehovah's mighty hand moves across the bewildered path to experience joy. When you grow weary, you will be sustained with renewed strength and be ready to thank God for deliverance. This chapter reminds me that God is capable of the impossible. If you keep hope alive, despair will not conquer.

REFLECTIVE SUMMARIZATION AND RESPONSES TO ACTION

Hope is the divine passport to travel to your next destination or your subsequent victory. What you do during your bumpy ride in life depends on how you see hope. Act by constant prayer, studying the word, and de-stressing to enjoy God's renewed strength. This forty-day journey is designed to plant hope so you can survive your daily confrontations, disappointments, frustrations, and the like.

The Point of Emphasis

No matter how complex your dilemma, hope is much deeper and broader.

The Relevant Question

Have you pondered God's blessings through the hope they bring?

A Prayer of Hope

Thank you, Eternal Spirit, for granting me the strength to keep close to hope in bewildered times. Hope gives me spiritual resilience to keep looking and maintain great anticipation of your guidance. Because of your grace and mercy, I conquered the beast of evil tactics to experience victory through your name. Amen.

PART TWO

Wisdom Pearls of Honest Living

The critical component of part two is to describe the DNA of negativity. The emphasis is on honest living and building integrity. Living honestly is a humanistic action of respect before God. Honest living reflects our character and involves recognizing God as the source of our existence. When one lives a dishonest lifestyle, it is useless and devalued by an authentic character. The dishonest lifestyle carries the DNA of negativity, lies, and unjust actions. We must all strive for an honest life, as it benefits us and glorifies God. Honesty builds respect, integrity, and a positive reputation. Honesty leads to having peace of mind amid many dishonest interactions with those we encounter. When one practices honesty, it pleases God. This section helps one to look beyond a world that lives in distrust and focus on the Eternal Spirit, the Creator, who shows grace and favor. The Pearls in this section embrace the righteousness of God so that the individual and the church can continue to be a resourceful support to all. This section serves as a reminder that honest living produces peace, humility, and integrity.

DAY 9

The Pearl of Justice Affirms Truth

But let justice roll on like a river, righteousness like a never-failing stream!
—Amos 5:24

When justice is done, it is a joy to the righteous but terror to evildoers.
—Proverbs 21:15

You must follow God's guidance on justice because it affirms truth. "Oh God, guide me to implement the Pearl of Justice toward others." The emphasis is that God will guide you to implement justice, as it is a fundamental and spiritual need for spiritual and social equality and equity. You are living in a world where justice is one-sided. Justice for some and no justice for everyone is a farce and a tragedy of injustice. Faithful justice is justice when it acknowledges that you are part of God's creation. The question is, How do you perceive what is justice? The Pearl of Justice challenges you to examine your lifestyle and the way you treat others. Into this fray, Amos points out a needed subject for righteous living. Amos's Scripture was the core of his message regarding divine justice. For Amos, justice is on a roll with an emphatic, righteous flow of life's equality streams. Your life is empty without the Pearl of Justice because justice is a requirement and criterion for spiritual enlightenment, growth, and strength. As you begin this day, a suggestive prayer: "Eternal God, embrace my heart, soul, and mind with anointed passion, advocating and implementing justice." Amos warns Israel of impending doom and the need for repentance. Reading and meditating on this passage will encourage you to practice a humble walk. You must understand God's judgment because God observes your actions and intentions. Amos sounded the justice alarm to remind the people that if repentance is not done, justice will roll like a river. Amos's message to Israel is to repent; if they do not, they will face judgment.

Amos was a minor prophet under Jeroboam II of Israel during the eighth century BC and a contemporary of Isaiah; his message advocated for equality and righteousness. This passage reminds us that God's justice is applicable today, just as it was in the eighth century BC. We should be encouraged to instill in others the importance of Jehovah's message of justice, which should flow like a river of life. Justice is translated as "judgment" in the King James version. It is God's judgment upon humanity that takes its course. However, everything is in God's hands because Amos was challenged to relay the message to Judah and Israel.

The world struggles to achieve equality because many perceive justice as one-sided. How can individuals understand the importance of unity? To adequately understand unity, we must view God's way of showing unity. Many on this earth lack the compassion to extend fair treatment to others. It seems so easy to advocate for injustice and overlook God's love. The psalmist says, "Blessed are those who act justly, who always do what is right" (Ps 106:3). When one begins a new day, one should consider treating everyone with love, compassion, and mercy.

APPLYING ROMANS 12:19

It would serve pastors and preachers well to encourage parishioners to advocate for equality. This passage in Romans challenges all to strive for a life of biblical integrity. There is no substitute for acts of justice, as they breed reciprocity. God requires and expects that we live in harmony. In many cases, that is hard for some people. Therefore, God is not telling us to do something beyond our capability, but to practice what we preach. The Pearl of Justice helps you to see the marvel of embedded truth. Many individuals want justice, but when it is time to implement it, they falter. We live in a dangerous world, and many do not wish for justice for all, but rather a one-sided coin that benefits them. Believers must follow the word and stand up for equality through love and compassion. The objective must be to let go of grudges and avoid evil. Many seek to get even because they live in a world were getting even is the norm. The apostle Paul emphasizes, "Do not take revenge, my dear friends, but leave room for God's wrath, for it is written: 'It is mine to avenge; I will repay,' says the Lord" (Rom 12:19). God is in charge and merciful, but God is also fair and just. There are keys in this verse that speak volumes. The first key is revenge as an act of God's nature.

DO NOT TAKE REVENGE

The key here is to keep peace and avoid revenge. Revenge leaves a negative mental mark that will haunt your conscience. It lacks merit and social grace. Simply put, social grace refers to the ability to interact with others respectfully. Don't be guilty by trying to get even and pay evil for evil (1 Pet 3:9; 1 Thess 5:5; Heb 10:30; see also Deut 32:35; Lev 19:18). Paul is saying that the Creator will render justice equally and honestly; that is authentic justice. In God's sight, justice is equality for all. Most importantly, justice is from God. We live in a society where people are angry, hurting, depressed, lonely, and disgusted because of injustice. Don't seek revenge from believers or unbelievers. It's not wise, and it's not beneficial. We must eradicate the gross odor of injustice and build justice with Christ. The second key in the verse is wrath.

LEAVE ROOM FOR GOD'S WRATH

It is impossible to handle what God does when badly treated or abused. It is a terrible feeling when you are lied to with inflammatory rhetoric, when it has spread like wildfire. God will not let any wrongdoing go unpunished. As you study the principles of this book, be honest and reflect on your conscience. God's wrath is much more dangerous than our evil. God's wrath is that he is against sin, iniquity, and vile behavior. He is holy and monitors evil activity because of his love for humanity.

The purpose of his wrath is to put things in perspective. The third key is "mine to avenge."

LEAVE ROOM FOR GOD TO AVENGE

God created us and knew our thoughts and actions. God says in Deut 32:35a, "It is mine to avenge; I will repay." When we observe God avenge, it is what God does that is for our benefit. He is willing and can pay. The main idea of this text is that the Creator will fight your battle. We fight our battles because of God's love and grace. Because of this divine protection, we should appreciate the Almighty's holy compassion.

FOLLOWING GOD'S EXAMPLE

I mentioned the Pearl of Love on day 1, but I use it here because it complements the Pearl of Justice. We were cut from God's mold to walk in his presence with dignity and spiritual pride. Following God is because of obedience and mature spiritual growth. It is wise to follow the path that Paul spoke about regarding Christ: "Follow God's example, therefore, as dearly loved children and walk in the way of love, just as Christ loved us and gave himself up for us as a fragrant offering and sacrifice to God" (Eph 5:1–2). Believers must replicate the above passage and live in the fragrance of high-intensity spirituality. God is well pleased when we maintain a fragrant relationship with the Lord and are fair and honest, showing compassion, respect, integrity, and equality to others. You will constantly be confronted with unjustifiable acts of injustice. These circumstances will not last; they prepare you for the next step. Participating in acts of justice pleases God (Prov 21:3). Trials and tribulations build character and provide spiritual strength and insight to see the road ahead by faith. You will not turn back when you follow your heart embedded in God's presence.

REFLECTIVE SUMMARIZATION AND RESPONSES TO ACTION

God's standards of justice are authentic. It is impossible to embrace some with justice and deny that others offend God. Following God's example sets the stage for believers and nonbelievers to engage in reciprocal interaction. Living honestly and showing equality to all pleases God. Trying to exact revenge on others violates God's word. The emphasis on implementing authentic justice represents the kingdom of God. Your action in the Pearl of Justice respects and fulfills God's divine plan.

The Point of Emphasis

We live in a world where justice is often one-sided.

The Relevant Question

How do you perceive what justice is?

A Prayer of Justice

Eternal God of mercy, guide my heart, mind, and soul to show justice to those who are treated unjustly. Help me to love those who are outcasts and to embrace them with your loving compassion, in your name. Amen.

DAY 10

The Pearl of Peace Comforts the Mind

Do not be anxious about anything, but in every situation, by prayer and petition, with thanksgiving, present your requests to God. And the Peace of God, which transcends all understanding, will guard your hearts and your minds in Christ Jesus.

—Philippians 4:6–7

Blessed are the peacemakers, for they will be called children of God.

—Matthew 5:9

The world is in a state of struggle, and peace seems far-fetched. In some places, it appears that peace is elusive because a war of bitterness and disrespect mars it. The above scriptures set the tone for peace advocacy. Situations will always be at the forefront of challenges. Paul makes it clear that the answer is to keep peace in your conscience. Take note of these words of a familiar saying: "If it's not one thing, it's another." The mind is lonely without peace. Peace solves problems by calming the nerves, alleviating emotional stress, and providing moments of deliberation.

Jesus urges his disciples to learn a positive lesson; he teaches, "Blessed are the peacemakers, for they will be called children of God" (Matt 5:9). The only way to live and implement peace as a disciple is by living the life of a disciple; peace is the central assertion for soul fulfillment. If peace is not on your mind, then the other option is war. You are either at war with yourself or others. I am reminded of a well-known hymn refrain, "It is well with my soul,"[1] by Horatio Spafford and Philip Bliss. Mr. Spafford lost his four daughters at sea. After much prayer, meditation, and reflection, the only deliverance to his grief was writing lyrics to a powerful church hymn, sung for over a century and a half. The Pearl of Peace is Jehovah's answer to hopelessness and frail moments in life.

In the Old Testament, the prophet Isaiah says, "And the effect of righteousness will be peace, and the result of righteousness, quietness, and trust forever" (Isa 32:17 ESV). Peace is laid out in God's word for your direction and hope, and hope is portrayed prophetically through Christ as a symbol of peace. The Hebrew word for "peace" is *shalom*. According to Strong, shalom means "safety, prosperity, well-being, intactness, and wholeness."[2] No worries; it sounds like wholeness is a sense of calm. The Greek word for "peace" is *eirene*. Strong says it means "peace, harmony, tranquility, safety, welfare, health; often with an emphasis on lack of strife or reconciliation in a relation, as when one has 'peace with God.'"[3] Humanity is constantly seeking comforting answers and solutions. Peace is not earned but granted by God's amazing grace in bewildering moments of pain. Remember, the apostle Paul testifies that "God can guard your hearts and minds in Christ Jesus" (Phil 4:7). Peace is the gem of comfort, a lifestyle of happiness and elegance. A comforting expression emphasizes that Jesus is our peace amid the dividing walls of hostility (Eph 2:14–22).

Those who seek to experience the road of peace seek a comforting pathway. It's a comforting pathway because "a mountain stream may begin as a trickle, but in time it can gather enough force to alter the landscape."[4] Regardless of the territory, there will always be significant obstacles set to test your faith. A dedicated disciple will always

---

1. Spafford, "When Peace, Like a River."
2. Strong, *Strongest*, 1968.
3. Strong, *Strongest*, 2008.
4. Yancey, *What's So Amazing*, xv.

overcome ruthless barriers, irrespective of the adverse life circumstances. Building a peaceful life is a road of trust in the God of mercy, hope, and faithfulness. God is eagerly awaiting requests for his blessings and comfort.

A MEANINGFUL STORY

I would like to share a meaningful story about what peace means to me. I was drafted in June of 1966 to join the US Army. When I opened the letter, I opened it with fear and trepidation. I opened the letter to report to the Naval Air Station in Jacksonville, Florida, in the fall of 1966. Soldiers in Vietnam were falling like flies because of an unpeaceful war. I had no choice but to report to the Naval Air Station. I had to defend my country for the sake of peace. I served in Korea instead of Vietnam. I was still in a combat zone. Being a soldier in a foreign country and maintaining a calm atmosphere and relationship with fellow soldiers was difficult. There were many close calls in Korea. My peace was to keep in touch with God, family, and friends. I hope my story will inspire you to trust God during trying times. God and Christ protected me and gave me hope in dire situations, and they will do the same for you. The military experience was a significant factor in living as a purpose driven disciple. I had a peaceful resolve because I lifted my eyes to the hills, and the hills were my focus on God. He did not let me slumber or sleep. In essence, God preserved my soul (Ps 121:1–13). My soul was at peace, and I had the comfort of mind and a heart of trust in God. The answer to all your circumstances will help you develop the life of a purpose driven disciple for the glory of God.

God wants you to be gentle, but most of all, to develop a closer relationship and fellowship. When we fellowship with God, we also fellowship with one another. Relationships and fellowship with God lead to peace. The apostle Paul says, "He will keep you firm to the end so that you will be free from all blame on the day our Lord Jesus Christ returns. God will do this, for he is faithful to what he says and has invited you into partnership with his Son, Jesus Christ our Lord" (1 Cor 1:8–9 NLT).

KEEPING UNITY ALIVE

Where there is unity, there is peace. However, there is always a gruesome rattle from Satan to interrupt peace and plot pain and misery. Since he is faithful and compassionate, you must be encouraged by what Paul said: "Whatever you have learned or received or heard from me, or seen in me—put it into practice. And the God of peace will be with you" (Phil 4:9). God's peace changes how you think, feel, and interact with others. All believers and nonbelievers must strive to live a peaceful life. However, believers are held responsible for being peacemakers. If you are a believer, you will understand the value and merit of what I am saying. The Pearl of Peace should become our consciousness and lifestyle as we touch lives. Peace must be the priority for living and be tagged by a faithful prayer life.

Jesus addressed the disciples regarding striving to become peacemakers: "God blesses those who work for peace, for they will be called the children of God" (Matt 5:9 NLT). The objective and goal of the believer is to remain peaceful in the face of all odds. The church must strive for unity and peace. Keeping peace is a requirement of the kingdom. One without peace is a miserable creature. There are several pertinent reasons why maintaining unity in the church and being a Christ-centered church can be so complex and challenging. We all have sinned and fallen short of God's glory. We allow Satan to block our intentions to forgive one another. Many have a superiority complex. Negative rigor, strife, and tension negate a loving transaction. Unity is at the crossroads of life, waiting for the opportunity of adoption to join a family of harmony. To preserve unity and peace, believers must ask the Holy Spirit to abolish negative actions that impede spiritual vigor.

A church that strives to keep unity is a church that is grounded in the Holy Spirit. It is a teaching church, a worshipping church, a social justice church, a church with a clear plan, a clear vision, and a clear mission. It does more than worship. It ministers to the needs of people, regardless of race or color.

THE FIGHT OF SPIRITUAL WARFARE

To fight the ongoing battle of spiritual warfare, you need to have a strong theology of peace. *My* theology of peace states that the Creator's passion encompasses my fragility, enabling me to attain hope amid hopeless situations. With the power of the Holy Spirit, I cling to God for guidance and a comforting resolution. A theology of peace validates your life as a disciple for living and implementing Wisdom Pearls, especially the Pearl of Peace. You need a solid and biblical theology of peace to navigate spiritual warfare effectively. Be on high alert and exercise caution in your movements. There are peacebreakers instead of peacemakers. A question and thought: Is peace the impossible reality? When peace seems to invade believers' consciousness, confrontations and antagonistic attacks are always in pursuit. Spiritual warfare is a constant battle of the mind to overthrow the spirit of calmness. It is on all fronts. The power and presence of God will drive believers to defend the Pearl of Peace adequately. Our defense depends on our spiritual maturity and faith when warfare attacks peace. Satan is the center of sadistic surprises that interfere with spiritual growth and peace in general. As stated earlier, Satan will appear disguised to divert attention from God and abolish your spiritual relationship and fellowship with God.

The apostle Paul declares the following about Satan's vile actions: "For Satan himself transforms himself into an angel of light. Therefore, it is no great thing if his ministers also transform themselves into ministers of righteousness, whose end will be according to their works" (2 Cor 11:14–15 NKJV). Jesus is our Savior and King and sets the importance of peace and happiness above detestable actions and intimidation. Therefore, spiritual warfare is a historical encounter against the spiritual realm. The lack of peace is a significant story because "the problem of history is the impotence of the good against the evil forces in history."[5] Believers must be an example to others, moving ahead with the drive to make their spiritually driven life fruitful.

COMMITMENT TO GOD TO ADVOCATE PEACE

Every time you show that peace is the way, God is pleased, and it is a sure sign that you are willing to abide by the word to encourage others to avoid trouble, disgust, and disrespect. There are characteristics regarding your spiritual walk that God monitors daily. One characteristic is having a humble spirit, and another is the spirit of prayer. Making peace

---

5. Niebuhr. *Human Destiny*, 19.

is significant because God provides spiritual backing and support. Jesus declares that he will give you peace. It is not the way the world gives it to you. Do not let your hearts be troubled, and don't be afraid. That is the authentic support available (John 14:27). With this pledge in mind, the commitment to peace is foundational in the word and theologically sound.

REFLECTIVE SUMMARIZATION AND RESPONSES TO ACTION

As an authentic believer, you aim to seek peace at all costs. It takes determination, love, integrity, and patience to arrive at a sensible resolve for a happy medium. Striving to eliminate tension and strife will always be beneficial. Whatever the task, strive to excel and move forward with a vital peace action plan despite obstacles. When and where the obstacles invade your space, your resolve is to follow the Scripture and be the peacemaker God calls you to be. Advocating peace is lifting the word to action and sharing with others what God is doing to unite individuals and countries.

The Point of Emphasis

Where there is unity, peace resides, accompanied by a positive message.

The Relevant Question

Is peace the impossible reality?

A Prayer for Peace

Everlasting God, here I am. I am a willing servant who desires to keep peace with all humans. If there is no peace, there is no joy. Instill in me a bubbling heart to encourage others to implement peace with all humankind, in Jesus' name. Amen.

DAY 11

The Pearl of Obedience Reflects Love

If you love me, obey my commandments.

—John 14:15 NLT

Only be very careful to observe the commandment and the law that Moses the servant of the Lord commanded you, to love the Lord your God, and to walk in all his ways and to keep his commandments and to cling to him and to serve him with all your heart and with all your soul.

—Joshua 22:5 ESV

Obedience is the genuine factor of honoring God's instruction. It is the moment to listen and find divine direction. Reflecting on obedience challenges everyone to make a sincere determination to love, walk, and keep Jehovah's commandments as servants. It is prudent always to obey God. You must remember that obeying God provides a spiritual safety net that is linked to keeping his commandments. When you break away from keeping the commandments, there is imminent danger. The Pearl of Obedience validates believers as genuine and authentic followers of Christ and worshipers of God. Obedience binds love through the obedient action plan, adhering to the compliant command. Love is essential for remaining obedient to his glory—obedience's biblical and theological foundation charts the path to fruitful living. Individuals who do not obey God live a toxic lifestyle of rebellion and defiance. It is urgent to remain focused on combatting attacks and distractions in the path of obedience. One of the Greek words for "obedience" is *hupakoé*, which means submissiveness and compliance (Rom 1:5).[1] You must remain obedient in your faith to your Maker and Savior. Obedience is the running thread from Genesis to Revelation. It emphasizes how God deals with his people. The love of God is seen in one's lifestyle of striving to keep his commandments in every action and interaction in life. Love encourages you to seek spirituality, to keep the commandments, and look for a transformative analysis of blending love and obedience to walk with God. Therefore, obedience becomes the apex of holiness and faithful honoring of the Creator. The law of Moses is the biblical and theological foundation of the guiding principle of authentic and faithful servanthood. John's Gospel links to the law of Moses to solidify the significance of implementing God's directive for obeying the commandments. If there is little or no obedience, then there is no validity to claim to live a godly life of the power and Pearl of Obedience. Obedience itself makes a profound statement of godly respect and reverence. Speaking of reverence, one cannot be genuine without evidence of a valid spiritual life. Deep down in your consciousness, you must consider God's words, as exemplified by Samuel, who conveyed a crucial message to King Saul regarding obedience and sacrifice. Here is the candor of the conversation: "But Samuel replied, 'What is more pleasing to the Lord: your burnt offerings and sacrifices or your obedience to his voice? Listen! Obedience is better than sacrifice, and submission is better than offering the fat of rams'" (1 Sam 15:22 NLT). Obedience far outweighs burnt offerings and sacrifices because the context touches and moves the heart of God. Obedience is better than sacrifice because it is deeply connected to God's reverential mandate. How are obedience and sacrifice related to honoring God?

Both must show humble submission, and the result is that God is expecting complete honor. You must not fall into rebellion and disappoint God's mandates. The danger is that rebellion can lead to a stark arrogance, which can damage your spirituality. Arrogance and

---

1. Bible Hub, "Hupakoé."

rebellion are closely associated for the same purpose of refusing to practice obedience. Arrogance is a proud behavior related to rebellion, characterized by an excessive sense of self-importance and a disregard for obedience. Obedience places one on a different plane and adds respect to the need to obey God, regardless of the situation and circumstances. Obedience is a humble test of faith that pleases Jehovah. When one decides to overlook obedience, it is often due to an inflated ego that focuses on self and exhibits negative behavior. Positive behavior helps one to implement Josh 22:5, be willing to undertake noble feats, and listen to the voice of God. Listening to the voice of God propels one's faith and trust, enabling one to remain faithful to the cause of Christ. Obedience helps believers live the life of a purpose driven disciple.

SERVING GOD

How one can serve God is a profound question. I propose that it is impossible to serve God without obedience. I say that because serving the Creator is linked with love. Serving is a significant factor in obedience. The Bible says, "Only fear the Lord and serve him faithfully with all your heart. For consider what great things he has done for you" (1 Sam 12:24 ESV). Obedience is a key success factor, and when obedience is followed, it brings God's favor. Serving the Creator through obedience is a humble action of love. Therefore, life is unsustainable without the obedience factor. The lack of compliance leads to the road of failure. When one decides to walk by faith, they live with a heavenly perspective and will use the Creator's grace for their journey. It is impossible to please God without obedience. Adam and Eve broke God's divine law by being disobedient in the garden of Eden (Gen 2:16; 3:11). "The whole redemption of Christ is restoring obedience to its place."[2] Implementing obedience helps believers reach their goal for eternity.

Paul was determined to press toward the prize of a higher calling, eternity (Phil 3:14). I am reminded of the apostle Paul's mention of Epaphroditus, a coworker and missionary, who cared for his needs (Phil 2:25–29). This experience serves as an example and a lesson in genuine obedience. That is why Paul said in his final exhortation to the Philippians that it is beneficial to always rejoice in the Lord, and because of obedience, the results will earn God's favor (Phil 4:4–7).

---

2. Murray, *Blessing of Obedience*, 11.

When obedient, believers will experience God's favor for spiritual development and will never lack his blessings. Paul shares a marvelous testimony of God's sufficiency. His travels in Macedonia and Thessalonica (Phil 4:15–16) confirm Jehovah's love, grace, and mercy, which is evident through the church at Philippi. Here is the profound testimony of God's providence: "And this same God who takes care of me will supply all your needs from his glorious riches, which have been given to us in Christ Jesus" (Phil 4:19 NLT). This verse encapsulates the essence of authentic sufficiency through obedience.

THE PURPOSE OF OBEDIENCE

The purpose of obedience is to remain in God's will. Obedience is necessary for spiritual growth. It is the reason for developing an intimate relationship with the Savior. And to keep us on track. All of us must be reminded that the eyes of the Eternal Creator watch us and watch over us. The prophet Isaiah appealed to Judah to acknowledge their condition and sins, and to come clean before God. Here is what is said: "'Come now, let us settle the matter,' says the Lord. 'Though your sins are like scarlet, they shall be as white as snow; though they are red as crimson, they shall be like wool. If you are willing and obedient, you will eat the good things of the land, but if you resist and rebel, you will be devoured by the sword.' For the mouth of the Lord has spoken" (Isa 1:18–20). God's compassionate love is guaranteed to release us and give grace for our wayward actions. That was the state of Judah's mindset. Today, we have the same opportunity to experience God's favor in forgiving our sins. Therefore, we must seek to remain obedient. Therefore, being obedient is never a mistake. It will always shine in your favor, because it is another way of telling the truth as you follow the divine command of God.

REFLECTIVE SUMMARIZATION AND RESPONSES TO ACTION

Obedience sets the stage for your spiritual walk and relationship with God. It is a practice to make sure you are honoring God in obedience. The objective of obedience is to remain in God's will regardless of the circumstances you encounter. It is a key factor in maintaining total compliance with Jehovah. Your response to this action should be to evaluate your relationship with the Creator and assess your spiritual standing. This Pearl reminds you to be determined to submit to God and be available to show sacrifice and obedience in the same vein. Seek to understand and implement the biblical and theological foundational principles stated in the Scriptures.

The Point of Emphasis

Obedience is the genuine factor of honoring God's instruction.

The Relevant Question

How are obedience and sacrifice related to honoring God?

A Prayer for Obedience

Everlasting Creator, I am deeply grateful for the spiritual strength that you have bestowed upon me, enabling me to live an honorable life. You have helped me to live by faith and trust in your grace and mercy, allowing me to live obediently. I sincerely seek your guidance to keep your commandments by obeying your word, following your will, and encouraging others in the body of Christ to live obediently. Help me to be committed to honoring your word and pleasing you in every way. Amen.

DAY 12

The Pearl of Contentment Revitalizes Your Outlook

But I rejoiced in the Lord greatly, that now at last your care of me hath flourished again; wherein ye were also careful, but ye lacked opportunity. Not that I am speaking of being in need, for I have learned to be content in whatever situation I am. I know how to be brought low, and I know how to abound. In any and every circumstance, I have learned the secret of facing plenty and hunger, abundance and need. I can do all things through him who strengthens me.

—Philippians 4:10–13 KJV

The Pearl of Contentment is the life that brings complete satisfaction. It revitalizes your outlook and refocuses your journey. This meditative Pearl of Contentment is designed to help you live close to Jehovah and develop an intimate relationship for a closer walk. It is a fresh start that de-stresses your spirit. It is a time when you do not complain but accept circumstances and situations as they are. Paul gives a classic lesson on contentment from the above Scripture (Phil 4:11–12). Contentment is relative to peace, producing the same objective, satisfaction. The Greek word translated as "content" in Phil 4:11 is *autarkés*. Autarkés is an adjective, and its literal meaning is self-sufficiency.[1] Self-sufficiency means being independent and adequately satisfied with one's resources. The above verse in the King James version has an intimate touch of words that gives a guided expression of profound thought. It is a test of heart, mind, and soul.

The Pearl of Contentment is a Pearl that connects us to trust and faith in God, enabling us to understand and accept life's challenges amid trying times, regardless of the difficulty. The apostle Paul undertook numerous missionary tours, and things were not always cooperative. However, Paul learned to adjust to opposition during challenging moments. He trusted God in all situations, and the church in Philippi. They always provided the necessary resources for Paul to survive. He said he knows what it means to be in need. The modern-day church must trust God for everything. There must be passion in the heart of believers for personal devotion. Personal devotion must be the essence of deep love for the Creator and appreciating how God makes a way when things seem dull and impossible. One of the running themes of this forty-day spiritual growth journey is *making everyday count* and making them count with each Pearl. Therefore, contentment is high on the list, regardless of the tides of anxiety. Don't give up because happiness is sure to come.

CONTENTMENT AND WORSHIP

Contentment is the authentic life that God seeks. It is life that one must eagerly apply to worshipping God genuinely. The Pearl of Contentment prepares you to worship God as you wade through the tides of anxiety before happiness is revealed; again, revitalization sets in for optimum action. Authentic worship is impossible without the mind and heart of contentment. One must have a free mind, heart, and purpose to please the Eternal Spirit through worship and spiritual edification. "For God is Spirit, so those who worship him must worship in spirit and truth" (John 4:24 NLT). This verse identifies genuine believers who have a heart for spiritual interaction and adoration of God through the Holy Spirit. In short, this verse means to keep worship alive. None of us can worship with clogged minds and hearts. Our minds need to be clear so

---

1. Bible Hub, "Autarkés."

that the Holy Spirit can minister to us, making personal contact with the God of grace.

Consequently, we must have satisfied minds as we worship truthfully and honor fully. Contentment breeds conversation with our Creator and Savior. It is a constant prayer to remain connected and relevant during authentic worship. While we worship the Holy Spirit ministers, and Jesus makes intercession for us because he is the living Savior, pleading for us with much groaning (Rom 8:26–27; Heb 7:25). When we are in our devotion, sometimes people move from "worship to praise." Regarding worship and praise, let me be clear with distinction. Praise and worship are related but different. Worship is bowing down and adoring God; worship is an intense attitude of heart, honoring the Creator. In Ps 96:9, the psalmist states, "Worship the Lord in the splendor of his holiness; tremble before him, all the earth." Praise is an initial expression of opening, and worship is entering the presence of God with spiritual integrity. Worship is more corporate, and praise is more personal.

For example, let us come and worship him. Praise is more of a personal interaction with what God has done; it does not have to be heard by others; however, when God has done something for you, there will be a grand expression of praise and hallelujah, which can't be hidden. No one can orchestrate praise; the direction of the Holy Spirit must do it. David danced before the Lord with all his might (2 Sam 6:14–22; 1 Chr 15:29). David seemed to be praising and worshiping in one setting. He went all out to praise God. Authentic praise is when one feels the direction and leading of the Holy Spirit. Therefore, one must be spiritually driven to praise and worship God.

THE POWER OF CONTENTMENT

The power of contentment is the message of mere satisfaction, and it is immanent in Phil 4:12–13. Paul says, "I know what it is to be in need, and I know what it is to have plenty. I have learned the secret of being content in any and every situation, whether well-fed or hungry, whether living in plenty or want. I can do all this through him who gives me strength." It is the prominence that what a believer has may not mean that many people are happy, but they fully accept their situation and learn to be as satisfied as possible. There is no time for complaint or compromise. Have you experienced the power of contentment? If you have, then you can attest the following statement: Contentment has a thread of deep faith and theology. It confirms total trust in the Creator and leaves no room for worry. The hymn "I Know Who Holds Tomorrow"[2] embodies robust contentment because true contentment has a driving energy to remain resilient through all opposition.

The title of that hymn assures that once saved, you will never be disappointed, because Jehovah will carry you to the end. It is the kind of power that does not allow one to be intimidated or manipulated, or for evil to have sway over one's mind. The fundamental principle of contentment is to draw closer to God in the long run, even amid challenging circumstances. William Barclay, in his book *In the Hands of God*, sums up contentment; he says, "Outward, onward and upward—these are the directions of the Christian's life."[3] An unsatisfied life does not experience the power of contentment because of a miserable life, and a wretched life can lead to dangerous and destructive behavior. When you are satisfied and calm, you will have joy. This kind of joy is joy that gives strength to a deplorable situation.

REFLECTIVE SUMMARIZATION AND RESPONSES TO ACTION

The main idea of contentment emphasizes satisfaction and peace of mind. If you are not satisfied and do not have a calm and peaceful mind, then be encouraged and know that Paul said that whatever state of mind you are in, accept and trust God. There is rejoicing when you have a calm spirit. You leave no room for worry, because you see things as they are.

The Point of Emphasis

Contentment is rooted in a deep faith and theology.

---

2. Stanphill, "I Know."
3. Barclay, *In the Hands of God*, 109.

The Relevant Question

Have you experienced the power of contentment?

A Prayer for Contentment

Thank you, Lord, for your blessing of contentment. Being content encourages me to live a spiritually driven life by heeding the Pearl of Contentment. Help me to accept my situation and live by trust and faith, so that I may continue to receive your blessing of a satisfied mind, regardless of my delicate circumstances. Amen.

DAY 13

The Pearl of Humility Builds Character

If my people, who are called by my name, will humble themselves and pray and seek my face and turn from their wicked ways, then I will hear from heaven, and I will forgive their sin and will heal their land.

—2 Chronicles 7:14

Humble yourselves in the presence of the Lord, and He will exalt you.

—James 4:10 NASB

Humility is the hallmark of the believer's relationship with Jehovah and others. The Pearl of Humility serves as the foundation for receiving God's favor while developing one's character. As believers, you must strive to recognize that humility is a fundamental core value that fosters self-awareness and helps you avoid a superiority complex. Humility is the core of your spirituality and leadership. It represents your character, and your character breeds integrity and honesty. It is impactful and tests your ability to realize when you are wrong and to admit it with humility. When that happens, genuine character touches the heart of God.

The Bible calls for character *to be in the right mind*. The right mind is described in Phil 2:4–5: "Let each of you look not only to his interests, but also to the interests of others. Have this mind among yourselves, which is yours in Christ Jesus" (RSV). Moreover, the right mind is characterized by humility. Don't do anything without humility because it is the cornerstone of your walk. It takes a severe believer to succumb to the Pearl of Humility. God has blessed this Pearl for a life of fruitfulness and purpose. This text is a message to God, posing a question in 2 Chr 7:14. It is a question that one should hold onto, acknowledging God's sovereign will and walking in humility. This text is a message of encouragement to obey and to live in humility. God spoke to ancient Jews, and this text applies to modern Jews and the modern-day church. Promises were made to the Jews through Solomon's message that he would honor his favor from heaven if they showed humility. When we claim God's presence, we must match our humility and prayer with fervor under the favor of the Creator. God blessed you with the spirit of humility; it comes with your spiritual anointing to remind you through the Holy Spirit to walk humbly before God (Amos 6:8). The question is, How do we live in humility? To live in humility is to live under the anointing and guidance of the Holy Spirit.

Paul encourages Timothy to "stir up the gift of God which is in you" (2 Tim 1:6 KJV). Stirring up the gift is the gift of the Holy Spirit that God gave you. In the case of Timothy, it was to stir up the gift of pastoral leadership. Stirring up the gift is associated with humility for the work of ministry. Humility is authentic when the gift of God is spiritually operative. God does not use those who live lofty lives because it is the opposite of humility. Jehovah seeks humility in his people to build character and reputation. Humility tells what one is and how one acts and interacts. It shows that one is willing to send a message of refraining from unnecessary confrontation. The Pearl of Humility demonstrates remarkable strength and compassion in even the most challenging circumstances.

THE SIGNIFICANCE OF HUMILITY

The significance of humility is the nature of the individual's heart, mind, and soul. It does not mean one is weak, but rather possesses the attitude of spirituality. Humility means being able to wait and remain patient during difficult times. It is an ongoing essential for spiritual growth and development. The test of humility is when one worships the Creator. Paul encouraged the church in Rome to practice humility through the guidance of the Holy Spirit. "Live in harmony with one another. Do not be proud but be willing to associate with people of low position. Do not be conceited" (Rom 12:16). This Pearl teaches and encourages us to push to love one another and never look down on others because we feel insignificant. It is essential to reflect and revisit our actions, considering how we can walk and live in pure humility. Humility is a chance to submit to God and humanity in a spirit of lowliness. Therefore, Murray says, "Humility is the bloom and beauty of holiness."[1] His statement affirms the actual birth of true humility; it is from the bosom of God that we are inclined to pursue this essential Pearl for authentic discipleship. True humility is a profound expression of love in its highest form. It charts the believer's course in life. It is the epitome of integrating spirituality, honoring and respecting God for the good of servanthood. Genuine believers must walk in humility, talk with humility, and lead with humility. One of the greatest servants of humility was Mother Teresa. She was a living legend for making statements about the ministry and mission of humility.

UNDERSTANDING AND APPLYING PHILIPPIANS 2:3-4

This passage is one of the most critical passages in Philippians. The difficulty of this passage is about vain conceit. It does not mean one should seek perfection, nor does it mean avoiding one's ambitions. It does not imply that avoiding vain deceit is easy. Paul encourages the church at Philippi to put others above themselves. It is difficult to put others above yourself because it seems you are leaving yourself out. There is much more to this passage. Let us examine the passage in an expositional manner to extract its meaning. "Do nothing out of selfish ambition or vain conceit. Rather, in humility, value others above yourselves, not looking to your interests but each of you to the interests of the others."

It is not healthy or wise to think about oneself as a way of self-elevation. Selfish ambition is the sign of a haughty spirit. A haughty spirit is the spirit of pride that supports superiority. A classic Scripture

---

1. Murray, *Essential Andrew Murray Collection*, 65.

on haughtiness is in Luke 18:10–14. Two men went into the temple to pray, a Pharisee and a publican; the Pharisee thanked God he was more religious than other people, and the publican beat upon his chest and did not look up to heaven. The Pharisee lacked humility because he believed he had reached a spiritual pinnacle.

Furthermore, the apostle Paul encourages the church to value humility and consider the interests and well-being of others: "Do nothing out of selfish ambition or vain conceit. Rather, in humility value others above yourselves, not looking to your own interests but each of you to the interests of the others" (Phil 2:3–4). Reaching out to them brings hope amid difficulty. To fully understand this passage, it is essential to investigate the Greek word for "vain conceit" or "vainglory." King James uses vainglory; we are using a verse from the NIV, which includes conceit. The Greek word is *kenodoxia*, meaning empty pride.[2] In essence, it is a false sense of pride with a haughty morality. It has no meaning, substance, or profundity. The above passages illustrates the nature of applying humility at its best. After exploring this passage, you will have the urgency to make an application as you cherish this Wisdom Pearl. This passage encourages you to keep the purpose driven disciple life at center stage.

HOW TO BUILD A CHRISTLIKE CHARACTER

Developing a Christlike character cannot be done by one's own volition. It can't be achieved through good deeds alone, but only by following the directions stated in Scripture. A Christlike character is essential for spiritual identification concerning your inner personality. Representing Christ is paramount to your godly lifestyle. Character is the complete story of your persona and the validity of your conscience. Many terms are used to describe the development of a Christlike character. Still, I propose five essentials to validate and develop a Christlike character: ethics, humility, integrity, justice, and love. These essentials are biblical. Jesus said Christian *ethics* is how you live, what you are, and what you do. It is your moral character. Jesus advocates that the ethical life glorifies God (Matt 5:44–45). The objective is to represent God genuinely. *Humility* is the key essential. James says, "Humble yourselves before the Lord, and he will lift you" (Jas 4:10).

2. Bible hub, "Kenodoxia."

The next important Pearl is *integrity*. Integrity is vital for spirituality; it is, in a sense, a part of ethics. The Bible emphasizes the importance of doing good regardless of your situation. You may have to suffer, but have a good conscience when you are slaughtered (1 Pet 3:13–18). *Justice* is one of the Pearls, but it is necessary to lift it here. As you build character, remember to implement justice. Jesus quotes Isa 61:1–2 in Luke 4:18–19.

The Spirit was on him because he had to preach good news to people experiencing poverty, release the captives, and give sight to the blind. Justice is treating all people the same. I discussed *love* at length in the first chapter. However, it fits this Pearl for greater significance. Genuine Christian character is strengthened by love. Jesus responded to the teachers of the law regarding the greatest commandment. He replied that the greatest commandment is to love the Lord your God with all your mind and soul, and the second is to love your neighbor as you love yourself. Jesus was direct with his answer. (Mark 12:28–31). Jesus embodied the above essentials during his ministry. God's will for us is to learn from Jesus' examples. He was interacting with his disciples regarding the anticipation of his death. Thomas confessed that they did not know what to do when the time came for him to leave them. Christ perceived that they needed hope; Jesus answered, "I am the way and the truth and the life. No one comes to the Father except through me" (John 14:6). Character building takes time. It does not happen quickly. There are necessary experiences that build our courage and faith. When it seems like you are sinking and drifting, remember the words of the psalmist: "I lift my eyes to the hills. From whence does my help come? My help comes from the Lord, who made heaven and earth" (Ps 212:1–2 RSV). Keep looking up and learning!

REFLECTIVE SUMMARIZATION AND RESPONSES TO ACTION

The life of a purpose driven disciple is a test that encourages one to change perspective for positive responses to action. It is necessary to implement the key essentials for building a Christlike character. A Christlike character identifies one who walks in humility and understands the significance of true spirituality. As a believer, you must follow the examples Jesus teaches and references in the Scriptures. Doing what Jesus did will always be beneficial and prudent for implementing the significance of humbleness.

The Point of Emphasis

Humility is a statement of genuine spirituality.

The Relevant Question

Have you grown in humility since your last negative encounter?

A Prayer of Humility

Thank you, eternal God, the God of the universe who executes sovereignty in the core of divine providence, for watching over me and guiding me to live humbly for spiritual growth and development. I seek the eagerness to be passionate in your name. It is my prayer to live in humility. Amen.

DAY 14

The Pearl of Honesty Is Pure Religion

Those who consider themselves religious and yet do not keep a tight rein on their tongues deceive themselves, and their religion is worthless. Religion that God our Father accepts as pure and faultless is this: to look after orphans and widows in their distress and to keep oneself from being polluted by the world.

—JAMES 1:26–27

The Pearl of Honesty confirms pure religion. God requires you to give him a religion unmixed with worldly additives. God is not interested in impure thoughts and actions. It is a vital spiritual essential for authentic growth. A disciple has no integrity without practicing honesty. God expects pure and faultless actions and never overlooks those who are disadvantaged. The purpose driven disciple encourages the genuine believer to live an authentic and honest lifestyle. The above verse is one of the spiritual benchmarks for living a purpose driven disciples life. James says that if the tongue is untamed, it will cause one's religion to experience a spiritual collision, leading to a total loss of purpose. James is honest and does not use the word religion loosely. We are responsible for ministering to and caring for the orphans and widows.

GOD GIVES FAVOR TO THOSE WHO PRACTICE PURE RELIGION AUTHENTICALLY

Pure religion pleases God because the Pearl of Honesty intertwines with integrity. Both terms focus on the same objective: being truthful in actions and behavior. The life of any believer will crumble without integrity and honesty. The Greek word for "honesty" is *semnos*, which means honorable and venerable.[1] The Bible teaches and emphasizes the importance of being truthful, avoiding lies, cheating, stealing, conniving, and deceiving (Lev 19:11; Exod 20:16). Practicing a life of dishonesty destroys character and damages one's spirituality. The following Scripture teaches how God feels about dishonesty: "He that worketh deceit shall not dwell within my house: he that telleth lies shall not tarry in my sight" (Ps 107:1 KJV). Honesty sets the stage for the spiritual walk and the spiritually driven life. An old proverb says "Honesty is the best policy." In this devotion, reflecting and thinking about the core meaning of honesty is essential. The word "honest" comes from the Greek word *kalos*, an adjective meaning that which is fair, right, and honorable.[2] Having a good heart and striving for spiritual purity are crucial in God's eyes (Luke 8:15). God created us to live honestly. That is why Adam and Eve were made in a state of innocence (Gen 2:4–25).

The spiritual life is useless without living honestly. Dishonesty lacks authenticity, credibility, and reliability. Therefore, God's will requires that people be honest. Dishonesty is stealing, taking something from someone without asking for it or buying it. Dishonesty serves no meaningful purpose in an authentic spiritual life. One must live and walk in the doctrine of truth as laid out by Christ. Jesus said, "Ye shall know the truth, and the truth shall make you free" (John 8:32 KJV). The Pearl of Honesty is contagious, and those who interact with honest folks will be inspired and encouraged to take positive actions. Religion is a way of life. Honesty is a way of life. Engaging with this subject prompts one's conscience to reconsider honest actions. James is the prime example of a servant who ministered to the tribes. His approach was honest. James was serious about getting people to live the right way. He realized that believers must maintain a contagious spirit, regardless

---

1. Vine, *Expository Dictionary*, 229.
2. Vine, *Expository Dictionary*, 229.

of their past trials and tribulations. James did not waste time embellishing and refining what he was going to say to the twelve tribes who were scattered abroad. His greeting refers to the Hebrew Christians outside Palestine. Their meeting place was the synagogue. These Jewish believers were plagued with problems testing their faith, and James was concerned that they were succumbing to impatience, bitterness, materialism, disunity, ceremonial defilement, and spiritual apathy. As a Jerusalem resident and a church leader, James no doubt had frequent contact with Jewish Christians from several Roman provinces. He was highly concerned and felt the need to encourage them in their need for faith. Their faith had weakened, and they were uncertain about their beliefs. They did not know the meaning of religion.

The apostle James was honest in telling them the truth about pure religion. They were entwined with contamination. Contamination has infiltrated the world's core, compromising its ability to function productively and vibrantly. It is poisonous and has affected individuals, families, institutions, governments, and churches. The church has the authority, ability, anointing power, and responsibility to change the world's course through a contagious evangelism, discipleship, and stewardship plan. The church must respond to the community's woes throughout the lifeline to rescue a drifter and wanderer. To know the truth is to walk the truth and be truthful.

A DISHONEST TRANSACTION

A dishonest transaction displeases God. One of the prime examples of dishonesty is illustrated in the lives of Ananias and Sapphira in the book of Acts, chapter 5. Ananias and Sapphira, a married couple, attempted to deceive the apostles by lying to the Holy Spirit, retaining part of the proceeds from the sale of their real estate (Acts 5:1–11). Their action was dishonest, impure, and dangerous—an impure act regarding their religion. Ananias could not bridle his tongue. He must have thought that the Holy Spirit was not listening. The early church in Jerusalem is the center of discussion. At the end of chapter 4, the decision was made concerning personal finances to be given to the church. Honesty and integrity were born from the same stock, and truth is the epitome of such essentials.

Therefore, Ananias and Sapphira devalued honesty and integrity by lying. They violated ethical actions and morality. Solomon succinctly states, "The integrity of the upright guides them, but their duplicity destroys the unfaithful" (Prov 11:3). Ananias and Sapphira lacked honesty and integrity, which is why they failed the truth principle. The upright follows the guidance of the Holy Spirit to maintain the spirit of honesty and integrity. Their case was a case of deceitful tragedy. *Honesty* and *integrity* balance the complexity of profound thinking because they are words that encompass the heart and the issues of life. Honesty rests in the minds of individuals who value and honor Jehovah amid the negative influence of cunning individuals. Honest individuals are knit to the heartbeat of God's presence. Servants of God must strive to maintain a life of authentic and safe words of conversation, especially in a world that is bewildered by wayward, sadistic actions designed to distract one from upholding integrity. Believers must be careful to avoid the tricks of character debasement from cunning individuals that can cause spiritual derailment and embarrassment. Jesus was candid with the disciples regarding the significance of a respectful life; he said, "I am the way, the truth, and the life" (John 14:6). This Pearl reminds all believers to make it a priority to begin each day with the spiritual anointing and seek to walk by faith and walk with honesty.

REFLECTIVE SUMMARIZATION AND RESPONSES TO ACTION

Living an honest life is pleasing to God. God expects genuine believers who practice purity. Avoid and stay away from the contaminated lifestyle. Ananias and Sapphira were terrible examples of impure religion. They had bad intentions and were not sincere about their actions and behavior. The bad choice they made was a deceitful tragedy that ended their life. Being untrue to the Holy Spirit causes danger that leads to destruction.

The Point of Emphasis

Honesty sets the stage for spirituality and the purpose driven disciple.

The Relevant Question

What do you think about the negative impact of dishonesty?

A Prayer of Honesty

This day, eternal God, is another day that I long to seek your face in righteousness and cry out to you for guidance and to experience your presence. Teach me and guide me in living with honesty. Jehovah God, thank you for instilling honesty in my heart, soul, and mind to live and walk in peace, in your name. Amen.

DAY 15

The Pearl of Dedication Is a Sacred Promise

Therefore, my beloved brothers, be steadfast, immovable, always abounding in the work of the Lord, knowing that in the Lord your labor is not in vain.

—1 Corinthians 15:58

Stay attached to God for some tremendous biblical vision for your life on this earth, and don't let go until you have it from his merciful hand. There are no substitutes for dedication. A life of dedication is a reminder to practice walking in the spiritual life. You must be spiritually prepared to survive the journey and meet the standards of the kingdom. This utmost reading on day fifteen is the essence of a genuine spiritual relationship of dedication for an authentic walk with God. Dedication is a theological word expressed in the above verses that tests your faith to inspire the discipleship journey. The more profound theological relevance lies in the custom of dedicated houses of prayer, Bibles, crosses, and pews used for worship, all for the glory of God. A higher level of dedication is following the above verses, in which we dedicate our bodies, minds, and hearts to the Creator.

Consequently, Biblical dedication is a move of God to believers to stay the course of life. It is well said in the book of James, "Count it all joy, my brothers, when you meet trials of various kinds, for you know that the testing of your faith produces steadfastness. And let steadfastness have its full effect, that you may be perfect and complete, lacking in nothing" (Jas 1:2–4 ESV). Leaning into this verse, it takes an insurmountable amount of faith to implement dedication. Consequently, dedication is a term associated with discipline, and only the Holy Spirit guides one to stay focused to please God against all odds. It is worth noting that the apostle Paul wrote to the church at Corinth. The redemptive fellowship of the church at Corinth was broken because of carnality. While in Corinth, Paul wrote to the church at Rome and was torn between the church at Rome and Corinth (Rom 16:23). He was dedicated to focusing on two churches.

Therefore, the spiritual lifeblood of the Corinthian church was being sucked dry while experiencing the gross sinful atmosphere of the Roman Colony. Paul's encouraging message to the church at Corinth was straightforward. His message was a theological liberation message; he says, "So then, dear brothers and sisters, be firm. Do not be moved! Always be outstanding in the work of the Lord, knowing that your labor is not in vain in the Lord" (1 Cor 15:58 ESV). These verses provided hope for spiritual renewal and dedication.

SPIRITUAL FORMATION

The Pearl of Dedication is a challenging characteristic of spiritual formation. It is essential to incorporate the following Scripture into your walk with Jesus. Paul says, "Do not conform to the pattern of this world, but be transformed by the renewing of your mind" (Rom 12:2). This verse clearly supports spiritual formation because it points to the challenge of discipleship and spiritual growth. The pattern of this world will fail in all attempts to derail your spiritual formation process. Spiritual formation is a synoptic term for discipleship and spirituality. All three emphasize a unified theological premise of spiritual growth. Your devotion is authentic when spiritual transformation draws you closer to God and fulfills your sense of purpose. Spiritual formation is the foundation for spiritual shaping and growing in Christ. It is further said that "spiritual formation is a process of being conformed to the image of Christ."[1] The apostle Paul challenged the church in Rome to be dedicated and "present their bodies a living sacrifice" (Rom 12:1a). What God expects of every believer is not difficult but is crucial for embracing and implementing the Pearls suggested in this book.

Paul was concerned about the Christians in Rome. He had a desire to get there regardless of any opposition. His dedication is set in these words, "For I long to visit you so I can bring you some spiritual gift that will help you grow strong in the Lord" (Rom 1:11 NLT). His encouragement was positive, and he wanted to see them make spiritual progress. I hope that those who read these words will be encouraged to focus on the Holy and embark on an intimate walk amid challenging circumstances and opposition, never compromising godly principles. One's conscience must become immersed in the Holy Spirit and look to Jesus as the author and finisher of our faith (Heb 12:2). It takes faith to maintain dedication and discipline. Dedication and discipline are inseparable realities. One must have a serious prayer life to authenticate a dedicated life. God is waiting and watching for spiritual growth to enhance daily function. Every believer must strive and seek a deeper spiritual walk with God. A closer walk with God ignites the passion for growing in the knowledge of our Lord and Savior, Jesus Christ (2 Pet 3:18). One cannot be dedicated without total surrender to God. Total surrender means leaving behind cunning and worldly actions to follow Christ. Worldly actions will leave you spiritually bankrupt. Andrew Murray says, "When God gives the Holy Spirit, his great object is the formation of a holy character."[2] The Holy Spirit is the source of spiritual growth for a meaningful and authentic lifestyle. Dedication is a life of prayer, Bible study, discipleship, stewardship, evangelism, and mission. God will always honor your dedication and passion for discipleship as you please him.

SOME KEY DEDICATED FAITH LEADERS

An intimate walk with God resonated with dedicated biblical characters who were faithful to their ministry. They had different challenges but maintained their devotion and lived as sacrifices. The Pearl of Dedication was a tangible reality in the lives of these biblical characters.

1. Mulholland, *Invitation to a Journey*, 25.
2. Murray, *Absolute Surrender*, loc. 218 of 1300.

Observing the following leaders leaves an indelible spiritual mark on the present-day believer, to know what it means to be a genuine believer. Their dedication was a sacred promise to glorify God. Through it all, the theological statement is, "keep moving and keep trusting." Their faith was unwavering and steadfast. Their relationship with God kept the fire burning as they walked with him. Let us look at some characters as spiritual examples.

Moses: A Liberator of the Old Covenant

Moses' challenge was to lead Israel out of Egypt. God was with him initially and called him from the burning bush for his intriguing mission (Exod 3:1–5). The bush burned but did not burn into ashes. God, in his sovereignty, burned Moses' conscience to prepare him to lead Israel from Egypt. Moses prayed for Israel (Exod 32:11). God took Moses to Mt. Sinai for personal reflection and reaffirmation to gain spiritual strength and encourage the people to see the divine mission of God. Moses was a relentless liberator destined to lead Israel from under the strict orders of Pharaoh. He stood up against the challenges and intimidation tactics of Pharaoh.

Abraham Was the Recipient of God's Covenant

Abraham was the father of the faithful. God directed him to leave his country and go to a different land (Gen 12:1). God made a covenant with him, and he was dedicated to waiting on God through all odds. When he left his home, he had to have been in a meditative state of mind. This experience required faith and trust. Genesis 15:6 tells us, "Abraham believed the Lord, and he counted it to him as righteousness." Righteousness was his spiritual mark of personal passion. His faith was the epitome of total dedication. Another example of a higher level of faith was when God told him to sacrifice his only son, Isaac (Gen 22:1–19). His dedication and faith were tested. Therefore, Jehovah showed up and honored his faith.

David: A Man After God's Own Heart

The challenge of genuine leadership was David's niche. He was a man after God's own heart. His faith and dedication pleased God. As a young boy, he defeated Goliath. His dedication and faith in God delivered him and Israel. The Bible says, "So David prevailed over the Philistine with a sling and a stone and struck the Philistine and killed him; there was no sword in the hand of David" (1 Sam 17:50 RSV). After David was crowned king, he had a shameful encounter with Bathsheba and her husband Uriah. David watched Bathsheba bathing through a window and assigned Uriah to the front of the battle, and had Uriah killed in battle (2 Sam 11:2–15). After those devious and sinful actions, he confessed before God. Psalm 51:1–2 sets the stage for his confession: "Have mercy on me, O God, according to your unfailing love; according to your great compassion, blot out my transgressions. Wash away all my iniquity and cleanse me from my sin." We must recognize that our dedication is the movement of the Creator within our faith, even in times of trial and trust.

Joseph Was Dedicated to Forgiveness

The life of Joseph was filled with compassion and forgiveness. Joseph was one of the twelve sons of Jacob and another dedicated and faithful servant. His life was not easy. Jealousy had a carnal grip on the family from his brothers. Joseph dreamed dreams and stated the intended meaning and outcome. They did not like their father's love for him, so they plotted to kill him, but it was foiled (Gen 37:18–36).

The Role of Deborah

The role of Deborah demonstrated stamina and pride. She did not have an inferiority complex to men. She was a unique woman in the Old Testament, and her presence was valuable. She was a prophetess, a wife, and a judge. God called her to deliver Israel. She had her close moments with God in her palm. She had a strong relationship with God and was focused on delivering Israel (Judg 4:4–10). She was called and committed to leadership. In Judg 4:6, "She sent and summoned Barak." She persuaded him to utilize ten thousand men from the people of Naphtali and Zebulun to complete the mission. She was confident, careful, committed, and compassionate. Her example paves the way for the modern-day church to emulate and cling to God with a passionate devotion.

Joshua: A Strong Warrior

A noted biblical character in the Old Testament was Joshua. He received his calling and charge from God after the death of Moses to cross the Jordan River into the promised land (Josh 1:1–5). God gave him specific directions: "Have I not commanded you? Be strong and courageous. Do not be frightened, and do not be dismayed, for the Lord your God is with you wherever you go" (Josh 1:9 ESV). Joshua stayed the course and kept himself under the manifold grace of God as a faithful, rooted, and devoted servant. In his powerful prayer he asked God in the presence of Israel to stop the sun over the Valley of Aijalon; the moon also stood still (Josh 10:12–13). His prayer was answered, and the sun stopped as nature watched the glory of God wink in eternity with a profound blessing of faith. As a result of his prayer, he accomplished great things for God. There is a need for more Joshuas today to spend time with God and be confident enough to ask God in faith for miracles. The test of his leadership is connected to his prayer life.

Daniel: A Prayer Warrior

We continue the list of biblical prayer warriors who implemented Pearls that also embody and edify the life of Daniel. In this context, Daniel was not slack when it came to prayer. Daniel was relentless about being a dedicated prayer warrior. His response was centered around the desolation of Jerusalem, a seventy-year captivity as noted in Dan 9:3–4. Daniel was a prime example of a devoted and robust prayer warrior for an intimate walk with God. You can designate a special time to be with God.

Jeremiah: The Weeping Prophet

Jeremiah was distinct: he was the weeping prophet. He was deeply concerned about the sins of Judah and grieved that Judah would not be saved. They needed a physician for their soul (Jer 8:18–22). The thread of internal consciousness continues with a prophetic word from Jeremiah. Based on Jeremiah's perspective, he had a complaint against God and felt that the word was not effective. He was experiencing a complex, ambivalent moment, but God moved and sealed his consciousness. After the sealing, a spiritual encounter magnified the presence of God. He concluded with his royal testimony that the word is like fire shut up in my bones (Jer 20:7–9). Jeremiah responded to the Creator with an ignited passion to utilize the Pearl of Dedication.

Jeremiah was dedicated and faithful to his calling. His testimony and dedication validated his faith: he was on fire with the word in his bones (Jer 20:9). He was locked into God's anointing, responding faithfully to deliver the southern kingdom of Judah. Therefore, he aimed to encourage Judah and affirm that there was hope during Jehovah's judgment (Jer 1:4–7; 16–17). Similarly, Elijah was not slack because he was poised and ready to move forward.

REFLECTIVE SUMMARIZATION AND RESPONSES TO ACTION

Dedicated servants are an asset to the body of Christ. I think the key biblical character and their commitment to God is anointed servanthood. There is no substitute for genuine dedication and discipline. God honors dedication to the work of ministry. Without total commitment, being an authentic, purpose driven believer is impossible. Dedication is not just about knowing, but also about doing and being. The biblical characters in this book provide the biblical, practical, and theological reasons for genuine dedication. They all had roles that matched their ministry. Therefore, dedication is the reason for living and practicing the faith given by God.

The Point of Emphasis

Dedication and discipline are inseparable realities.

The Relevant Question

How willing are you to maintain dedication amid difficulty?

A Prayer for Dedication

Lord Jesus, I pray that you would provide me with the strength to conquer all trials, oppositions, and pains so that I, in your name, can be a living witness to your will. Guide me with your Holy Spirit to be a genuine disciple. Give me the courage to move forward and handle heartaches of all kinds, so I can walk by faith and glorify your name. Keep me alert to be dedicated and focus on your sovereign grace as I live as a purpose driven disciple. Keep me focused and committed to prayer, worship, and being a genuine servant who brings pleasure to the Father. Amen.

PART THREE

Wisdom Pearls That Honor God

Part three describes and discusses the significance of honoring God. It explains believers' commitment and reputation. The Pearls of honoring God make a statement regarding the autobiography of God. It is the character and personality of God's nature. Adoration, sacredness, and holiness are spiritual terms that belong to the God of Abraham, Isaac, and Jacob. There are other attributes of God, such as omnipresence, omnipotence, omniscience, holiness, mercy, and infinitude. The previous attributes are just a sprinkling of his glory. Those terms are congenial to the nature of God and must be revered with humility and spiritual passion. Honoring Jehovah God is more than just expressions of words; it must connect to your actions and being. Believers must cling to God's presence and worship with spiritual dignity. Honoring God is unlike any other duty and responsibility. When you understand the meaning of persevering and applying Old and New Testament theology, acknowledging God's dominion, providence, sovereignty, and glory, it leads to spiritual edification.

DAY 16

The Pearl of Trustworthiness Breeds a Positive Reputation

A man who makes a vow to the Lord or makes a pledge under oath must never break it. He must do exactly what he said he would do

—Numbers 30:2 NLT

Do not lie to one another, seeing that you have put off the old self with its practices and have put on the new self, which is being renewed in knowledge after the image of its creator.

—Colossians 3:9–10

Living a life of trustworthiness brings pleasure to God. Making a vow to the Lord is an honorable act not to be broken. Every one of the Wisdom Pearls mentioned in this book is an essential factor for authentic living. Consequently, the Pearl of Trustworthiness is central to the other Pearls, including honesty. Your reputation is your bond. It charts the course of your life because it is your mouthpiece. What you say and do goes before you and speaks for you. However, the Pearls of Honesty and Trustworthiness are made in the same place, emphasizing the same significance, but with slight differences. The following is a credible example: returning a borrowed book is a sign of honesty. Trust says I trust you to return the book. If one is lax regarding trustworthiness, one's spiritual walk with God is weak and insignificant. You are responsible for monitoring your spiritual walk. Scripture is the authentic and divine communication breathed out by God (2 Tim 3:16); the words came directly from God as our source. Every believer must embrace the spirit of trustworthiness because God's sovereignty in your life acknowledges genuine trustworthiness.

The above scriptures confirm that it is a disdainful and deceptive motive to lie to one another and deliberately break a covenant vow to the Lord. Trustworthiness is closely tied to your intimate relationship with God, as you cultivate integrity, honesty, and loyalty. I share this Pearl as a reminder that trustworthiness is a spiritual challenge and a must for believers who value the sacred life. An attempt to live the holy life encompasses a strong constitution to help you when you falter. Max Lucado says, "God did not emphasize Israel's strength. He emphasized his."[1] The encouraging hope is that the same holds for the present-day believer. God emphasizes his strength and demonstrates it simultaneously. However, this Pearl is the epitome of your spiritual worthiness to be strong as you mature and follow the dictates of the Holy Spirit.

A SOLID FOUNDATION

Trustworthiness is the foundation of how we achieve spiritual maturity. God expects you to cultivate your spiritual integrity and focus on building trust and respect. Therefore, stretch your conscience, live a compelling life of reliability, and never be guilty of unwavering actions. The Pearl of Trustworthiness signals that God is watching and monitoring all actions. It is a solemn word that represents the fiber of our nature. None of us should ever cling to having a reputation. God's word serves as a model for living a life of trustworthiness. A noted phrase, "Your word is your bond," has been used to separate the truth from a lie. A profound biblical reference that solidifies the sanctity of trust is evident: "Again, you have heard that it was said to the people long ago, 'Do not break your oath, but fulfill to the Lord the vows you

---

1. Lucado, *Unshakable Hope*, 5.

have made'" (Matt 5:33). Making a vow to the "Lord is your bond." God and people watch you. What you say is held accountable. If your word is not good, your promise crumbles and crashes on the opposing point of reality. Words devoid of meaning are empty, hollow, and vacuous. Trustworthiness is required because people evaluate and assess our actions and promises.

BEING PASSIONATE ABOUT PERSONAL TRUST

It is essential to have a passionate push to trust. Since trustworthiness is a critical factor for an authentic relationship with God, it is a gem that shines and glows with confidence in what others expect, as well as God. Making every moment count with God is your passion to build spiritual credibility with God. The question comes to mind: Can God trust you? Only you can answer that. It is a question of integrity. Walking in the presence of God with a confident attitude of implementing and applying trust is an honorable act of passion. Biblically, we must live with the principle of trust because "the omnipresence of God appears in the activities of nature, it appears in the supervision of providence, it appears in the voice of conscience, and it appears in the conquests of righteousness."[2] I concur with the above quote as I refocus my passion for trustworthy righteousness. Trustworthy righteousness is being passionate about being genuine about honoring and obeying God in your spiritual walk. As you become passionate about trustworthiness, you will mature in faith. When you go to bed at night, you must rest with a trustworthy mind. When you wake the next day, you should wake with the burning passion to make the day trustworthy. Trust is a Pearl that wisdom shines through brightly.

THE BEST PRINCIPLE OF TRUSTWORTHINESS IS CONFIDENCE

The significance of walking with God is to have confidence in knowing that you are doing the right thing. The more confidence you have in yourself, the closer you are to understanding the challenges of life. Challenges cross your path daily and knowing where your priorities lie

---

2. Boothe, *Plain Theology for Plain People*, 23.

is essential amid opposition and, often, scandalous attacks. Through all of that, remain in the lane of trust. Confidence is your friend because it can be harnessed for spiritual growth and development. It allows you to access your assurance and abilities. When you have confidence, you can encourage others to appreciate their skills and qualities. Your confidence gives you the courage to respect the lens of reality and speak and live the truth. Confidence is not about being superior, but about being humble and genuine when faced with challenges that require confidence. "Don't be afraid, for I am with you. Don't be discouraged, for I am your God. I will strengthen you and help you. I will hold you up with my victorious right hand" (Isa 41:10 NLT). Conversations and interactions embrace confidence with courage. The best way to identify confidence is trustworthiness.

Faith is the most credible act of confidence; without it, life is inadequate, hopeless, and deplorable. Trustworthiness is not about impressing others, but rather about how you interact with and treat them. Many believe trustworthiness is a one-way interaction to build rapport, but it is a reciprocal process to establish genuine relationships. Paul speaks an incredible word to balance a slippery lifestyle in Titus 2:7; he says, "Show yourself in all respects to be a model of good works, and in your teaching show integrity, dignity." Do your best to know that God will trust your endeavors to interact with others with steadfast loyalty, love, and integrity. These actions will genuinely represent your biblical and theological foundation. Another point to consider is avoiding entanglement with harsh attitudes that impede respect from others. Many people are fighting from within, which causes anxiety about not trusting others. Therefore, you can develop the spirit of living with courage. The renowned theologian Paul Tillich says that courage is self-affirmation "in spite of that which tends to prevent the self from affirming itself."[3] The Pearl of Trustworthiness challenges you to examine yourself and assess your state of mind. God is keeping tabs on the actions of all believers to show that the spirit of truth is foundational for honoring God.

There is no substitute for your word of honor. The worst thing is when others cannot and will not trust you. When others can't trust you, certainly God will not. The following metaphor is both truthful and timeless, making it a valuable teaching tool. It is the degrading

---

3. Tillich, *Courage to Be*, 32.

side of the mountain where the slippery slope never ends. It is where and when trust has been violated; it leaves an indelible mark of a despicable reputation. Therefore, a spirit of trustworthiness is better than sapphires, pearls, and gold. When you live with an attitude of trust, people will eagerly seek you out for a gracious interaction. When trustworthiness embraces God and others, your life is a spiritual treasure of hope and happiness. Trustworthiness will penetrate the consciousness of another and ignite the passion of joy and peace. Remember, your trustworthiness precedes you and creates a positive mental model. It is best said that "A good name is to be more desired than great wealth; Favor is better than silver and gold" (Prov 22:1 NASB).

TRUSTWORTHINESS MATTERS NOW

Now is the time to be truthful. The question is, When will you start being trustworthy? The time is now to delete the procrastination habit. People are searching for trustworthiness. An untruthful life is in danger with God. Many in the world lack the Pearl of Trustworthiness. Therefore, it behooves all to evaluate their state of heart and strive for earnest trustworthiness. The Bible declares, "But the fearful, and unbelieving, and the abominable, and murderers, and whoremongers, and sorcerers, and idolaters, and all liars, shall have their part in the lake which burneth with fire and brimstone, which is the second death. Because liars will not see the kingdom of God" (Rev 21:8 KJV). Some lie so much that they think their deceitful words are actual. It is their devious DNA. In essence, they can't be trusted. Untrustworthiness is their true nature. Trustworthiness matters because the world needs a reset on what is true.

When there is more trust, there is less hesitation to trust. God is watching and waiting for faithful and fruitful living. I remember a gospel song, "I Want to Live So God Can Use Me."[4] God can't use us if we are untruthful. Now is the time to prioritize trustworthiness and please God by living and applying trustworthiness because it matters. We, mature believers, set the example for our children and others who need to know the way. It is time to refocus and reaffirm our lifestyle to be prepared for eternity.

---

4. "I'm Gonna Live."

REFLECTIVE SUMMARIZATION AND RESPONSES TO ACTION

One day, all of us will stand before God. Take this time to meditate, pray, and ask God to anoint your mind with the Holy Spirit and live trustily for his glory and your benefit. Be encouraged and live a trustworthy life now. People are seeking trustworthy individuals from all walks of life. Walking in the presence of God encourages you to understand genuine trustworthiness. Remember, Matt 5:33 teaches the danger of breaking an oath. It is an unwise action. Trustworthiness is saying and doing what you declare. This chapter on the Pearl of Trustworthiness presses you to act and be genuine in your walk, talk, and action.

The Point of Emphasis

The spirit of trustworthiness is better than sapphires, pearls, and gold.

The Relevant Question

How can you live peacefully in an untrustworthy world?

A Prayer of Trustworthiness

Gracious God, thank you for the precious moments of walking with you in trust, having been saved by the blood of your Son, Jesus. My trust is in you. Help me to cultivate trust with others and encourage them to appreciate the value of trust in a world where many people are often untrustworthy and need love, forgiveness, and hope. Amen.

DAY 17

The Pearl of Perseverance Is a Strong Anchor

Not only so, but we also glory in our sufferings because we know that suffering produces perseverance; perseverance, character; and character, hope. And hope does not put us to shame, because God's love has been poured out into our hearts through the Holy Spirit, who has been given *to us*.

—ROMANS 5:3–5

Spiritual strength is staying on the challenging course in life. Perseverance is your experience that signifies what it means to see through a dark tunnel with a tiny light. Light brings hope to a hopeless situation. This experience is when you glory in your sufferings through the spiritual production line to reach hope. The Pearl of Perseverance charts the course before you for eternity. This Pearl confirms that true believers are spiritually connected to God and seek to live by faith until the end. It helps to sustain you as a purpose driven disciple in maturing and preparing for eternity. Expect to encounter challenges that push you to the max. Don't give up. Stay on the track and finish the course. The Pearl relates to a genuine believer's relationship with God.

A strong doctrine is vital for a deep constitution undergirded with a biblical foundation and a theological perspective. You must become spiritually saturated in this doctrine. The doctrine of the perseverance of the saints is one of the most popular articles of faith. It is theologically sound as the doctrine of the perseverance of the saints. It furthers the doctrine that the saints will persevere until the end because they are God's elect. It is popular because it is the anchor of your faith and salvation, and another name for eternal security. Perseverance is to stay the course against all odds through suffering and pain. It is wise never to allow sadistic and satanic actions to interrupt your relationship. The term *perseverance* surrounds itself with faith and determination to focus on the Creator for power to hold on through this life. Faith is an integral asset for those who trust Jehovah God, walk by faith, and persevere. Grace is included in perseverance and makes a case for our eternity. The term is a viable theological doctrine that guarantees and assures the eternal place and position with Christ. As you engage in this devotion, remember that true believers must continue a meaningful, authentic, and personal relationship.

An old gospel song, "Lord, Keep Me Day By Day,"[1] has perseverance significance that is at the heart of God's grace; this song includes grace, perseverance, and faith. It speaks to African Americans, Africans, Caribbeans, and any other ethnic group or culture that identifies with their struggles. Believers must embrace perseverance as part of God's grace and sovereignty. No encounter influences to shatter the strength and joy of persevering to the end. It is a theological testimony to continue daily perseverance every day we wake from sleep to experience another segment of pushing forward. Focus on spiritual strength regardless of the pain when difficulty evades your territory. The perseverance of the saints is part of the articles of faith and is one of the most popular. It is a theology that drives the believer's faith toward eternity. Knowing that God has your back, front, and all over, inside and out, is comfort. The word matters profoundly: "And without faith, it is impossible to please God, because anyone who comes to him must believe that he exists and that he rewards those who earnestly seek him" (Heb 11:6). Pleasing God is implementing the spirit of focusing on what matters. Don't let the world make you feel your beliefs and relationships are useless. No matter the details of your circumstances

---

1. Williams, "Lord Keep Me."

or situation, don't forget Job's determination to persevere. He experienced intense suffering, and God restored him (Job 42:10–17).

SOME PROMINENT BIBLICAL CHARACTERS WHO PERSEVERED

As a point of reference, I will share two prominent characters in the Bible who persevered until they attained their goal. Job's plight and pain open with his epic of pain, sorrow, and disappointment. His story sets the stage for handling pain and sorrow with determined faith. Job 1:1–21 records the details of his life and painful situation. He was from the Land of Uz. The Bible says, "He was blameless and upright; he feared God and shunned evil" (Job 1:1). Let us single out this portion of the verse for foundational purposes: he was blameless, meaning God had no issues with him. He lived right and feared God.

A marvelous biblical highlight is that he avoided an evil lifestyle. His perseverance pleased God, but God required more from his vibrant faith. God had more for him; the same is true in our walk with him. Testing time was for Job. He received the news in different segments about losing his livestock and children. Through all these disappointments, Job did not complain. A profound theological statement is, "At this, Job got up and tore his robe and shaved his head. Then he fell to the ground in worship" (Job 1:21). He worshiped and praised God by shaving his head. He honored God through his devotion. It sounded like he connected to the modern-day hymn before it was written: "It Is Well with My Soul." He was tested, and Jehovah assured him of his perseverance. He had nothing to worry about because God reached through eternity and calmed his fears, sorrows, and pain in the archives of eternity. What encouragement it is for the present-day church.

The second example is the miracle recorded in Luke 8:42–27 that describes the story of the woman with the issue of blood. She was the epitome of genuine perseverance. Her mind was made up, and she pressed through the crowd. Because of her blood problem, she was determined to get to Jesus. She did it with character and hope. Her mind was made up. Let us summarize the woman's plight: this incredible event recounts the story of a woman who suffered from a chronic issue of blood for many years. The woman's makeup and spiritual DNA vacillated between the triangle of faith, fear, and frustration. She was persistent and fearful of the leaders in her day, but she pushed her way. These miracles are examples showing how beneficial it is to walk by faith making perseverance an essential response to God's intervention. Through her faith, she encountered Jesus and persevered; he healed her and gave her a new lease on life. In an act of profound compassion, Jesus referred to her as "daughter" to signify her place in his family. She persevered from an outcast to recognition. This miraculous incident also served as a powerful metaphor for the redemptive power of Jesus' sacrifice on the cross. Moreover, it demonstrated Jesus' divine authority and ability to resurrect Jairus's daughter instantaneously, further reinforcing his position as the Son of God and protecting her from any potential backlash from the Jewish community. This pericope is a vibrant theological statement of a genuine Pearl that reflects the resurrection's relevance of deliverance. When healed, she crossed the barriers of culture, rules, and sin to receive her deserved wholeness. She was included in the doctrine of the perseverance of the saints. The blood of Jesus stopped her flow of blood before he shed his blood on Calvary. This story should remind you to keep looking upward with eternal anticipation. How often do you think about eternity? It is essential to think about it because this earthly journey is temporary. That is the reason for perseverance. The apostle Paul is a credible character who persevered.

The eternal encouragement from Paul to the church at Philippi states, "I press toward the mark for the prize of the high calling of God in Christ Jesus" (Phil 3:14 KJV). Thinking about the mark to achieve the prize of eternal life is a spiritual comfort. It is helpful and relative to anticipate the new heaven and the new earth (Rev 21:1–4). Paul shares a testimonial affirmation, and he says, "We are experiencing trouble on every side, but are not crushed; we are perplexed, but not driven to despair; we are persecuted, but not abandoned; we are knocked down, but not destroyed, always carrying around in our body the death of Jesus, so that the life of Jesus may also be made visible in our body" (2 Cor 4:8–11 ESV).

REFLECTIVE SUMMARIZATION AND RESPONSES TO ACTION

The Pearl of Perseverance is a reminder of the theological relevance of eternity. The perseverance of the saints affirms eternal security. Engaging in the story of Job and the woman with an issue of blood solidifies how credible it is to build on our relationship. The grace of God includes perseverance. It is the foundation, and the theological emphasis is a driving factor for spiritual finality. When you persevere, it is for a specific goal or objective. There is no substitute for walking with perseverance, it is a call of responsibility.

The Point of Emphasis

Perseverance is to stay the course against all odds through suffering and pain.

The Relevant Question

Are you dealing with an enormous challenge that requires your perseverance to be tested?

A Prayer of Perseverance

Almighty God, I humbly enter your presence to request the continued assurance of the perseverance of the saints. I pray for your guidance and confirmation for eternal finality under perseverance. I strive to please you with unwavering perseverance to meet your standards of holiness. Help me minister to others and assure them that perseverance is confirmed while traveling this eternal journey. Amen.

DAY 18

The Pearl of Sanctification Is a Genuine Identity

May God himself, the God of peace, sanctify you through and through. May your whole spirit, soul, and body be kept blameless at the coming of our Lord Jesus Christ.

—1 Thessalonians 5:23

If we confess our sins, he is faithful and just and will forgive us our sins and purify us from all unrighteousness.

—1 John 1:9

There is no focus greater than focusing on God's spirit and the process of sanctification. Sanctification is a theological term that distinguishes between genuineness and falsehood. There is no way to fake sanctification or consecration. This Pearl stands apart from many others in this book mainly because it is the authentic identification of salvation. It involves your actions and behavior after salvation. Sanctification is a widely used theological term that encompasses five significant views on sanctification: Wesleyan, Reformed, Pentecostal, Keswick, and

THE PEARL OF SANCTIFICATION IS A GENUINE IDENTITY 107

Augustinian Dispensationalism. They are all similar but different. Your salvation and change of heart hinge on sanctification and regeneration. For clarification, sanctification and regeneration are distinct processes. The Greek word for "sanctification" is *hagiasmos*, meaning "holy," "consecration," and "set apart.[1] "Sanctification is an ongoing action based on maturity. Being set apart is our intention to follow the direction of the Holy Spirit, authenticating our identity and relationship with Christ. The Greek word for "regeneration" is *paliggenesia*, which means new birth or renewal.[2] It is a one-time action. Your life is changed forever through the work of the Holy Spirit.

The writer of Hebrews expresses the critical essential of eternal life: "Make every effort to live in peace with everyone and to be holy; without holiness, no one will see the Lord" (Heb 12:14). In simple terms, no holiness, no heaven. J. Robertson McQuilkin says that a person is forgiven so that the result of sin, eternal punishment, is done away with.[3] I concur with the above quote because, after sanctification, the real work begins. May the God of hope guide me as I ponder this theological essential today for encouragement. Another day has arrived, and it's time to experience an even greater blessing. Now is the time to ask God what your purpose and focus are for today. How does the term *sanctification* speak to your walk with Christ? It should talk about volume and awaken your spiritual appetite. There is no way to be blessed other than acknowledging the work of the Holy Spirit in sanctification. The blessing is to reflect on the power and presence of God. It is time to sit in his divine presence and be mesmerized by your spirit and soul in his divine space and presence. Confession and repentance precede sanctification. God is waiting for your confession and repentance to initiate the work of sanctification. The work of sanctification in your life hinges on the working of the Holy Spirit, regardless of your condition or situation. God's forgiveness searches your soul to prepare you for eternity. The Bible states, "Jesus gave his life for our sins, just as God our Father planned, to rescue us from this evil world in which we live" (Gal 1:4 NLT).

Consequently, *sanctification* is a term that I believe is credible and authentic because it values your soul for eternity. This word is a

---

1. Strong, *Strongest*, 54.
2. Strong, *Strongest*, 2046.
3. McQuilkin, "Keswick Perspective," 158.

valuable Pearl that brings peace. It is relevant to the term *confession*. Confession is humbly recognizing your sinful state of mind and moral predicament. The above verses confirm that God does the sanctifying work of salvation through grace, love, and mercy. Sanctification should impel you to take urgent action to communicate and interact with God to purify your soul for eternity. I must take a praise break from the previous sentence and say hallelujah for sanctification. Before sanctification, we were heavily burdened with the weight of sin, destroying us and preventing us from experiencing heavenly treasures.

JESUS: THE ROOT OF SANCTIFICATION

The road to sanctification comes through Jesus. He is the blueprint and pattern from which you were cut. Our Savior is the root of our sanctification and spiritual growth. Jesus' life as a Palestinian Jew was in opposition to the Palestinian culture. He grew up in Nazareth, a village in Galilee. The phrase has been said, "He was the man from Galilee." His motive was to show a new way against his Jewish identity. In short, the Messiah paved the way for righteousness through sanctification. He shares a poignant and relevant Scripture to make his point regarding consecration. In the Gospel of John, he says, "Sanctify them in the truth; thy word is truth. As thou didst send me into the world, so I have sent them into the world. And for their sake, I consecrate myself, that they also may be consecrated in truth" (John 17:19 RSV). I tag the above verses as the theology of a high priestly prayer. The spiritual significance of sacred devotion encompasses the Holy. Jesus' consecration was the highest level of God's holiness. Jesus' message was to impress upon the disciples the importance of consecration.

God is holy, which serves as a reminder of what Isaiah acknowledged. Isaiah's mesmerizing attention was arrested in awe as he experienced a higher level of worship, one that brought him closer to holiness. Isaiah's level of consecration connects to Jesus' consecration. He acknowledged God's Hebrew name, Yahweh. His testimony was that in the year King Uzziah died, he witnessed the Lord high and lifted up (Isa 6:1–5). Isaiah's commission was to go to the people and proclaim to them the message. He said, "'Woe to me!' I cried. 'I am ruined! For I am a man of unclean lips, and I live among a people of unclean lips, and my eyes have seen the King, the Lord Almighty.'" (Isa 6:5). He was a committed servant who did not feel adequate and capable. He was a ruined person in both thought and action. He and Judah lacked consecration but later received the atonement (Isa 6:6). God, in his wise providence, is the only one who can and will purge our unclean lips.

It is a sacred moment of spiritual communication when you become intense in your moments with the Master. Jesus was adamant about his disciples receiving the message of sanctification. He wanted them and the rest of his world followers to live the sanctified life. John 17 is a priestly prayer that he prayed for his believers. The root was in the consecration of his life. If Jesus consecrated himself to God, we should do the same. Jesus' consecration was not marred by sin because he was sinless; instead, because he was both human and divine, he provided the perfect pattern to follow. Our sanctification identifies us as being freed from sin, as Jesus was the example and provision for us to overcome it. The vital truth about John 17 is that Jesus prayed for unity long ago for the body of Christ.

SPIRITUAL COMPLIANCE MEETS GOD'S STANDARDS

The first letter to the Thessalonians specifically brings the purpose and genuineness of sanctification to center stage. This letter confirms the significance of maintaining a sanctifying life. What a Pearl to reflect and implement to identify with the sanctity of righteousness. Sanctification is a state of holiness that implements love. It is the perfect love for pursuing the Wisdom Pearls in this book and activating and implementing the passion for meeting God's standards. Paul, the writer of 1 Thessalonians, provided the church with a positive biblical lesson on living a life that is well-pleasing to God, emphasizing the importance of rejoicing and avoiding evil (1 Thess 5:22–24)—the context of 1 Thessalonians points to the day of the Lord and the second coming of Jesus.

A life focused on Jesus is a prudent decision, especially in these times we live in. Paul's profundity and fluidity in 1 Thessalonians leave a message of hope for those he wanted to see. "Now may the God of peace himself sanctify you completely and may your whole spirit and soul and body be kept blameless at the coming of our Lord Jesus Christ (1 Thess 5:23 ESV). This verse reminds believers to ensure their lifestyle is in spiritual compliance before the coming of the Lord Jesus.

Make no doubt about it: he is sure to come, and when he comes, he is looking for a church without spot or wrinkle and without the stain of blemish (Eph 5:26–27). It is incumbent upon believers to value the doctrine of sanctification and represent God's kingdom in a world of people whose minds are dominated by impassioned feelings and who practice ideology at its extreme.

If you are guilty of practicing ideology, this Pearl of Sanctification will press the point of getting your house together for spiritual identification. The question is, Are you in compliance with the Creator's standards? Only you can answer that question. God honors spiritual identification as a way of life, as seen in the Old Testament. The prophet Ezekiel states, "Then the nations will know that I the Lord sanctify Israel when my sanctuary is in the midst of them for evermore" (Ezek 37:28). Since Yahweh was with Israel, he would grant spiritual favor under his divine providence.

GROWING THROUGH SANCTIFICATION

Growth through sanctification is a path to spiritual sanctity. It is to spend quality time with God to maximize potential spiritual growth. Emphasis entails reflecting on God's grace, favor, and compassion. The goal of sanctification is to defeat rebellion with perfect love and holiness in the Almighty. In short, it is the salvific sacrifice of Christ for your redemption. Therefore, sanctification is the powerful work of the Holy Spirit that uses regeneration to indwell us for the growth process. Being anxious about regeneration, the foundation of sanctification leaves an indelible mark that empowers you to act responsibly. It requires that one fully understands its core significance. Sanctification is more than separation from the world. It is associated with an integral union with Christ. "Paul sees union with Christ as a core doctrine of the Christian faith and a crucial aspect of what it means to grow as a Christian."[4] The time has come for the church to take a radical turn with a theological consciousness of being a creative agent for God. A creative agent for God has a goal in mind and an action plan to implement the union with Christ for maturity. It is prudent to practice sanctification because it is a continued reality. The spiritual life is empty without realizing the importance of sanctification. Therefore, the term purification is a

---

4. Grant and Hughes, *1 & 2 Thessalonians*, 60.

significant factor in your spiritual resolve. It is the same as sanctification in cleansing your sinful defilement through the washing of the blood at salvation. Reflecting on this process causes you to think about your past sins and move to a new life of deliverance.

REFLECTIVE SUMMARIZATION AND RESPONSES TO ACTION

Every believer must take valuable time to reflect on the process and experience of the Holy Spirit's work in regeneration to appreciate the Pearl of Sanctification. There is no sanctification without the new birth. After sanctification, you must seek to maintain a viable relationship with God. You must refrain from worldly distractions and press toward the mark of a higher calling in Jesus Christ. The end goal is to see Jesus.

The Point of Emphasis

Our Savior is the root of our sanctification and spiritual growth.

The Relevant Question:

How does the term *sanctification* speak to your walk with Christ?

A Prayer for Sanctification

Today, I pray in the name of Jesus for the open door to eternal life. It is pleasant to experience sanctification with joy and confirmation. Help me, Lord, to know that I now live in another world of hope and reality. I don't have to worry about eternal residence and the future. Amen.

DAY 19

The Pearl of Confession Renews the Soul

Have mercy on me, O God, according to your steadfast love; according to your abundant mercy blot out my transgressions.

—Psalm 51:1 ESV

If you declare with your mouth, "Jesus is Lord," and believe in your heart that God raised him from the dead, you will be saved. For it is with your heart that you believe and are justified, and it is with your mouth that you profess your faith and are saved.

—Romans 10:9–10

The Pearl of Confession renews the soul because it is a potent remedy for a wounded soul. When one procrastinates, ignores, or overlooks confession, it only worsens and deteriorates one's character. Therefore, the injured soul shows weakness and flaws. God knows your imperfections and shortcomings. It is left up to you to seek redemption for a new and promising lifestyle. This spiritual Pearl demands attention regarding what God requires for spiritual resolve. The longer you procrastinate about acknowledgment, the more it allows Satan to attack.

If you have not succumbed to the first or second time Satan attacks, then Satan takes mulligans to achieve his goals. A *mulligan* is a golf term that means you get a chance to redeem yourself when you make an error and have a lousy shot. In this case, when you err as a believer, God allows his grace and favor for your spiritual renewal.

The strength of your devotion is a sign of genuine confession. In simple terms, this Pearl is a serious conversation about your shortcomings. Pray to God to get out of your worldly straitjacket where you are bound, crushed, miserable, and ruined. There is good news! The purpose of confession for the unbeliever differs from that of the believer. The nonbeliever is pleading for the opportunity to be saved, which leads to the prayer of admission of sin. "Lord, I am sorry for my sins and acknowledge that I have wronged your sacred presence; I accept Jesus Christ as my Savior." The believer's confession is the reconciliation of wrongdoing against God, and a resolution is needed. "Lord, I confess that I have done wrong today and am not comfortable ignoring the fact that I need forgiveness." The above Scripture, Rom 10:9–10, explains what the apostle Paul was saying to God. He made a heartfelt declaration to plead for salvation. Confession breaks the barrier of sin and opens the door to spiritual prosperity. The writer says, "Whoever conceals their sins does not prosper, but the one who confesses and renounces them finds mercy" (Prov 28:13). This verse is straightforward concerning the danger of concealing sins. There is no way around coming face to face with your sin. The spirit of God and confession are intertwined to awaken the sinful nature.

The Bible clearly explains the benefits of living by God's word. God's words transform, inspire, inform, and change the direction for a new nature. The new nature is the scope of systematic theology, whereas it is the doctrine of salvation, precisely the term of regeneration. In simple terms, having been born again, anew. The Bible supports the concept of what happens after admitting sins. Jesus instructed Nicodemus regarding how one can be born again. He stated that you could not be born again when you are old (John 3:4). In John 3:3, Jesus uses the phrase "born of water and Spirit" to mean born again. He answered Nicodemus's question regarding how to enter the kingdom of heaven. He told Nicodemus that he "must be born again" (John 3:3). To be born again means confession precedes being born again.

If you are pondering spiritual setbacks and attacks, God has a plan for your life and is waiting for you to make a grave move to make a difference. No matter the situation, there is hope. A powerful expression of hope is given by Moltmann: "To believe means to cross in hope and anticipation the bounds that the raising of the crucified has penetrated."[1] The message of the crucified solidifies the salvific experience. God's grace is available in the process of the redemptive plan of salvation. Jesus shares a model of the theology of confession by stating, "I tell you, whoever publicly acknowledges me before others, the Son of Man will also acknowledge before the angels of God" (Luke 12:8). God acknowledges confession because of faith, dedication, commitment, and obedience.

A NEW CREATURE

Suppose you are stumbling in the dark. God desires you to be a stronger disciple, and if you are not, take the time to confess your sins and upgrade from misery to mercy. Your lifestyle does not have to remain weak and insufficient. You are a new creature. To be a serious believer, take advantage of what the apostle Paul called "a new creature." He alerted the church at Corinth of what it means to change: "Therefore if anyone is in Christ, he is a new creature; the old things have passed away; behold, new things have come" (2 Cor 5:17). Becoming a new creature is a new road to travel. It's like going to a restaurant with a variety of healthy options. After being saved, there is a new appetite. You crave spiritual food. When you confess a priority, you level up to look forward to spiritual blessings in heavenly places, as recorded in Eph 1:3–11.

I MUST LEAVE THE OLD LIFE

The teaching of the Bible affirms that the new life sets a new standard for your life. You have a new GPS to guide you and encourage you to accept the new way of living. You will encounter new ideas and gain fresh spiritual insights. Your decision to make the Bible your guide is a remarkable turn of events. Confession sets the stage for this complete

---

1. Moltmann, *Theology of Hope*, 20–21.

change. The new life will be challenged and tested by trials and opposition. The Bible tells us that James was concerned about those converted Jewish Christians (Jas 1:1). After their confession and conversion, James was serious about getting them to live right. He realized that believers must keep a contagious spirit regardless of their past trials and tribulations. James did not waste time embellishing or elaborating on what he would say to the twelve tribes scattered abroad. His greeting refers to the Hebrew Christians outside Palestine. Their meeting place was the synagogue. These Jewish believers were being tested in their faith, and James was concerned that they were succumbing to impatience, bitterness, materialism, disunity, ceremonial defilement, and spiritual apathy. As a Jerusalem resident and a church leader, James undoubtedly had frequent contact with Jewish Christians from various Roman provinces. He was highly concerned and felt the need to encourage them in their need for faith.

REFLECTIVE SUMMARIZATION AND RESPONSES TO ACTION

Have you come to a place where you know that confession is good for the soul? If not, it will make you think that you have to leave the old life behind. You are now changed and set for a permanent change. Confession points to a new life, one of experiencing God through spiritual blessings. It is essential to rectify wrongdoing, and be honest before God, and leave the old life. God wants to see action, rather than intention, which is what matters. Admission of guilt affirms that you are walking from the entanglement of a miserable life to spiritual enlightenment.

The Point of Emphasis

You will experience new ideas and new insights.

The Relevant Question

Do you know that God is waiting for your confession?

A Prayer for Confession

Today, Eternal God, I come with the passion for knowing the value of confession. Bless me with the spiritual insight to appreciate and understand the significance of confession. The Pearl of Confession reminds me to remain spiritually compliant and confess all wrongdoing. I pray to get closer to you and meditate on the power of confession. Amen.

DAY 20

The Pearl of Grace Is Sufficient

But he said to me, "My grace is sufficient for you, for my power is made perfect in weakness."

—2 Corinthians 12:9

By judging others, we blind ourselves to our evil and to the Grace which others are just as entitled to as we are.

—Dietrich Bonhoeffer

Every moment spent with the Master is a cherished moment. The good news is that grace is sufficient. It is adequate because believers gain spiritual growth by Grace. The Bible says, "But grow in the grace and knowledge of our Lord and Savior Jesus Christ. To him be glory both now and forever! Amen" (2 Pet 3:18). Thank the Creator for providing his son as the entrance to grow in grace and knowledge. God saved us by his grace so that we could benefit from and experience spiritual growth. Paying attention to the Pearl of Great Price is critical, as noted in Matt 13:45-46. The Greek word for "grace" in the above passage is *charis*, which means the state of kindness and favor toward someone.[1] It is non-deserving because grace is sufficient.

Grace will capture your attention and prompt you to think about God in ways you may not have before. As you reflect daily, you are given favor because Grace is in action. *Favor* is the theological word expressing God's action for your actions. You can't thank the Creator enough for grace. These Wisdom Pearls will excite you to think about the comprehensiveness of God's grace and mercy. He created you for worship and to grow spiritually for his glory. You, as a believer, must study to show yourself approved unto God, which means growing spiritually (2 Tim 2:15). Growth is impossible without study, prayer, and practice. You wake daily from your sleep in God's grace. Now, start the day for another round of experiencing spiritual growth. Grace and mercy are the twin towers of God's sovereignty, and he grants both for his purpose in our lives. When you went to sleep last night, it was bed grace; when you woke up this morning and went out of the home, it was ground grace; if you flew in an airplane, it was astronomical grace; if you boarded a ship and sailed the sea or the ocean, it was water grace; if you boarded a train, it was rail grace.

However, as you travel, grace surrounds you. My primary aim is to focus on what Paul experienced and how he handled opposition and challenges, as outlined in this text, so that your spiritual growth can be effective. What was in Paul's mind when he penned these veracious words in this passage? They stem from the previous verse regarding the battle with the thorn in the flesh. "Therefore, to keep me from becoming conceited, I was given a thorn in my flesh, a messenger of Satan, to torment me" (2 Cor 12:7b). This thorn in the flesh moved him to focus on God's deliverance. He was given favor from God to withstand the thorn's agony, pain, and anxiety. It was painful but, in the end, he prevailed. Considering the myriad problems in the Corinthian church and his issues, he was determined to share nuggets of truth and wisdom. Paul left Athens and came to Corinth, reasoning in the synagogue, testifying to the Jews that Jesus was the Christ, teaching the word, and baptizing (Acts 18:1, 4, 8, 11). God granted him the grace to write the second Corinthians' letter of gratitude to encourage the saints. Grace is God's favor that provides strength and hope during complex and

---

1. Strong, *Strongest*, 2074.

challenging encounters. It takes grace and spiritual growth to conquer opposition.

This Pearl has sufficient power to sustain you through your weaknesses. The twentieth-century theologian Reinhold Niebuhr offers a different perspective on grace, stating, "Grace represents, on the one hand, the mercy and forgiveness of God by which he completes what man cannot complete and overcomes the sinful elements in all of man's achievements."[2] When you experience sinful elements, hardship, pain, and anxiety, the Creator protects your shortcomings. Furthermore, Paul defends his ministry with meekness amid the weapons of warfare and the waging of war in the flesh and against strongholds (2 Cor 10:1–6). You must be growing as a disciple driven by the Holy Spirit to mature into a stronger and better believer. To face all of that is with grace and strength from God. Grace is never depleted. However, you don't deserve it, but it is divinely granted and permitted. There is nothing you can do to repay God for his bountiful blessings of extended grace. His grace is expressive of his compassion and patience. All of us are on borrowed blessings of grace that we will never deserve. It means that we will never pray enough to thank God, because exhaling and inhaling are signs of extended grace. Praise his holy name!

HOW DO YOU UNDERSTAND GOD'S GRACE?

How you understand grace relates to your appreciation for what God has done and is doing, as well as your perspective on the future. Paul's experience with his culture proved that grace is sufficient. Some Jews' lack of concern was evident when he reached Rome and was placed under house arrest around AD 60 to 62. He defended his position regarding Christ as the Messiah and was granted freedom after two years (Acts 28:16–30). His freedom is another way of explaining and understanding grace. As you read about Paul's dilemma, you will see how God's action prevailed. Some Jews would not give in, but God's unmerited favor rested on the apostle wonderfully. Those experiences and having survived the shipwreck confirm the power of a compassionate God. The question is, Do you understand grace? Some may say, probably, but it is too much for the human mind to understand fully. Grace is about who God is rather than what we say or do. It is

---

2. Niebuhr, *Human Destiny*, 98–99.

about what God does. Grace is the unmerited favor of God. The Pearl of Grace shares many encounters in the Old Testament.

Therefore, we must reflect on Paul's experiences and encounters, as well as those in the Old Testament. God protected and preserved Joseph from the attacks of his brothers, who sold him (Gen 37:12–36). Ultimately, Joseph was appointed as the prince of Egypt (Gen 42:6–8). The most profound act of favor shows Israel's deliverance from Egyptian bondage. Moses stretched out his hand over the sea as a symbol of favor, and the Egyptians pursued them. The Israelites, however, walked on dry land through the Red Sea (Exod 14:21–29). You, as well as others, have Red Sea experiences that we need to cross. Jehovah will send Moses to lead you through the Red Sea.

Moses could be a coworker, sibling, child, spouse, or neighbor. The Old Testament occurrences that warranted divine favor reveal compassionate deliverance. Our understanding of grace is what we can comprehend. The Pearl of Grace reminds you that deliverance is still available regardless of circumstances. Undoubtedly, Jehovah does more than what you can retain. It is mind-blowing and mind-baffling to comprehend. Remember the old gospel song "Precious Lord, Take My Hand."[3] When you know God is leading you through your pitfalls and Lodebar, then you are on the road to understanding the purpose and nature of grace as it strengthens you. The town and story of Lodebar is found in 2 Sam 9:4–5 and 17:27. "The name 'Lodebar' is often interpreted to mean 'no pasture' or 'no word,' suggesting a place of desolation or barrenness."[4]

GOD, THE CENTER OF GRACE

Jehovah God is the central factor of your existence. When you are not thinking about what is happening around you, Jehovah's plan is at work. The apostle Paul says, "God saved you by his grace when you believed. And you can't take credit for this; it is a gift from God. Salvation is not a reward for the good things we have done, so none of us can boast about it" (Eph 2:8–9 NLT). When God grants grace, it is the moment to focus on the flavor that protects you and strengthens your maturity. Believers must know that God is the center of grace,

---

3. Dorsey, "Precious Lord."
4. Bible Hub, "Lodebar."

preparing them to value their relationship for effective worship and witness. God's act of favor is your response to praise him. It must be noted that the Holy Spirit is right there to advocate for you when you face episodes that rattle your foundation. Paul writes words of hope: "And the Holy Spirit helps us in our weakness. For example, we don't know what God desires of our prayer. But the Holy Spirit prays for us with groanings that cannot be expressed in words" (Rom 8:26 NLT). Knowing the focus and central factor of grace confirms that grace is sufficient. Therefore, this Pearl shines brightly and becomes the theme of your testimony, encouraging others to persevere through spiritual struggles.

The Holy Spirit intercedes in the same way as grace does. The Greek word for "intercession" is *huperentugchano*, which means to make a petition or intercede on behalf of another.[5] Interceding is representing you to help you in your dilemmas. It is blessed that the Pearl of Grace is bestowed as a double indemnity that includes God and Christ. John's Gospel says, "The Word became flesh and made his dwelling among us. We have seen his glory, the glory of the one and only Son, who came from the Father, full of grace and truth" (John 1:14). Knowing this about the divine favor brings peace and comfort. Therefore, it builds courage and faith to conquer all obstacles. Grace is the message of salvation to save the world from fleshly demons. Knowing you have been saved is God's act of compassion and favor. It is what keeps us above the deep and treacherous waters of life.

The words of Charles Spurgeon regarding grace speak loudly and are a viable summary of the essence of grace. He said, "Divine mercy has intervened and provided a plan of salvation from the Fall." Grace is that plan of "another covenant, a covenant God the Father made with His Son Jesus Christ, who is appropriately called the Second Adam because He also stood as the representative" of humanity.[6] God expects you to cherish and appreciate grace and live a well-pleasing life, growing in maturity. It is honorable to reflect on the covenant and the meaning of God's grace. At this moment, you should be full of joy and tears that express thankfulness to the God of Abraham, Isaac, and Jacob. Truthful living is confirmation you can share with others regardless of fragile lives, because there is enough grace for all.

5. Vine, *Expository Dictionary*, 267.
6. Spurgeon, *God's Grace to You*, 8–9.

REFLECTIVE SUMMARIZATION AND RESPONSES TO ACTION

You will never fully understand God's excellent grace because it is far too comprehensive to comprehend. This Pearl will encourage you to pray and focus on understanding the significance of grace. The apostle Paul affirms that his circumstances reveal that Jesus is full of grace and truth, and that his grace is sufficient. Grace is never depleted; all you need to do is express appreciation for the fact that grace is vital. God is the center of grace, the focal point of all interactions and experiences as you experience God. Experiencing God involves spiritual growth as you mature.

The Point of Emphasis

Grace is the fundamental factor for your existence.

The Relevant Question

Do you know that grace is a never-ending factor in your life of growth?

A Prayer for Grace

Thank you, Eternal Spirit, for your favor during my most difficult moments. Help me, Jehovah, to grow in grace and knowledge of Jesus and fulfill your promise and will. Your favor lifted my burdens, calmed my fears, and gave me strength to continue my earthly assignment. I desire to continue being a recipient of spiritual strength that propels my spiritual walk to be upright, as I appreciate your amazing grace. Amen.

DAY 21

The Pearl of Friendship Matters

Anyone who withholds kindness from a friend forsakes the fear of the Almighty.

—JOB 6:14

There is nothing on this earth more to be prized than true friendship.

—THOMAS AQUINAS

Friendship matters because it fills the void left by unrighteous actions. Moreover, Jehovah's favor is needed for the genuine and kind execution of friendship. May the Lord of hosts instill in you through the Holy Spirit the ability to share true friendship with others. He will reveal his marvelous blessings of choosing friends who reciprocate in kind. In this chapter, I propose encouraging individuals to value quality time with the Creator, thereby developing a deep spiritual anchor and cultivating a credible reputation through a friendly lifestyle. Friendship is an asset that can be demonstrated in both good and challenging situations. However, there is a lesson from Job that helps to bond a meaningful friendship. He says anyone who withholds kindness from a friend is making an unwise action. Friendship seeks to maintain kindness that lasts. No matter the circumstance, befriend someone and help them have a good day. Genuine friendship matters in all areas of life, and it matters because it is the strength of building community. A community lacking friendship, trust, and love will derail before the foundation is laid. Job shares encouraging words to build a better friendship for the glory of God.

FRIENDSHIP THAT LASTS

Friendship seeks to maintain a robust relationship that lasts through the rubble of toxic indignation. True friendship will last because it focuses on character, respect, and generosity. In this context, character refers to the behavior that nurtures your spirit for longevity and a vibrant relationship. Solomon says, "The righteous choose their friends carefully, but the way of the wicked leads them astray" (Prov 12:26). However, you must carefully choose your friends, those who genuinely like the company you keep, not always partying, but sharing life. It is someone you can relate to, with whom you build a sense of integrity and a friendship that bonds.

Think about unfriendly encounters you have experienced. In those moments, it might feel like the world is against you. However, by faith these challenges can be seen as ways in which the Trinitarian Godhead, understood as Father, Son, and Holy Spirit, is helping you become stronger for what lies ahead." Not everyone can be your friend, but you can still be friendly to them. Your friendliness is based on the word of God, no matter how you are treated. The Bible says, "One who forgives an affront fosters friendship, but one who dwells on disputes will alienate a friend" (Prov 17:9). The ideal gesture is to show friendship and be friendly. It can become the norm for community interaction and relationships.

UNDERSTANDING THE IMPACT OF FRIENDSHIP

Friendship is not bound by color, race, religion, or class because it transcends the cultural, racial, and religious divides. The famous words of Rodney King, "Can't we all just get along," bind the community to blend thoughts and unite for social and emotional support in pursuit of equal justice. Understanding friendship is like a magnet that draws, inspires, and encourages. Therefore, it becomes the sweet core of the community. Further friendship is vital for successful interaction because it bears the fruit of compassion with everyone. The fruit of compassion is in Jesus, which calls for spiritual humility. Spiritual humility has its roots in Jesus, the true vine. The vine that dresses everyone and encourages spiritual growth to abide in Christ and spread the fruit of friendship (John 15:1–12). We need Christ for intimacy and to prevent spiritual demise. Emphasis is to abide in Christ because "abiding in Christ also works in us the fruit that can provide an answer."[1] These daily readings challenge the integrity of genuine friendship. The Pearl of Friendship is a fruitful compass that guides you to keep extending it as a model for all to follow. Moreover, it embodies peace and justice, self-evaluation, and the unity of the circle of love. A wisdom truthful nugget: "Walk with the wise and become wise, for a companion of fools suffers harm" (Prov 13:20). It is a good idea to pray for your friends constantly. Authentic friendships are built to last, enduring the test of trials and tribulations.

The Holy Spirit will guide you to make this a constant concern. Genuine friendship has no age, cultural, or ethnic barriers because it is rooted in biblical principles and the foundation of compassion. It grows deep over time and survives any tensions or disagreements that occur. Let's be clear: it will take a severe misunderstanding or disappointment to disrupt the relationship. Sometimes, it depends on the person or persons and the circumstances for it to come to an end. Ruth and Naomi had a close bond when Ruth became friends with her mother-in-law. "But Ruth replied, 'Don't urge me to leave or turn back from you. Where you go, I will go, and where you stay, I will stay. Your people will be my people, and your God will be my God. Where you die, I will die, and there I will be buried. May the Lord deal with me, be it ever so severely, if even death separates you and me'" (Ruth 1:16). Naomi and Ruth were dear and dedicated friends. Their relationship had value and merit.

---

1. Murray, *Essential Andrew Murray Collection*, 247.

A THEOLOGY OF FRIENDSHIP

The theological meaning of *friendship* is embracing kindness in the face of mistreatment and rejection. When most church congregants hear the word "theology," they think it is exclusively for seminarians, pastors, or Bible college students. Those servants use the term, but to be clear, they encourage the laity to appreciate the significance. Theology is the study of God. Every believer has a theology of God, Christ, and the Holy Spirit. If you walk by faith, it's your theological root and identity. When you pray and study your Bible, you advocate an authentic theology. To alleviate your concerns, let's examine the theology of friendship. It is a strong bond you have for someone, and it shows affection and trust in a genuine relationship. The apostle Paul admonishes the Thessalonians to help one another and build each other up, helping them gain confidence, courage, and respect for each other (1 Thess 5:11). This Scripture is a foundational passage to support an adequate and sound theological perspective on helping one another. God's will is for us to be supportive and serve each other without any strings attached. Serving each other and being willing to inquire about their needs is a remarkable response. Solomon says, "Two are better than one because they have a good reward for their toil. For if they fall, one will lift his fellow. But woe to him who is alone when he falls and does not have another to lift him! (Eccl 4:9–10 ESV). The above Scripture is God's design for a theology of friendship, as it outlines what God requires for us to imitate this sacred bond.

FRIENDSHIP ATTITUDES

The frame of mind determines the outcome of an actual relationship. There will be times when genuine friendships are tried and tested. The danger of any friendship is listening to others who are jealous of your relationship. Under no circumstances should you avoid those who are negative. The devil is on the prowl to destroy authentic friendships. A true friend is a jewel that never tarnishes because the fire will never prevail. The Bible says, "One who has unreliable friends soon comes to ruin, but there is a friend who sticks closer than a brother" (Prov 18:24). We can only trust a friend with a positive attitude and a life of prayer. Also, it is best to have an open conversation and discuss issues and disagreements. This action tests attitudes and behavior. Every friend needs social graces; don't take things for granted because you have a genuine friend. Honest friends will last. For example, I had several friends for over fifty years, and we never argued; we only had mild disagreements. Our secret was that we never had a superiority complex or used bravado to strengthen our relationship. We did not see the necessity of being braggadocios and impressing each other.

REFLECTIVE SUMMARIZATION AND RESPONSES TO ACTION

The honest action that friends can show is to continue trusting each other, regardless of the difficulty or circumstances. The genuine relationship will last through the test of fire, temptations, and trials. Keeping a positive attitude is a sign of an authentic relationship. Some will try to break up genuine relationships. Many scriptures support friendship. One must have a dedicated passion to execute and apply the significance of relationships. The Bible is right when it says being a true friend is the same as being closer than siblings. Take the encouraging statements from this day and demonstrate your kind actions to present friends and add new friends to your profile of kindness.

The Point of Emphasis

A true friend is a jewel that never tarnishes.

The Relevant Question

How devoted are you to your friends?

A Prayer for Friendship

My Lord and God, thank you for the day I read this Pearl. Help me be more friendly to those who show me affection. Give me the strength and patience to be a faithful friend in these times we live in. Help me, through the Holy Spirit, to gain proximity to you through meditation, prayer, and the word. I pray that you will please endow me with the ability to befriend others in your name. Amen.

DAY 22

The Pearl of Wisdom Is an Insightful Treasure

How much better to get wisdom than gold, to get insight rather than silver!
—Proverbs 16:16

Be wise in the way you act toward outsiders; make the most of every opportunity. Let your conversation be always full of grace, seasoned with salt, so that you may know how to answer *everyone*.
—Colossians 4:5–6

Experiencing wisdom involves righteousness, prayer, and insights. People cannot teach wisdom, but they can be encouraged because of God's divine nature. Wisdom emits spiritual rays of righteousness, offering insights into the profound wonders of God. The Hebrew and Greek words for "wisdom" are nearly identical; the Hebrew word is *chokmah*, meaning wisdom, skill, and learning.[1] The Greek word for wisdom is *sophia*, which means wisdom (either secular or divine).[2] In essence, wis-

---

1. Strong, *Strongest*, 2437.
2. Strong, *Strongest*, 2061.

dom is to understand principles. I suggest meditating on the following Scripture: "God has united you with Christ Jesus. For your benefit, God made him to be wisdom itself. Christ made us right with God; he made us pure and holy, and he freed us from sin" (1 Cor 1:30 NLT). That Scripture, along with others, is a profound statement regarding the righteousness of wisdom.

Wisdom speaks the truth in any situation. When Satan's barrage of opposition creates uncertainty, God turns the Pearl of Wisdom loose to make its poignant point (Ps 37:30–31, 39–40). Prayer is another factor that helps believers experience the Pearl of Wisdom. Never feel that your prayer doesn't matter. Spurgeon says, "May we not draw some comfort from the thought that our prayers never are intrusions."[3] The prayer of trust strengthens the cord that binds wisdom insights. Trust in the Lord with the completeness of your heart is the answer to wisdom insight (Prov 3:5–6). I believe that the Pearl of Wisdom has the virtue of divine construction. The question comes to mind: What is wisdom? Philosophy is strong on wisdom because of its emphasis on "the love of wisdom."[4] Despite the immense spectrum of wisdom from various philosophies, many consider wisdom to be well-accepted as authentic and original from multiple perspectives. Some believe that wisdom is genuine because psychological traits are connected to the intellectual ability to solve difficult situations. Wisdom provides merit during high-tech meetings in the corporate world. During these high-tech discussions, godly wisdom will ignite the insightful treasure and reveal settling answers to the truth.

Four well-known books in the Bible teach wisdom as an insightful treasure. They are classified as the wisdom literature: Job, Ecclesiastes, Proverbs, and Psalms. Each book presents the ancient world in a unique way and offers guidance on living a godly life. Job is filled with handling suffering, while Ecclesiastes focuses on valuing time and the significance of life. Proverbs structures streams of wisdom on the validity of authentic guidance, and Psalms advocates viewing the world through the lens of poetry to combat suffering through faith, patience, and fortitude. Wisdom is applied through the above books to view life from a positive perspective, rather than dwelling on pain and depression. Encourage others to recognize the wisdom in you and see

---

3. Spurgeon, *Daily Wisdom on Prayer*, 16.
4. Cowan and Spiegel, *Love of Wisdom*, 2.

how you can make a difference in their lives. When this happens, this action encourages you to keep encouragement alive.

PURSUING WISDOM

One must seek sensible and wise thoughts to formulate authentic statements that lead to wisdom. Solomon received the spiritual endowment of wisdom from the Creator. He was an example of what wisdom can do for those who pursue it. He affirmed that silver and gold do not match up to the insight of wisdom. Pursuing wisdom is an excellent fulfillment because wisdom is from the mind of God. J. I. Packer says, "Wisdom is, in fact, the practical side of moral goodness. As such, it is found in its fullness only in God. He alone is naturally and entirely and invariably wise."[5] Anyone who walks and talks their faith shows that the wisdom treasure is full of value and merit. The pursuit of wisdom is a sensible and passionate desire that yearns for spiritual growth and eternal fulfillment. The book of Revelation mentions and describes the pearly gates in heaven: "And the twelve gates were twelve pearls, each of the gates made of a single pearl, and the street of the city was pure gold, like transparent glass"(Rev 21:21 ESV). Wise thinking and preparation are to focus on the pearly gates. Appreciate the symbolism of the gates as they represent entering the finality of your new eternal home. Too many individuals focus on unwise thinking, focusing on the land of the living. Wisdom constantly shows the way and reveals better arrangements for eternity.

It strives to interpret and explain situations and circumstances. Prayerfully seek wisdom and make the most of its value. A person with a self-serving arrogance will find it challenging to appreciate wisdom. A person with a humble spirit values the merit of wisdom. Pursuing wisdom refreshes and revitalizes a clogged mind and a wounded spirit. Wisdom is one of the gifts of the Spirit as found in 1 Cor 12:8: "To one there is given through the Spirit a message of wisdom, to another a message of knowledge by means of the same Spirit." Every believer is equipped to use wisdom for the good of the spiritual walk. Some are in the body of Christ with the spiritual gift of wisdom and knowledge. They possess the divine skills to understand complex situations and provide credible advice for informed decisions. Solomon was the

---

5. Packer. *Knowing God*, 90.

wisest man during his era. He continued to pursue wisdom. After he offered his burnt offering, a choice had to be made, and God asked him to choose what he wanted. He then asked God for more wisdom (1 Kgs 3:4–5). Believers today must do as Solomon and request more wisdom. It is an act of stern humility. Pursue God through the power of prayer and the Holy Spirit to accentuate the Wisdom Pearl as the rays of an insightful treasure. God blesses those who pursue wisdom amid opposition.

WALKING IN WISDOM

Walking in wisdom pleases God. It pleases God because conversations initiate positive communication between individuals and God. When we walk in God's wisdom, we show dedication and respect for God's sovereignty and providence. There is an adage that people make wise statements to garner attention to themselves, and that is not the wisdom this book advocates and presents. Using wisdom is essential for developing an intimate relationship with God because we reach a higher respect as we honor God. We don't have to pretend or try to impress others by adding to viable and sensible discussions that add value to conversations. The almighty word says, "If any of you lacks wisdom, you should ask God, who gives generously to all without finding fault, and it will be given to you" (Jas 1:5). James was sincere and frank about the lack of wisdom. The source to go to is God because he is the answer that provides spiritual support. Walking in wisdom is living up to God's standards.

Focusing on the Creator is imminent as you walk in wisdom. Walking in wisdom is trusting in the Lord with all your heart and not relying on your understanding. Acknowledge Jehovah God, who will make your paths straight (Prov 3:5–7). There is no substitute for walking against wise thoughts, decisions, and ideas. As you go through life, treat this Wisdom Pearl of insight as a valuable treasure.

REFLECTIVE SUMMARIZATION AND RESPONSES TO ACTION

Wisdom is an experience that helps one to see God's direction with hope. It makes one appreciative to honor God by walking in and pursuing wisdom that aids the body of Christ. Wisdom is following God's plan and will. It matters to cherish the insights of wisdom as a Pearl that shines with rays of righteousness and prayer. Pursue wisdom to leave a lasting impression and help build others' faith through wise decisions as they journey on a viable spiritual walk. Remain on track, stay in your lane, and value your spiritual insights.

The Point of Emphasis

Wisdom offers insights into the deep wonders of God.

The Relevant Question

Did you know God blesses the pursuit of wisdom?

A Prayer for Wisdom

Eternal God, thank you for this reading and meditation on your divine wisdom. I desire to understand and share wisdom for your kingdom. As a servant, allow me to help the body of Christ share sensible conclusions of thought. I need you every moment to grow in knowledge and wisdom for your glory. Amen.

DAY 23

The Pearl of Hospitality Is a Comforting Presence

Do not neglect to show hospitality to strangers, for thereby some have entertained angels unawares.

—Hebrews 13:2 ESV

People will forget what you said, forget what you did, but people will never forget how you made them feel.

—Maya Angelou

Entertaining angels unaware is a mark of believers. Doing so demonstrates genuine hospitality to strangers and leaves a lasting impression of warmth and inclusion in a foreign setting. Because of this jewel of a Pearl, I will share this mark in detail later in the chapter. It is a passionate and comforting presence that demonstrates compassion at its highest level. The Pearl of Hospitality brings peace away from home to a place where welcome opens the door of immediate friendship. This action lingers in the receiver's heart, changing anxiety into an ambition to succeed in the race from the welcome mat in a strange setting.

Hospitality is likely part of God's decisive will to "show hospitality to one another without grumbling. As each has received a gift, use it to serve one another, as good stewards of God's varied grace" (1 Pet 4:9–10 ESV). However, this gesture welcomes not only strangers but also anyone who needs the welcome mat of love.

People will never forget what you did as much as what you said. The Bible teaches that hospitality must be used thoughtfully and as a gift. Moreover, as a believer, you possess the essence of divine reality, representing God's agape love. The following passage emphatically clarifies the significant use of hospitality: "Therefore, as we have opportunity, let us do good to all people, especially to those who belong to the family of believers" (Gal 6:10). In essence, one should serve others without seeking gratification. The church must be authentic and genuine and practice high-level hospitality. Hospitality breeds kindness, appreciation, and credibility. It is the rightful path for inspiration and endearment. It is one of the spiritual gifts (Rom 12:13). It has the passionate glue of love that sticks and embodies compassion for serving others.

DON'T OVERLOOK THE PEARL OF HOSPITALITY

It's time to remove spiritual blinders and focus on the Holy Spirit for guidance in comforting others. You can't be blind and show hospitality. Honestly, many churches and individuals are succumbing to self-aggrandizement, neglecting the ministry of hospitality. Meditatively, I think about the impact and message of this Pearl. It exclusively represents God's character because it is a moral attribute of God. Life is valuable and must be lived with worth. Hospitality strives for a relationship that bonds through the spiritual substances of comfort, compassion, encouragement, love, and peace of mind. God trusts us to step up and show quality hospitality with new joy.

More likely, individuals are seeking this kind of nurture and care, whether at home or abroad. Churches have many opportunities to embrace people from all walks of life. Church leadership must provide a welcoming environment for visitors seeking a new place to worship. From the pulpit to the pew, all must go to work with a compassionate spirit of warm embrace. The danger is to be trapped in tradition and overlook using your ministry gift to inspire someone. To inspire others, constantly seek the presence of God to put you on the spiritual track of sharing compassion, kindness, and love. It is not necessary to overdo it and scare people away. Therefore, the strength of this Pearl is the positive presence of kindness across cultural groups and ethnicities. Why does God require genuine hospitality? It is necessary because it is one of the spiritual elements that meet his obedience and directive in Heb 13:2. It is a faithful saying: "If your church is not reaching and attaining new people, some inward-focused barriers may exist."[1] When you overlook hospitality, you and the church may be on a spiritual derailment and risk spiritual demise. If that happens, there will be a need for resurrection. Believers must meditate, study the word, and stay alert so God can use their gift for an effective and wondrous act of inspiration. Trust and faith are urgent for God to have the courage and fortitude to embrace and influence humanity.

SHINING THROUGH HOSPITALITY

When hospitality matters in your life, you will shine. The Bible says, "Let your light shine before men, that they may see your good works and glorify your Father in heaven" (Matt 5:16 NKJV). When Jesus gave his disciples these words of encouragement, he revealed a life-changing opportunity to make a lasting impact on the world. Good works fit being kind and generous to all needing an affectionate embrace. Sharing lights for God's glory is one of the greatest accomplishments in ministry. During Jesus' ministry, he remained the epitome of hospitality. He healed, encouraged, and provided hope for the lonely. He shines in our dark spaces daily. The Bible declares, "The Son is the radiance of God's glory and the exact representation of his being, sustaining all things by his powerful word. After he had provided purification for sins, he sat down at the right hand of the Majesty in heaven" (Heb 1:3). Christ's mission delivered us from darkness to experience light. Light keeps us on the right course to grow and experience God's glory.

    Our paths are illumined to express and appreciate God's inherent majesty. Praise God for this day because light is the package deal for sustainability. To witness good works is a testimony that represents

---

1. Gentile and Nixon, *Art of Hospitality*, 6.

the Almighty God. We sing, "This little light of mine, I'm gonna let it shine." Shining your light does not mean having a braggadocio spirit but instead blessing others and glorifying the Father. Your bright light will shine a beacon of hope in a dark and dim situation. The motivation is to appreciate the light and comfort that those who see it as a symbol of God, faith, and hope derive from it. The Bible says, "The people dwelling in darkness have seen a great light, and for those dwelling in the region and shadow of death, on them a light has dawned" (Matt 5:16 ESV). Many individuals on the streets, in stores, schools, and corporations eagerly await a welcome mat. Be a light of hope and witness the grace of God at work in you and others. When you bow in the presence of God, your heart is open to the movement of God to bless you with moments of opportunity to shine.

OLD TESTAMENT CHARACTERS WHO PROVIDED HOSPITALITY

The foundational example of the Pearl of Hospitality began in the Old Testament. We share this gesture from King David: David's welcoming of Mephibosheth to eat at his table was a remarkable moment and interaction (2 Sam 9). What an encouraging pericope, as seen in Gen 18:1–15, when Abraham and Sarah's generosity spread like wildfire in their land. They shared a meal with traveling visitors. This gesture of love is what God wanted, and they met the challenge unequivocally. Here is a meaningful act of love in the face of death: the prophet Elisha provided a meal to the Aramean army that had been sent to kill him. This situation was an act of faith over fear (2 Kgs 6:22). Also, the Shunammite woman provided genuine hospitality to Elijah with a room on the top of her and her husband's home (2 Kgs 4:8–10). God shows favor by providing necessities from his providential care.

NEW TESTAMENT CHARACTERS WHO PROVIDED HOSPITALITY

The foundational example of hospitality in the New Testament begins with the redemptive Christ. Jesus' action plan was comprehensive through his miracles and parables. His spiritual and social imprint was his ministry. His unusual gesture was when he went to Zacchaeus's house and ate with sinners. A word of wisdom is "Please don't overlook outcasts" (Luke 19:1–10). Hospitality is demonstrated at Peter's house, where Jesus healed Peter's mother-in-law. She was hospitable to Jesus amid her fever (Matt 8:14–15). As Jesus was anointed in Bethany, much complaint came from the disciples. Priority was about economics rather than hospitality (Matt 26:6–10). Martha opened her home to Jesus to rest from his travels. The Master encouraged Martha not to worry but to focus on more important things, as Mary did (Luke 10:38–41).

We emphasize engaging, inspiring, and encouraging others to remember what Paul says: "Have this mind among yourselves, which is yours in Christ Jesus" (Phil 2:5 RSV). To further amplify and advocate hospitality in the New Testament, the apostle Paul did not fall short of how the mark of hospitality helped shape the early church. He strongly emphasizes the significance of showing hospitality as one of the marks of a Christian. He says, "Contribute to the needs of the saints and seek to show hospitality" (Rom 12:13 ESV). In short, to be dedicated and obedient, we are encouraged to follow Jesus' example and make hospitality impactful. Jehovah gets the glory when we make the uncomfortable comfortable. People of all walks of life genuinely seek hospitality.

REFLECTIVE SUMMARIZATION AND RESPONSES TO ACTION

Whatever you do, don't let your hospitality flame die. The Pearl of Hospitality is a jewel of opportunity to demonstrate marvelous hospitality to strangers and people from all walks of life. Cross-cultural opportunities should never be an excuse for overlooking hospitality. The goal is to break through any possible barriers and change discomfort to comfort. It is wise to utilize the mark of hospitality for the glory of God. Jesus provided examples during his ministry of the importance of comforting those in need.

The Point of Emphasis

You can't be blind and demonstrate hospitality.

The Relevant Question

Why does God require genuine hospitality?

A Prayer for Hospitality

Almighty God, I bow down in humble submission to your holy name. Bless me with the passion to demonstrate a spirit of kindness in welcoming others who need affirmation or comfort. Keep me under the shadow of your grace and mercy as I extend your hospitality to your people. Help me to abide by your guidance, let go of myself, and utilize the image of your moral attribute of hospitality in your name. Amen.

PART FOUR

Wisdom Pearls That Glorify God

Glorifying God emphasizes the reason for worshiping God through spiritual action. These Pearls provide an overview of spiritual health. Spiritual strength comes from spiritual health. Every moment of a believer's life is an opportunity to satisfy God. Seeking to grow spiritually must be the prime factor that pleases God. Whatever happens during your spiritual walk, the Almighty provides the foundation for sustainability. As you focus on the sublime majesty of Jehovah, there is a high expectation to know and see where God leads. As you read this section, you will be encouraged to understand why spiritual markers matter.

DAY 24

The Pearl of Fruit Is a Relationship Factor

I am the vine; you are the branches. If you remain in me and I in you, you will bear much fruit; apart from me you can do nothing.... This is to my Father's glory, that you bear much fruit, showing yourselves to be my disciples.

—John 15:5, 8

The Pearl of Fruit is a relationship factor between the vine and the branches. The setting of this passage in John 15 is dark. It is just before Jesus is crucified. He is just preparing his disciples for ministry during their weakness so they can be comfortable when he leaves them. Therefore, abiding in the vine gives strength, courage, and focus to see the big picture of your spiritual journey.

Because of Jesus' passion for his disciples, he began his upper room discourse with the venerable image of the vine and branches, *a favorite reference to Israel in the Scriptures he knew.* As the prophets so often lamented over Israel, Israel repeatedly disappointed God by failing to be fruitful. If Jesus had not set the tone and prepared the way, his disciples would have failed like Israel, and if we, as his disciples today, do not take the gospel seriously and stay connected to Jesus, we will fail. Jesus was very concerned about his believers. He was concerned because he knew how difficult it would be without his guidance.

This parable of the vine and the branches shows a union between Jesus and his followers. He taught them what it takes to live when he is gone. Bearing fruit is a mark of believers, and Jesus requires you to bear good fruit. Some will turn out bitter as natural fruit grows on healthy trees and becomes juicy and tasty. The same holds for spiritual fruit. God's will is for spiritual fruit to be succulent and flavorful. The positive and fruitful lifestyle pleases God and encourages others to duplicate it. The challenge is to circumvent Satan's desire to tempt you to bear bad fruit. Bad fruit is not loving and the opposite of the nine qualities of the fruit of the Spirit. Matthew 7:15–20 alerts us to "beware of false prophets," observing their camouflage and the bad fruit they produce. Jesus says, "Every good tree bears good fruit, but a bad tree bears bad fruit.

STAYING CONNECTED TO THE VINE

A good tree cannot bear bad fruit because it is connected to the vine. A good tree is a spiritual blueprint that guides us through rugged experiences. This Pearl is about spiritual survival, and Jesus is the central focal point because he is the true vine. It is wise to know that bearing fruit is a spiritual refreshment for the soul, mind, and body. Therefore, the branches depend on the vine for nourishment and refreshment. It is the guiding factor for remaining in the vine. Nothing can be accomplished without guidance from the sap of the vine. Every believer must show the marking of fruit in their lives. No fruit, no favor. God monitors fruit activity. Start this day with a fruit connection that will be real and personal. Jesus says, "You did not choose me, but I chose you and appointed you so that you might go and bear fruit—fruit that will last—and so that whatever you ask in my name the Father will give you" (John 15:16). When you plug into the vine (Jesus), it is a power plug that spiritually energizes you for a fruitful relationship. A fruitful experience with the vine is a loving experience that reminds you to call out to God for power to do ministry. The aim is to remain in the vine, and remaining in the vine solidifies and guarantee continuing relationship and fellowship. It gives the branch a reason to bear fruit. Fruit bearing is the ability and encouragement to gauge the spiritual barometer for a higher level of relationship. This Pearl is vital and is an acknowledgment to review the theology of fruit-bearing as emphasizing relationship and fellowship. Staying connected to the vine is the spiritual wattage of the Holy Spirit that powers you with the light to shine in dark places.

THE FOUNDATION FOR FRUIT BEARING

The key to fruit bearing is essential for spiritual growth, and the connection is foundational. Fruit bearing is to bear the fruit of the Spirit. Our fruit bearing is to adhere to Jesus' teaching, and he says to abide in him. You bear the fruit once you abide in Jesus, the vine. The fruit Jesus requires and expects us to bear in Gal 5:22–23 is love, joy, peace, patience, kindness, goodness, faithfulness, gentleness, and self-control. These nine essentials serve as a clear directive and guide for fruitful living and fulfilling the fruit of the Holy Spirit. Bearing fruit starts with the right attitude, which is to think optimistically about the fruit of the Spirit.

The Pearl of Fruit has vital questions to ponder. Are you bearing his fruit today? This spiritual guide is an encouraging factor for such action. Review the above nine qualities of the fruit of the Spirit. What are you doing since you have been saved? Where do you stand with Jesus today? Are you on the right road? I want to challenge each of us to take a serious look at what Jesus means and what it means to stay in the vine. You may be living a false sense of life with no purpose. Do you desire to remain in the vine and bear fruit for the kingdom of God? If so, then make it a priority to value the nutrition that the vine supplies. Take the time to ask God for direction and focus on bearing good fruit. Here is what Paul said to the church in Colossae about fruit: "So that you may live a life worthy of the Lord and please him in every way: bearing fruit in every good work, growing in the knowledge of God" (Col 1:10). This Scripture emphasizes the spiritual life of a believer. Paul admonishes and alerts the church in Colossae to implement fruitful living because bad fruit indicates a negative outcome. Consequently, the outcome dictates an unfruitful lifestyle. Every unbeliever is on a different path from the believer. They do not abide by the vine when living loosely and are subject to support bearing bad fruit. There is no relationship between a person whose tree bears bad fruit and a person whose tree produces good fruit. Certainly, there is no relationship with the Lord. Consequently, the flesh builds a divide and cuts off nourishment because the flesh problem is against godly principles. You cannot please the flesh and abide in the vine because "the flesh must be directed toward death. Having fallen victim to the world, it can do nothing other than live in hostility toward God."[1] A vital thought is that the Roman passage is difficult and describes two lifestyles, the Spirit and the flesh—*sarx*, for sinful nature,[2] and *penuma*, for the Spirit.[3] The Spirit and the flesh are diametrically opposing principles for living. One will have to decide on one's lifestyle or which fruit to choose, good or bad. Every moment with the Eternal Spirit is a sacred moment to excel spiritually because your spiritual identity charts your life course.

Such a one may look very spiritual, indeed, to those who see them, but the heart of one who follows this fleshly approach to God is sin's stain, guilt, and God-hatred. Their life is conflict and death, and they cannot stay in the vine. Those not staying in the vine for fruitful living are dying and withering away. Use this day to prioritize this sacred moment as a fruitful branch in God's kingdom. The concluding question is: "Are you sure you are in the vine?" If you are, don't hesitate to blossom with meaningful fruit representing a loving Father who supplies all you need according to his glory (Phil 4:19). Jesus said he is the vine, and his Father is the vinedresser (John 15:1 RSV). He keeps us fresh with the anointing of the Holy Spirit. We who live in the vine have a purging experience from the power and guilt of sin to keep going. Through the Holy Spirit, being able to battle sin and survive is at a higher level of purging and cleansing through the word.

REFLECTIVE SUMMARIZATION AND RESPONSES TO ACTION

Reflecting on the vine and the branches brings hope to be a participant in helping to contribute to the kingdom of God. The branches are essential factors for bearing fruit. Emphasis is on total connection and developing a relationship with the vine for the authentic spiritual

---

1. Käsemann, *Commentary on Romans*, 219.
2. Strong, *Strongest*, 2058.
3. Strong, *Strongest*, 2052.

walk. Having the mark of a believer is a relative factor for meaningful living. It is a genuine essential for righteousness in action. This book has motivational principles designed for practical living. The objective is to use discernment to determine the difference between good and bad fruit.

The Point of Emphasis

A good tree cannot bear bad fruit because it is connected to the vine.

The Relevant Question

Are you abiding in the vine?

A Prayer for Fruit

Everlasting Creator, thank you for the Pearl of Fruit from your presence to provide strength and courage to abide in the vine. It is a powerful connection and relationship that encourages the soul to be happy and bear fruit for your glory. Thank you for allowing a wretch like me to be on your timetable to add to the fruitful ministry. Thank you, God, for the presence of the Holy Spirit to guide me through serious times in the face of false prophets while bearing good fruit in your name. Amen.

DAY 25

The Pearl of Spirituality Is Enlightenment

The righteous will flourish like a palm tree, they will grow like a cedar of Lebanon; planted in the house of the Lord, they will flourish in the courts of our God. They will still bear fruit in old age, they will stay fresh and green, proclaiming, "The Lord is upright; he is my Rock, and there is no wickedness in him."

—Psalm 92:12–15

And I said to the man who stood at the gate of the year:
"Give me a light that I may tread safely into the unknown."
And he replied:
"Go out into the darkness, and put your hand into the Hand of God.
That shall be to you better than light, and safer than a known way."

—Minnie Louise Haskins

God knows the heart and mind of the righteous. He desires that we flourish like a palm tree. In essence, he expects us to grow deep in the roots of his presence. He knows that you experience distractions every day. The only solution is to depend on his divine presence. Believers don't have to live as a recluse when experiencing the courts of God. The Pearl of Spirituality authentically warms the heart of the Almighty through the sacred search for the meaning of life. Spirituality keeps the heart full of hope for guidance and bright hope because the aim is to love the Lord with your complete heart (Deut 6:9).

The psalmist emphasizes that he aims to grow deeply with spiritual roots that get God's attention. Spirituality is associated with every Pearl, as it searches for the sacred that matters in life. Each Pearl drives one to search and flourish for enlightenment. Today, your spirituality is a deeper dive for anchoring down in solid roots and trusting in the God who directs you through dark spaces. No matter the challenges, circumstances, and temptations, you have reasons to strive for a viable foundation. What is your life like, and how are you acting based on what Jesus has given you? God is interested in your spirituality. Do your best to comply and satisfy God by being alert. Make spirituality your goal; it is walking in the presence of God, seeking guidance from the sun's rays that give enlightenment for a dim journey. This journey to spirituality aims to unleash the rigid tension of anxiety, suppression, or disappointment to give hope for stability.

THE NEED FOR FLOURISHING

The need to flourish is a sign of spiritual development and a walk with God. There is never a time to think about giving up due to impending challenges, opposition, and setbacks. The psalmist provides robust assurance that the righteous will prosper and be successful and flourish like deeply rooted palm trees (Ps 92:12). When you walk deep in God's presence, you are destined to grow with favor. Unknown attacks of spiritual warfare will challenge your walk and testimony. You need God's spiritual guidance to navigate times of testing. Take the apostle Paul's advice: "Finally, be strong in the Lord and his mighty power. Put on the whole armor of God so that you can take your stand against the devil's schemes" (Eph 6:10–11).

I was encouraged by the above engaging poem "The Gate of the Year" by Minnie Louise Haskins.[1] It is contextually associated with the Pearl of Spirituality. God blessed the body of Christ with this engaging

---

1. Wikipedia, "Gate of the Year."

Pearl. Spirituality is needed for your relationship and fellowship with the Creator. As we tread the unknown, God makes the reality of reason and existence real through his holy presence. We are still walking through this Pearl because to be spiritual is to be authentic. For further authenticity and relevance, the Greek word for "spirituality" is *pneumatikos*, an adjective described by Bauer "as in the sense in one breath spiritually, in a spiritual manner caused by or filled with the spirit."[2] I define spirituality this way. Spirituality reveals the condition and strength of the believer's heart through the power of the Holy Spirit. It affirms that the big picture is to value spiritual health for a lasting relationship with God. Believers benefit from maintaining an authentic lifestyle that aligns with God's expectations for flourishing and growth.

A ROCK OF DEFENSE

Believers need to use wisdom to effectuate the closeness to the Rock that guides and sustains hope in old age in the courts of the Lord. A reminder from the psalmist: "The Lord is my rock and my fortress and my deliverer, my God, my rock, in whom I take refuge, my shield, and the horn of my salvation, my stronghold" (Ps 18:2 ESV). Walking in the strength of the Lord means having total focus, dependability, and trust in a strong shield. Reminiscing on this day affirms that Jehovah is the authentic Rock. Any evil opposition and confrontation give the courage to wade through fears of defeat. They will come, day after day, week after week, month after month, and even into the twilight of the end of the day. Be encouraged and bolster your fortitude to garner heavenly safety. Take a moment to trust and act through meaningful, fervent prayers for righteous protection. Jehovah provides a massive covering of protection from any type of enemy onslaught. The assurance is applying total focus and maintaining a purposeful life in a distracting world.

MAKING SPIRITUALITY MEANINGFUL

Making spirituality meaningful is a direct attack on the wiles of the devil. (Rom 6:10). Satan does everything to disrupt your spiritual

---

2. Bauer, *Greek-English Lexicon*, 679.

walk. That is because the evil one is carnal. We must observe what Paul said to the Romans regarding carnality: "For to be carnally minded is death; but to be spiritually minded is life and peace. Because the carnal mind is enmity against God: for it is not subject to the law of God, neither indeed can be" (Rom 8:6-7 KJV). There is a difference between a carnal thought and a carnal mind. The natural mind means to have a heart for carnal things, to be agreeable to sensual ways, to approve of carnal values, to have a purpose for carnal goals, and to walk sensually to please the flesh. The spiritual person is the opposite of the carnal life (1 Cor 2:14-15). The two lives are on two different spectrums. This Scripture is a Scripture about spirituality.

Paul is alerting the church in Rome to watch out for carnality because its objective is to promote the carnal lifestyle. The carnal lifestyle strives and lives on a negative presence. A negative presence prevents spiritual nourishment. Every unbeliever is carnally minded, and every believer is spiritually minded. When carnally minded, there is a lack of a daily spiritual agenda. This Pearl on Spirituality prepares you for victory over the craftiness of spiritual warfare. Its purpose is to practice and function aggressively to defeat negative interruptions. God requires you to consider fulfilling your spiritual purpose and building your capacity. Building capacity is thinking biblically; the Bible says, "Like newborn infants, long for the pure spiritual milk, that by it you may grow up into salvation" (1 Pet 2:2). As a believer, your spiritual walk and growth are essential for spiritual vitality because they enable you to build and identify with a meaningful theological foundation. This principle is an inspiration for continued development. Paul's encouragement, "Do your best to present yourself to God as one approved, a workman who has no need to be ashamed, rightly handling the word of truth" (2 Tim 2:15 RSV). God wants your best, and it is the only way to live with a spiritual purpose for growing through the word.

A LASTING EXPERIENCE

Your spirituality is a lasting, inward, and experiential process, a reminder that God creates life and that life with the Holy is significant and even more incredible with the divine. It is a lifetime journey to effectuate change. This lasting relationship undergirds your faith and earns God's favor. Your experience and interaction with God will have a profound impact on your spiritual development. When you effectuate change, you take charge of your life under the divine umbrella of everlasting covenant and covering. Your experience with God is what drives you to continue the journey of steadfastness and growth in the sacred. Be ambitious about growing in faith, hope, and love. Develop a habit for the light at the end of the tunnel of your pursuit of God. These Pearls affirm that your spiritual walk is a testimony of your total commitment that binds you to God's power, presence, and providence.

REFLECTIVE SUMMARIZATION AND RESPONSES TO ACTION

This spiritual growth guide is a meaningful experience that effectuates authentic, deep spiritual engagement with God. Spirituality is a lasting relationship that binds one's pursuit of God through the challenging terrains in life. It is a blessing to earn God's favor during your walk. The objective is to maintain open lines of communication as you seek more spiritual nourishment for personal growth. The Pearl of Spirituality assures you will flourish in the deep rivers of inspiration and information to benefit from your testimony. The spiritual action plan involves seeking signs of being drawn closer to God for spiritual intimacy and striving for daily meditation of total surrender.

The Point of Emphasis

When you walk deep in God's presence, you are destined to grow with favor.

The Relevant Question

Are you in the sacred search for a meaningful spirituality?

A Prayer for Spirituality

Eternal Lord, I take this valuable moment to thank you for allowing me to walk in your presence and experience your fellowship as I seek the sacredness of your power in my life. Oh God, I need your fellowship and guidance for my spiritual identity. Make and mold me as your servant while I meander through life's rugged terrains. Help me understand the impact of remaining connected to the divine. Give me the strength to stay focused on you and see the light at the end of every tunnel, even the most challenging tasks. Amen.

DAY 26

The Pearl of a Gentle Tongue Is a Discipline Factor

Let no corrupt communication proceed out of your mouth, but that which is good to the use of edifying, that it may minister grace unto the hearers.
—Ephesians 15:29 KJV

A slip of the foot you may soon recover, but a slip of the tongue you may never get over.
—Benjamin Franklin

The Pearl of a Gentle Tongue is a blessing from God to practice discipline. Use it, adore it, and cherish it. It is a blessing because it creates a safe environment for ministering to others when used correctly. The wise counsel from the apostle Paul makes sense: avoid corrupt communication, for it is of no benefit. The tongue is essential for positive edification and encouraging others to make a difference. Proverbs 15:4 says, "The soothing tongue is a tree of life, but a perverse tongue crushes the spirit." What an encouraging biblical truth that Solomon compares the tongue to the tree of life.

The tree of life is a theological emphasis on eternity (Rev 22:2). Solomon put his spiritual weight on the tongue to emphasize the validity of a wise tongue. A gentle tongue falls under godly wisdom. When I say *tongue*, it is more than the physical tongue; it is the reflections that come from the inward thoughts, ideas, and speech tone. It is good to pray and meditate before speaking. Don't speak out of emotions that cause negative, intriguing excitement. The premise and purpose of this reading is to share significant factors for speaking compassionately. Pertinent factors will be shared from this study that represent compassionate conversation from believers. You must strive to be strong when the tongue desires to be unruly. Sin causes an unruly tongue. James discusses an unruly tongue that humans cannot control. It is full of deadly poison and full of evil. We bless God with our words, but we also speak blessings and curses with the same tongue and words (Jas 3:7–12); *cursing* not in the sense of profanity, but God uses believers to show his wrath on the evil one. Remember, it is not what goes in a person's mouth but what comes out that defiles the person (Matt 15:11). Defilement is a profane action. The reason is to seek God's guidance for personal devotion.

FAITHFUL FACTORS OF WISE WORDS

Here are five essential factors to identify the value of a gentle tongue:

1. The power of wise words.
2. The passion of wise words.
3. The practice of wise words.
4. The persuasiveness of wise words.
5. The perfection of wise words.

These faithful factors will build the discipline to connect confidently with people. Mostly, people are waiting for wise words that can redirect and power their spiritual journey. The first factor is the *power* of wise words. The tongue's power has two roads, which explain its focus and intent. You must choose which road to use in conversation, death or life. When one uses the power of the tongue to hurt and disrupt, that is a death sentence for one's character. They are of no use to God because they use power for self-gratification. When it is used to glorify God, it is beneficial for life. Wise words bring many benefits; they increase posting on social media and encourage individual interaction. They affirm relational comfort and spiritual well-being. Wise words reduce the propensity for paranoia. They give a calming effect on any anxiety. The power of the tongue avoids evil to see good days (1 Pet 3:10). Solomon describes the power of the tongue this way: "The tongue has the power of life and death, and those who love it will eat its fruit" (Prov 18:21).

The second factor is the *passion* of wise words. The passion for wise words is a deep desire to communicate with kindness and comfort. Therefore, you must have an impetuous passion to use wise words. A passionate spirit is no desire to speak bitterness. How will you respond to bitter communication? Bitterness can make you bitter if you reciprocate. In the name of Jesus, keep me from bitter talk. Prayer is the answer through the Holy Spirit to conquer bitterness. Paul emphasizes dropping any malice or anger. Bitter communication has no merit or value for peace. Bitterness leads to further sin. The Holy Spirit empowers one to fight sin and the sin of thoughtless words. The purpose of the ministry of the Holy Spirit is to convict one to live a life of spiritual happiness. The work of the Holy Spirit is to convict individuals. Don't allow bitterness, anger, and slander to flow from your mouth (Eph 4:31).

The third factor is the *practice* of wise words. We need a reason to practice wisdom talk. Simply put, ask God to give you the strength to implement positive actions. James's encouragement, "If you are wise and understand God's ways, prove it by living an honorable life, doing good works with the humility that comes from wisdom" (Jas 3:13 NLT). I remember what Mama said, "Practice makes perfect." Continue doing and saying what will leave a lasting impact on you and others.

The fourth factor is the *persuasiveness* of wise words. Most people desire encouraging words. Persuasive words of wisdom impact others and inspire them for many reasons. Wise words unlock hopeless situations, enabling you to move forward with positive thinking for promising results.

The fifth factor is the use of wise words lead to effective communication. Therefore, it is impossible to achieve absolute perfection in spoken language. All of us are incapable of being language perfectionists because of our faults and shortcomings. When some things are said, they could be expressed more effectively. Speaking correct English is one thing, and speaking from the heart is another. It is vital to choose the proper words and phrases when in conversation. Different words affect people differently. God's word is the foundation and practice for spiritual living. The Bible says, "The one who knows uses words with restraint, and whoever has understanding is even-tempered" (Prov 17:27). A word of caution: don't allow the influence of words to cause you to get out of character. It is wise to keep focusing on prayer as the link to God to use the right words for every occasion, even if it's small talk.

As a believer, have you ever thought about how to use words with meaning? If not, the reason could have been that we were more concerned with pleasing the flesh than following the guidance of the Holy Spirit. Paul admits the following action: "My message and my preaching were not with wise and persuasive words, but with a demonstration of the Spirit's power" (1 Cor 2:4). He did not use persuasive words. Still, he leaned heavily on the demonstration and dependability of the Holy Spirit. The ineffectiveness of our talk and life is a lack of spirituality. You must know the significance of the tongue and its influence. Don't allow sin to influence unwise conversation in all endeavors, as this of personal sin and guilt. The Holy Spirit is the only one who can convict individuals of sin. I suggest continuing the path and guidance of the Holy Spirit to tame the tongue.

RESPECTFUL COMMUNICATION EDIFIES INDIVIDUALS

The Eternal Creator did not create the tongue for ruthless and degrading conversation. The Pearl of a Gentle Tongue guides sensible thoughts and respect for those around you. Respectful conversation is a form of healthy communication that fosters curiosity and attentive listening, thereby building relationships and promoting spiritual growth. One of the most famous and engaging Bible verses about communication is in Paul's letter to the church in Ephesus. He says, "Do not let any unwholesome talk come out of your mouths, but only what helps build others up according to their needs, that it may benefit those who listen" (Eph 4:29). This verse teaches wisdom in a nutshell. It's truth travels everyone's path, those possibly meandering thoughts, the opposite of edification.

Corrupt communication spoils a great moment. It ruins the moment with useless guile that leads to no good. The purpose and emphasis of the tongue is to create a safe environment. Believers must treat the Pearl of a Gentle Tongue carefully and seek to speak kind words, especially in heated confrontations. A gentle tongue symbolizes thoughtful and respectful communication, as well as a word of wisdom. Many people struggle to control their tongue because they allow their ego to get in the way. Then, the devil takes the ego on a destructive flight path to a perilous outcome, all to make an egotistical point. To avoid that entanglement, you must stay under the influence of the Holy Spirit, and you will avoid the flight path of a satanic outburst of the tongue. Those outbursts are damaging to your psyche. Damages will leave you ineffective for present and future conversations.

REFLECTIVE SUMMARIZATION AND RESPONSES TO ACTION

Reflecting on this day with a gentle tongue has encouraged positive and meaningful action. You must strive to avoid bitterness and malice through an engaging conversation. Avoid reciprocating with unwise blows that damage relationships. Edification inspires others to adopt a positive mindset. It is suggested that a plan of action be devised through prayer and practice using wholesome words to communicate without outbursts. Think biblically and theologically about the state of the tongue.

The Point of Emphasis

Bitter communication has no merit or value for peace.

The Relevant Question

How will you respond to bitter words?

A Prayer for the Tongue

In Jesus' name, help me be a better servant of effective communication. I need the guidance of the Holy Spirit to keep me on the right path, speaking kind words of compassion to all I encounter. Give me the strength to overlook those who may speak unkind words to agitate a negative response from me. In your name. Amen.

DAY 27

The Pearl of Compassion Is a Touch of the Heart

Blessed be the God and Father of our Lord Jesus Christ, the Father of mercies and God of all comfort, who comforts us in all our affliction, so that we may be able to comfort those who are in any affliction, with the comfort with which we ourselves are comforted by God.

—2 Corinthians 1:3–4 ESV

Another day has come to appreciate the Pearl of Compassion from the heart of God. His powerful touch lingers, and you will desire to hang on to the impact of his mercy. Compassion depends on God for the healing touch of love, grace, and mercy. The apostle Paul graciously shares the above Scripture to affirm the touch of God's heart. God blesses and bestows the Pearl of Compassion in believers' hearts, and at salvation, it is an experience that will always remain. Since God blessed you with mercy and consolation, you must eagerly pass the compassionate baton to others, relieving them of their stress and grief. The genesis of this forty-day journey focuses on the above Scripture as the point of departure to feel the divine touch and care of the Father. This action of the Father extends mercy before we ask for compassion.

Paul writes in a tone of feeling God's heart of pity. It is simply an act of grace using deep pity for you.

Three key words in the above Scripture carry a vibrant theological emphasis, making this reading both valuable and spiritually significant. The words are *blessed*, *compassion*, and *comfort*. These words unite a robust experience of God's presence. The apostle Paul was thinking about the praise and worship of the God of all comfort. The Greek word in this passage for "blessed" is *eulogétos*, which means "blessed" or "praised" and is used specifically to praise God.[1] Both "blessed" and "praised" express the same appreciation for God. Compassion comes from the Greek word *oiktirmos*, the root word *oiktir*, meaning "compassion" or "pity." Thayer says "compassion, pity, mercy."[2]

Every believer must cultivate humility and appreciation, for God dwells in our hearts with mercy, compassion, and pity. There is no slack with Jehovah's mercy and no end. That is why Paul makes an assuring statement of faith: "God can do exceedingly, abundantly, above all we ask or think" (Eph 3:20 KJV). Whatever you're believing in, whatever you're dreaming about, God is going to take that and make it bigger, better, and more rewarding than you've ever imagined. Compassion comforts the mind and heart and consoles you for eternity.

SHOWERS OF BLESSINGS

While we are weak, frail, and undeserving of his mercies, we are blessed before we ask. No matter the depths of your perplexities and afflictions, God provides ways to minister to your needs and issues. This gospel song reminds you of his abundant blessings: "He Looked Beyond My Fault."[3] God's blessings are flowing now as you read this volume, and the Bible attests that there are more blessings and mercies than you can handle. To all believers, have you seriously thought about the abundant mercies of God? Do you get excited about more blessings of his mercy? Or have you thought about the depths of his mercy? Those questions should stimulate your mind and cause you to leap for joy, receiving never-ending blessings. On the cross, Christ suffered to give compassion meaning. It was compassion for our sins and the sinner.

1. Bible Hub, "Eulogétos."
2. Bible Hub, "Oiktirmos."
3. Rambos, "He Looked."

Oh God, thank you. Jesus died before deteriorating from the power of sin. The power of sin has no match for the mercy of God. The book of Lamentations affirms a theological tenet about mercy: "The steadfast love of the LORD never ceases; his mercies never come to an end; they are new every morning; great is your faithfulness" (Lam 3:22–23 ESV). These verses reveal the covenant of mercy, love, and grace, offering believers hope amid stress, grief, disappointment, and opposition. The relevant question is, Oh God, am I living with genuine compassion? That question shifts the needle of assessment for how to treat others.

APPRECIATING GOD'S MERCIES

Appreciating mercies is a humble action of love. Knowing that mercies are fresh every morning girds one to walk deeply in faith while experiencing them. Love and mercy are inextricably bound, for mercy is needed every day for an adequate supply. Because of the agape love of the Father, mercies keep coming our way. We should appreciate God's compassion. The prophet Zechariah says, "This is what the Lord Almighty said: 'Administer true justice; show mercy and compassion to one another. Do not oppress the widow or the fatherless, the foreigner or people experiencing poverty. Do not plot evil against each other" (Zech 7:9–10). Living with appreciation for the mercy of God is like fresh water flowing from the bosom of God. Like Niagara Falls in New York where the water continuously flows, God shows his compassion as the symbol of showers of mercy flowing to give hope in an uncompassionate world. Believers should take a praise break and shout hallelujah because praise is the celebration of God's deliverance! We should be open to the leading and anointing of the Holy Spirit for guidance when we are under judgment like Judah for idolatry and immorality. (Mic 6:1–16). God's mercies worked for Judah; undoubtedly, the same opportunity stands for the modern-day church because his mercies run deep. God's mercies are abundant. They continue to arrive and flow in every day.

This Wisdom Pearl of Compassion encourages one to stand tall in the presence of Christ, as Christ represents believers who emulate the tender heart of God. Compassion is translated as a tender heart. The Father's heart responds to the most resounding cry for consolation. The African American tradition has an old saying, "God may not come when you want him, but he is always on time." That phrase is theologically connected to people of color: faith, hope, and dependence on God. It also confirms God's mercy, which believers must embody with faith to extend mercy to others. When this happens, it glorifies God.

THE SIGNIFICANCE OF THE SPIRITUAL GIFT OF COMPASSION

The Pearl of Compassion and mercy are spiritual gifts. The significance is that compassion draws one to cling to pity. All believers are expected to have compassion and mercy, as they are supported by God's word (Matt 5:7). Showing mercy is essential for effective ministry. A profound example of mercy is when Jesus went through Jericho, and people cried out, saying, "Lord, have mercy on me." God responds to cries seeking compassion. They were crying for compassion (Matt 20:29–34). You do not have to have the gift of mercy or compassion to console a person. Everyone desires sympathy for their problems.

Some believers are blessed with the spiritual gift of compassion. Compassion is listed in Rom 12:6–8: "We have different gifts, according to the grace given to each of us. If your gift is prophesying, then prophesy in accordance with your faith; if it is serving, then serve; if it is teaching, then teach; if it is to encourage, then give encouragement; if it is giving, then give generously; if it is to lead, do it diligently; if it is to show mercy, do it cheerfully." The spiritual gifts show how Christ ministers to believers. Believers must seek to discover their gifts. However, one may not have the gift of compassion, but as a believer, one must have a heart for helping and showing compassion and mercy. There are many gifts in the body of Christ. They all have different functions for nurturing and ministering to individuals. People need to connect to the message of gifts for their lives. God made us all different. We are different because we have other purposes for the body of Christ.

In Rom 12:6, the phrase "having gifts that differ" highlights the variety of gifts used in today's church. The gift of mercy is not the same as the gift of miracles. Having the gift of mercy is the extraordinary ability to show compassion to others delicately. It is extreme empathy for those suffering from spiritual and emotional stress. The one who has this gift will know how to minister to others. This gift is connected to the beatitude in Matt 5:7. The gift of miracles is the ability to perform influential works that transcend nature's physical and natural laws. The person with this gift is not the originator of the miracle, but the recipient, through God, to be able to minister to others. However, those in affliction need a miracle, and God is open to releasing them from their stressful plight. The large and boisterous waves of life will move when God shows compassion.

REFLECTIVE SUMMARIZATION AND RESPONSES TO ACTION

It is challenging to honestly think about the essence and essential of showing compassion to others who seek pity for their problems. There is no substitute for having a tender heart for the destitute, stressed, and emotionally drained. It is essential to take action to help people cope with the heavy burdens they face. Those with the spiritual gift of compassion and mercy have a unique ability to serve in a needed ministry. What God did for Judah is open to the modern-day church. When one waits and trusts, one will see the waves of life moving in the opposite direction.

The Point of Emphasis

God responds to the most resounding cry for consolation.

The Relevant Question

Do you get excited about more blessings of his mercy?

A Prayer of Compassion

Thank you, Lord, for this day. Give me a tender heart to have deep compassion for those who struggle with pain. Help me through my plight and pain to minister to others and implement what your word directs. I can only be stronger according to your will. Praise your name and hallelujah for the desire to praise your name and give you the glory. Amen.

DAY 28

The Pearl of Servanthood Is a Five-Star Ministry

When he had washed their feet and put on his outer garments and resumed his place, he said to them, "Do you understand what I have done to you? You call me Teacher and Lord, and you are right, for so I am. If I then, your Lord and Teacher, have washed your feet, you also ought to wash one another's feet.

—John 13:12–14

Servanthood does not nullify leadership; it defines it. Jesus does not cease to be the Lion of Judah when He becomes the lamblike servant of the church.

—John Piper

Authentic servanthood embodies the Trinitarian Godhead through a five-star ministry. The Pearl of Servanthood must focus on valuable ministry and spiritual intimacy that pleases God the Father, the Son, and the Holy Spirit. The Trinitarian Godhead expects nothing less than the best. Whatever you do when showing servanthood as a believer, it must be done with class. Servanthood, like all the Pearls in this book, has a glowing sparkle of going beyond. Moreover, the above verses teach that servanthood, at its best, inspires believers to practice servanthood humbly. The example is set in stone. Jesus' example demonstrated that washing one another's feet defines who you are (John 14:1–17).

Service is needed in the body of Christ. Humility and compassion exhibited Jesus' love for the disciples. He showed an example of leadership and servanthood. Theologically speaking, servanthood is closely tied to the spiritual gift of service. It is found in Rom 12:6–7: "We have different gifts, according to the grace given to each of us. If your gift is prophesying, then prophesy by your faith; if it is serving, then serve; if it is teaching, then teach." Whatever your gift is, integrate it to aid others and make a difference. Here is a powerful example of why it is vital to serve when people require help: Jesus clearly stated the condition of the harvest. That is why he went through the villages teaching and proclaiming the gospel. The Savior sensed helplessness and advocated that *laborers* are needed (Matt 9:35–38). In every city, town, and state, help is needed. The disciples were bewildered and had no idea that Jesus would demonstrate an unusual, humble act of love. This five-star act of servanthood transformed their perspective on and understanding of what it means to be a servant. Jesus changed the intent and direction of the disciples. The Bible says, "For even the Son of Man did not come to be served, but to serve, and to give His life a ransom for many" (Mark 10:45). Serving was the primary objective of the Savior because he realized the need for this humble ministry. Thank God for this ministry because people of all cultures cry for servanthood at its best.

Servanthood encourages the believer to take action to demonstrate God's genuine love for others. Serving others is essential because it is deeply rooted in theology and the principles of servant leadership. What a blessing that, despite our inadequate service, we can provide excellent service to humanity in the hands of God. Where there is no service, the ministry is badly missing. You seek the best service possible when traveling by air, land, or sea. On the airline, whether you are in first class or economy, you want the best service. You feel better when served with positive passion. When you travel by train in coach, business, first class, or sleeper, great service gets your attention. The same holds true on a cruise. The same holds for the kingdom of God; make it your goal to emulate Christ's example of humble servanthood. Many are searching for a church with individuals who are passionate about giving five-star service. Five-star service extends from the pulpit to the pew. You can be impactful, inspiring, and informative for those who are seeking kingdom service. The objective is to put servanthood at center stage.

SERVANT LEADERSHIP

May God reveal the importance of true servanthood. Servanthood and leadership are intimately intertwined to accomplish the sacred task of meeting people's needs, helping during the greatest need of dire situations. If you see a need, act on it for the glory of God. When Jesus takes residence in our lives, things will never be the same, because a new direction and emphasis take over, leading to rapid transformation. Therefore, the heart becomes full of authentic servant leadership. Jesus clearly states the reason for service: "He sat down, called the twelve disciples over to him, and said, 'Whoever wants to be first must take last place and be the servant of everyone else'" (Mark 9:35 NLT). In this context, Jesus becomes Lord of your life and provides the reason for understanding the significance of authentic servanthood. Servant leadership connects to the lordship of Jesus. The lordship of Jesus is the reason for the theological emphasis on the value of servanthood.

When leadership is executed positively, people can sense the presence of genuine service in their ongoing circumstances. David was a good example of a strong leader regardless of his episode with Bathsheba. A lesson from David's' leadership of the nation of Israel: his leadership started when he was young, as he cared for the sheep with five-star leadership. Moreover, he exemplified great courage with passionate servanthood (1 Sam 16:11; 17:34–35; Ps 78:70–72). Another example of David's leadership occurred when he was in the Cave at Adullam, and four hundred men came to be with him, calling him their commander (1 Sam 22:1–2). It takes love, courage, and determination to implement authentic servanthood. You must love people, the church, and the world to implement five-star servanthood. What does your servanthood look like? It should resemble Christ as the master-servant leader, as well as other biblical figures. When love is genuinely given, it has a spiritual touch that embraces God's presence. God's presence is sacred, and the lordship is sacred. Therefore, "sacred leaders have an amazing gift of helping people experience the depths of God himself."[1]

WE PLEASE GOD BY SERVING OTHERS

Serving others touches the heart of God. You can't comfort others without having a strong connection to God. Your serving makes a difference no matter the difficulty. The Pearl of Servanthood is challenging and comforting because it takes courage to help someone who may be prideful and feel unstable. It is comforting when you have served them, regardless of how they feel about Christ over culture. When Jesus washed the disciples' feet, he saw humility over feelings and tense emotions. Servanthood is humility and compassion. He aimed to leave a message of gratitude. Servanthood aims to reveal the genuine heart of the church. A lack of serving is a church on track for spiritual derailment. As a believer, it is wise to take a deep dive into implementing this spiritual giant, having a heart, eye, and ear to people's needs. You must be willing to be an enslaved person for Christ. It's a deep commitment to untiring kingdom work. Your conscience must become stained with a biblical charge of filling needs and comforting hearts. Having the willingness to work until the results of the service rise. It's about meeting needs. The Bible says, "He will meet all of your needs according to his riches in glory" (Phil 4:19). There is no substitute for service. Therefore, show love, tenacity, and integrity.

REFLECTIVE SUMMARIZATION AND RESPONSES TO ACTION

God is a blessing for all our blundering and bickering. The objectives of the believer must include the main point of helping where the need exists. Emulating Jesus is the profound guide to genuine servanthood. This spiritual guide emphasizes the grand significance of servant leadership. One must be willing to become an enslaved person for Christ, representing the compassion of the Messiah. A wise encouragement: do your best to represent serving God's kingdom for his glory.

---

1. Olson, *Discovering Your Leadership Style*, 93.

The Point of Emphasis

The Trinitarian Godhead expects nothing less than the best.

The Relevant Question

What does your servanthood look like?

A Prayer of Servanthood

Almighty God, grant me the serenity to accept your directive and develop a sincere passion for genuine servanthood. Create in me the steam for serving and the commitment to passion. Anoint me for this sacred service of serving people of all walks of life. Guide me in every moment and every step so that I may help others feel valued and important. Help me understand how impactful the church's serving ministry is in adequately representing your kingdom. In your name, I pledge to emulate the examples of your Son, Jesus, for your glory. Amen.

DAY 29

The Pearl of Silence Is Listening to God

Be silent before the Lord, all humanity, for he is springing into action from his holy dwelling.

—Zechariah 2:13 NLT

Be still, and know that I am God. I will be exalted among the nations, I will be exalted in the *earth!*

—Psalm 46:10 ESV

God directs and mandates you to honor his presence by using quality time to receive late-breaking news of spiritual guidance. It is his will that you follow his biblical guidelines for holistic and fruitful living. The news is to spend time with God and listen attentively in awe of his holiness as he guides you with his providential sovereignty. Take a praise break, "Praise his holy name!" How beautiful it is to sit in silence before the Lord. It is the prime time of spiritual nourishment. The more you think about being in the divine presence, the more you gain encouragement and experience the powerful anointing.

The prophet Zechariah marks a valuable precedent for being silent. God alerts the people that the land of Judah will be his possession and encourages Jerusalem to shout and rejoice! because he is on the way to living with them (Zech 2:10–13). The present-day church awaits to experience its holy dwelling. It is a time to disengage your thoughts and listen further to the Holy. Quiet time with God demonstrates respect for the doctrine of God's *sovereignty*. It is also an act of obedience and prudence as a reminder that silence precedes worship. It is vital to listen to the Creator amid the grave hustle and bustle. Listening to God requires the discipline of humbleness. You must train yourself to listen to God as much as or more than crying out to God. God hears the cries of the voice of listening as well as speaking.

LISTENING TO GOD BUILDS YOUR INTIMACY

The depth of understanding silence lies at the heart of Ps 46:10 (also see Hab 2:20; Rev 8:1; cf. Ps 61:1). God is exalted and will be exalted in the earth among all nations. These references highlight and emphasize what it means to abide in stillness, waiting on the move of God. The psalmist confirms the reason to listen to God. When you listen to God, you are demonstrating humility by receiving all directions and assignments that align with God's will. Silence changes your focus from your busy lifestyle, allowing you to turn your attention to God. It is necessary to honor his presence as you grow in knowledge. Honor and respect the Creator's presence, sovereignty, and providence. When in silence, give God your full attention for spiritual growth and development.

What a reason to evaluate your daily routine as you grow in intimacy. God created this Pearl for spiritual intimacy and focus for spiritual growth. It is a time of shaping and molding for a greater spiritual walk. This Pearl is a reminder of the potter and the clay. God invited Jeremiah to the potter's house to witness the molding and shaping of clay. This experience involves accepting silence to hear God speaking (Jer 18:1–4). Spiritual shaping and molding are vital because they shape and mold you for spiritual intimacy. During your silent moment with God is a time of comfort, nourishment, and strength. You are in the presence of the eternal fountain of life. The Bible explains, "Teach me, and I will be silent; make me understand how I have gone astray"

(Job 6:24 ESV). Silence is the turning wheel for a greater opportunity to hear what God must convey to a meandering saint adequately.

Silence has two significant purposes. The first is to spiritually bond and benefit from connecting to God. Second, you need to practice when to talk and when not to, but you also need to hear God speaking and listen to others to evaluate life's circumstances. The time is critical that we understand that there is "a time to be silent and a time to speak" (Eccl 3:7b NASB). The Creator monitors your eager ambition to hear spoken words. Silence leads to genuine worship. The Bible teaches, "God is spirit, and those who worship him must worship in spirit and truth" (John 4:24 ESV). Worship is impossible when one is distracted, and there is no spiritual connection to reverence Jehovah. God is spirit, and that is the sacred moment for silence. We must recognize our helplessness and lack of godly attention to the Creator. Oh, how frail and broken we are when constantly on the go. Stop! Take time and give God time for fellowship.

You must enter God's presence as an empty pitcher before a flowing stream. The symbolism of an empty pitcher relates to your soul needing to be refilled, refueled, and refreshed. Listening builds a credible relationship and anointing. The more you listen, the more God pours into you to mend your brokenness. God's presence dictates listening and gaining access to be a greater witness. I will share a biblical vignette for the ultimate act of silence: God utilized his silence in heaven to make a statement of prophetic significance when the Lamb opened the seventh seal (Rev 8:1). The opening of the seals occurs in Revelation 5–8, which reveals the second coming of Christ. This prophecy reveals the impact of the impending apocalypse, which marks judgment and the prophetic power of moving to succumb to total silence in heaven for half an hour. Revelation teaches that believers must value the Pearl of Silence and devote themselves completely to God. Sitting, meditating, and quietly waiting on God is the gateway to his presence. Quietness with God builds spiritual credibility as maturity brings confidence in spiritual growth. It is not how long one waits in quietness; it is the quality of hearing what God says to your spirit. When you sit quietly in the presence of the Holy, you benefit from presence and power.

THE POWER OF SILENCE

Silence is the power that comes from listening attentively to God. The Bible states that Jesus speaks to the Father, representing our frailties and weaknesses. That is power in full force. Romans 8:34 says, "Jesus is at the right hand of God interceding on our behalf." Our silence grows more profound than we can imagine because Christ cares. He stands vicariously in our stead: "But if anyone does sin, we have an advocate with the Father—Jesus Christ, the Righteous" (1 John 2 ESV). No matter our circumstances, we must never cease to be silent before God, because Jesus will always be our advocate (Heb 7:15; see also John 14:16, Heb 9:15). Being before the Lord in humble submission shows ultimate respect for the Creator. It reveals that we are willing to pursue the deeper relationship that God requires. A deeper relationship prepares you for what lies ahead.

The good news is that you are covered vastly. This coverage includes the Holy Spirit praying for you with groanings that can't be spoken (Rom 8:26–28). It is double indemnity; Jesus and the Holy Spirit pray for you. That is the benefit of the power of silence. Since double indemnity is a life insurance term, we have life assurance in Jesus and the Holy Spirit. Not only do Jesus and the Holy Spirit hear our groans, but God also hears them and does not overlook our groans and pain. "God hears the prayers of the righteous" (Prov 15:29). Silence before God is a spiritual privilege to listen to Jehovah. The first letter from Peter affirms the same: "For the eyes of the Lord are on the righteous and his ears are attentive to their prayer, but the face of the Lord is against those who do evil" (1 Pet 3:12). When God keeps watch over us, it encourages us to move forward in the power and anointing of the Holy Spirit.

The power of silence rewards unique benefits from listening to God. However, the aim is not to forget God's message to the prophet Zephaniah. The message was to be silent before the Lord because the Lord had prepared a sacrifice for guests (Zeph 1:7). The modern-day believer and church model the prophetic message of Zephaniah. What is an appropriate guide and encouragement to practice and engage in silence? The question is, How badly do you want to experience the power of silence before God? The goal is to begin experiencing the benefits of godly silence.

LISTENING TO GOD IS A MEANINGFUL RELATIONSHIP

Listening to God demonstrates patience and perseverance in sustaining oneself until divine results emerge. A relationship with God must be authentic. The Bible states, "After the earthquake came a fire, but the Lord was not in the fire. And after the fire came a gentle whisper. When Elijah heard it, he pulled his cloak over his face and went out and stood at the mouth of the cave" (1 Kgs 19:12–13). When you settle down and focus on hearing God's voice, you are eager and excited to raise your antennas for a relationship connection. I propose two benefits that authenticate a robust and meaningful relationship with the Holy. The first benefit is strength. Godly strength is the spiritual defense against and means to conquer spiritual warfare. Spiritual warfare is accurate, and to conquer, sitting quietly in God's presence is an overt preparation for duty. The purpose of spiritual warfare is to attack your faith so that you would succumb to the devious craft of satanic activities. Moments with God will prepare and preserve you for battle. I am reminded of what God told Joshua: to be strong and courageous, never to tremble or give up, because he had his presence and power wherever Joshua went (Josh 1:9).

The second benefit is anointing. Receiving the anointing through the Holy Spirit is a primary spiritual defense against the enemy. As a result of sitting with Jehovah in silence, you are blessed with the opportunity and privilege to pray. The more you listen, the more you hear the voice of the Lord God. The signs of anointing through silence affirm a strong faith, a vibrant prayer life, a sense of purpose, and a sense of obedience that manifests wisdom. This affirmation gives one confidence and courage to walk in the presence of God and pursue a more meaningful relationship. The hands of God are active during the moments of complete silence. Therefore, silence before God confirms one sense of calling for authentic intimacy with the Creator. Regardless of distractions, stay the course and watch the hand of God guide you. The prophet Isaiah says, "For my thoughts are not your thoughts, neither are your ways my ways, says the Lord. For as the heavens are higher than the earth, so are my ways higher than your ways and my thoughts than your thoughts" (Isa 55:8–9 RSV). This verse affirms the Pearl of Silence in the lives of believers and encourages one to continue respecting God's sovereignty. When this happens, remember that "the Lord will fight for you; you need only to be still" (Exod 14:14). Be confident and persevere to be still against all odds. Stillness before the Creator is a sign of honor, adoration and worship. Listening before God is the art of learning to appreciate the fullness of Spirit. The Spirit helps us when we are weak (Rom 8:26). Stillness before God is a true test of growing in the Spirit. You must be eager to wait on God's power to move through the Holy Spirit and his protection to embrace your feebleness

REFLECTIVE SUMMARIZATION AND RESPONSES TO ACTION

Sitting quietly in the presence of God is an honor for believers. During the moments of silence, God desires to develop a lasting personal relationship. It is essential to block all distractions and give total attention to God. The meaningful action is to pursue spiritual fellowship to fully experience and respect God's sovereignty through the power of silence. The prophet Zechariah emphasizes the need for significant action to implore God for spiritual refreshment. It behooves believers to break away from the overwhelming daily distractions and seek a vibrant prayer life and a sense of purpose to authenticate their divine calling.

The Point of Emphasis

The hands of God are active during moments of silence.

The Relevant Question

How badly do you want to experience silence in God's presence?

A Prayer of Silence

Eternal God, here I am in humble submission to you. Help me constantly respect your sovereignty and guide me in all my ways. Anoint me with your Holy Spirit to develop a stronger relationship. I pray for understanding the power of silence as I grow spiritually in intimacy. I'm reminded of the old church hymn "Guide Me, O Thou Great Jehovah."[1] Keep me under the shadow of your wings. Use me for your will. Amen.

1. Williams, "Guide Me."

DAY 30

The Pearl of Conviction Is a Positive Reality

They said to one another, "Surely we are being punished because of our brother. We saw how distressed he was when he pleaded with us for his life, but we would not listen; that's why this distress has come on us."

—Genesis 42:21

For the word of God is alive and active. Sharper than any double-edged sword, it penetrates even to dividing soul and spirit, joints and marrow; it judges the thoughts and attitudes of the heart.

—Hebrews 4:12

Conviction brings everything full circle. God has a strategic plan for the process of conviction. The Pearl of Conviction is a valuable response to eternity, meaning that the Holy Spirit monitors the reality of the seriousness of conviction. It is an eternal gift given and ordained by God for a more significant response, yielding better results and changing direction for a new path in life. This Pearl is the voice of God, urgently speaking to convince us of the need for a significant redirection. A major change is brewing on the path of eternity. Don't get caught in the throes of life's unpleasant vicissitudes. God is passionate about providing you with a better opportunity to see the big picture of eternity. Keep focused and value God's word. It is the action for a permanent change that highlights an authentic lifestyle. Oh, what assurance that the Holy Spirit significantly impacts change. It connects with the word. The Holy Spirit is the change agent for accepting conviction, which convicts of sin (John 16:7–11). The Holy Spirit moves upon individuals and convicts those with strong evil thoughts and a ruthless, wicked lifestyle. The Pearl of Conviction is the attention-getter for a better lifestyle, and you can change your address from sin to salvation. That action is the big picture and purpose of this Pearl. This devotion promotes a positive outlook on reality. It prompts your conscience to reflect on your character and behavior.

The purpose of this Pearl is to reflect on your situation and circumstances. The relevant question is, How do you respond to the conviction of the Holy Spirit? As a believer, your response is to reevaluate your spiritual walk and meditate on its spiritual status. When you cry for release, God is there to answer your plight. The Pearl of Conviction includes God's grace and the direction of the Holy Spirit. It acts to convert from negatives to positives. Remember, the writer of Hebrews reminds us that the word of God is alive and sharp, and it has the penetrating power to get attention to respond to how it speaks to the mind and heart to move positively (Heb 4:12). Conviction is a persistent, driving reality check to move in the right direction. It pierces the heart, soul, and mind. Genesis shares the pericope of Joseph and his brothers. The situation was a family saga that brewed over time. After much sadistic plotting, Joseph's brothers came to a positive reality concerning their treatment of Joseph, who received blessings amid bitterness. Thank God for orchestrating this story for his glory, revealing a hostile scheme. While they planned to wreak havoc, God diverted their intended havoc to healing through conviction (Gen 42:21). Again, conviction serves as the exit sign at the door of condemnation, prompting a change in direction before the final step of ruthless condemnation is taken.

The Pearl of Conviction carries a heavy theological emphasis on listening to one's conscience, which speaks to moving with possibility and initiating change. Your lifestyle and interactions can lead to misfortune and mistakes, which in turn generate adverse consequences. However, the Holy Spirit works to redirect your steps for the better. The Trinitarian Godhead—the Father, the Son, and the Holy Spirit—are in union regarding the Pearl of Conviction. The Holy Spirit ministers to believers, guiding them on the path of joy and peace.

THE PURPOSE OF CONVICTION

The purpose of the ministry of the Holy Spirit is to convict one to live a life of spiritual happiness. Therefore, the purpose of conviction is to adhere to the direction and leading of the Holy Spirit. What is the role of the Holy Spirit's work? A significant role of the Holy Spirit is to convict. The work of the Holy Spirit is to convict individuals of personal sin and guilt. You must be serious about your conviction and not be swayed by others to do what they do; hold fast to your conviction. The strong and the weak in Rom 14:13–23 describe how believers must be examples to those who are weak. Conviction is a strong exhortation of faith and passion governed by the Holy Spirit. Therefore, "mature Christians must limit their liberty for the weak and for church unity."[1]

You must be willing to follow the guidance of the Spirit and be prepared and willing to bear the infirmities of the weak, which is a spiritual consideration for encouraging others (Rom 15:1). The Holy Spirit continues to convict individuals of sin. The Bible teaches, "And when He has come, He will convict the world of sin, and of righteousness, and judgment (John 16:8 NKJV). Preachers can preach week after week, but the work of the Holy Spirit moves upon the hearts of individuals living in sin. When we evangelize, the work will be done by the Holy Spirit.

THE POWER OF CONVICTION

The power of conviction is the work of God through the Holy Spirit, lifting one from the bottomless pit of sin. God's voice leaves a lasting and memorable urgency to move with positive reality, to take a check of personal action, and to maintain a viable relationship with the Almighty. What a new and better direction that adds value and

---

1. Pate, *Romans*, 300.

purpose to life. The experience of this action draws us closer to God and encourages and inspires participation in kingdom work. Conviction leads one to practice being the world's light and never cease to let it shine before humanity. In the words of Isaiah, "Arise, shine; for your light has come, and the glory of the Lord has risen upon you" (Isa 60:1 ESV). *The power of conviction* guides the conscience to act by morality. It aims to reveal the truth about a large-scale experience. When convicted, you have much to share about God, Christ, and the Holy Spirit. What a blessed, impactful encounter when you experience the power of conviction; it presses you to tell the truth and do what is right.

Jesus' teaching to the disciples on the Mount of Olives (Matt 8:1) is an important context for conviction. He further encourages, "And you will know the truth, and the truth will set you free" (Matt 8:32 NLT). It reveals that you desire to live a new life in the presence of God. When you are led to permanent change, it is a change that completely represents Christ, and you will tell the truth, not just in one instance, but continuously. Conviction is a lifetime experience that builds character and courage. Courage is knowing that you are on the right path. However, your conviction is deep because you stand on the power and principles the Holy Spirit teaches. When you walk in the power of the Holy Spirit, you have unwavering faith to live the principles of the power of conviction. The Bible teaches, "Be on your guard; stand firm in the faith; be courageous; be strong" (1 Cor 16:13). The four principles, *be on guard*, *stand firm*, *be courageous*, and *be strong*, in this verse confirm that one's conviction has a tight grip on being a disciple. The tight grip is a grip that matches one's faith theology to walk in conviction and please the Almighty. This Pearl captures the mind of individuals and makes them ponder the power of conviction. Conviction makes you think about your lifestyle and look in your mirror introspectively as your life is driven spiritually.

REFLECTIVE SUMMARIZATION AND RESPONSES TO ACTION

This devotion emphasizes the importance of listening to your heart and being true to God's voice of conviction. It is significant to hear what the Almighty has to say. It is prudent to assess the state of your spiritual mind personally. When God speaks, he speaks with power through the word to make a difference. I urge believers to make it a priority to continue to pray for guidance to live a lifetime of honest action. As a disciple of Christ, be excited about the power and purpose of conviction.

The Point of Emphasis

Conviction is the exit sign at the door of condemnation.

The Relevant Question

How do you respond to the conviction of the Holy Spirit?

A Prayer of Conviction

Oh, Merciful God, thank you for your work of conviction. Your power draws my finite mind and heart to walk with you. You have challenged me to meditate on my actions and determine the condition of my heart, soul, and mind. You touched my heart to live the life of realizing and accepting your powerful conviction and urged me to speak the truth and move with positive reality. In Jesus' name. Amen.

PART FIVE

Wisdom Pearls That Please God

Wisdom Pearls that recognize God's sovereignty are a potent statement about God's providence. This section makes a glorious statement about the importance of pleasing God in all spiritual endeavors. The purpose of worship is a meaningful factor that pleases God, highlighting the significance of discipleship. The layout of praise in this section speaks volumes to its meaning and how it differs from worship. This section is not exclusively about worship, but rather provides nuggets that outline the purpose and define worship. Believers must please God with a deep passion for discipleship, evangelism, missions, and the significance of prayer in a life of resilience. God is pleased when all factors in this section edify the believer and please God.

DAY 31

The Pearl of Worship Shows Adoration

Lord, you are my God; I will exalt you and praise your name, for in perfect faithfulness you have done wonderful things, things planned long ago.

—Isaiah 25:1

The time has come for a revival of public worship as the finest of the fine arts.... While there is a call for strong preaching there is even a greater need for uplifting worship.

—Andrew W. Blackwood

Jehovah longs for pure worship from his children. You were created to worship God. It is wonderful to know the significance of authentic worship. Worship nourishes the soul while meeting the eternal criteria for transformation for a deeper relationship with the Holy. The spirit of worship impacts you with the truth that authenticates true worship for all aspects of life. It is a blessing because Jesus taught the disciples this genuine Pearl of Worship so they would get a meaningful start in life. His care and concern for his disciples were to make sure they understood how worship connects to God. God is drawn to your sincere spirit of worship. This day's encouragement to worship will awaken your consciousness and prompt you to reflect on spiritual admiration and adoration for the Almighty. It also makes you think about eternity and the presence of God.

Reverence is his ultimate will to please him with utmost passion. God is omnipresent (present everywhere), accessible for worship at any time and from anywhere. Therefore, his omnipresence and omnipotence (all powerful) are linked to worship. The phrases *God is spirit, is loving,* and *is good* have often been quoted passionately by believers to show reverence and adoration. Some may not be aware of the whole spiritual significance of the phrases. They are attention-getters that captures the mind to think about connecting pure worship with God. Too many people are somewhat confused about what worship is. They attend different churches and have different views, methods, and ideas about worship. Those ideas relate to styles of worship. Regardless of the styles, God must be the main factor for spiritual elevation. Some believe that worship should be loud, while others prefer it to be soft and quiet. The psalmist says, "Make a joyful noise to the Lord, all the earth!" (Ps 100:2 ESV). Joyful means happy and cheerful, and noise means loud.

THEOLOGY OF WORSHIP

For this reading and reflection, here is an example of a theology of worship: A biblical theology of worship is grounded in the word of God: "As the deer pants for streams of water, So my soul pants for you, my God. My soul thirsts for God, for the living God. When can I go and meet with God?" (Ps 42:1–2). You must come to God in holy reverence and awe, expressing your humility as you render your ultimate adoration. Worship is the response to the Creator as he sits in his divine nature, guiding his creation in the splendor of his sovereignty, grace, and providence. Honor and respect the Biblical proclamation that God is spirit, truth, holy, and just.

CONNECTING TO GOD

Worshippers must feel and connect to the leading of the Holy Spirit to connect with God. I yearn for spiritual reciprocity; God feels my needs, and I sense God's gentle, still voice. God oversees the worship experience. There is a chapter on praise, in which the difference is explained. Praise and worship are not the same, but they relate. Praise is an expression of what God has done for us. It is a way of letting our feelings flow. Worship is about our state of mind and heart. It reveals what we think about the Creator. How difficult is it to discipline worship time with God? Where your heart is is the question. Only God knows the heart and how it is prepared for worship. It could be both styles: at times, it may necessitate a loud and excited style, and at other times a serene and quiet one. Regardless of the method, God seeks true worship. Please remember that worship can't be orchestrated. It must be spontaneous, as evidenced by the action of the Holy Spirit. It is a move of God and not humanity. Authentic worship shows adoration because God created you to worship him. Your spiritual life is unbalanced and devoid of proper worship of the Creator. If you miss the spiritual mark, worship is not part of your daily plan with God. The Bible declares that worship is connected to God; it says, "God is spirit, and those who worship him must worship in spirit and truth" (John 4:24 ESV). God helps us understand and know the significance of worship. By God's will, he will direct us in avenues as we experience opportunities to worship him.

THE ALMIGHTY IS WORTHY

A longing desire to express God's worthiness is a sacred act. Seek to worship God at anytime, anyplace, and anywhere. Worship in meditation is a method that brings happiness and joy, just you and God. Take a moment to bow down, as it shows adoration. The three Hebrew boys are a prime example of the conviction to worship Jehovah. The Bible declares, "Shadrach, Meshach, and Abednego replied to him, 'King Nebuchadnezzar, we do not need to defend ourselves before you in this matter. If we are thrown into the blazing furnace, the God we serve can deliver us from it, and he will deliver us from Your Majesty's hand" (Dan 3:16–17). You must exhibit a strong adoration, like that of the three Hebrew boys, regarding authentic worship. All bowing must be before Jehovah.

When you refuse to serve other gods, you are protected with power and God's promise. Make worship your ultimate objective to please God. After worship, the anointing of the Holy Spirit will impact your heart, mind, and soul. You will have to say, Hallelujah, praise God! A thorough examination of worship in the book of Revelation reveals the prophetic significance of worship. The apostle John says, "You are worthy, O Lord, To receive glory and honor and power; For You created all things, And by Your will they exist and were created" (Rev 4:11 NKJV). John, on the island of Patmos, shared a vital spiritual point on the sacredness of worship. The sacredness of worship in this chapter centers on the twenty-four elders bowing down to worship the Almighty (Rev 4:10–11). They begin their praise with the words, "You are worthy." Thank God for the book of Revelation. It unlocks and reveals the mystery of worship in heaven. That is why I said earlier that worship focuses on eternity. That means worship is only temporary on this side but everlasting in heaven.

Earthly worship is merely a dress rehearsal for the permanent worship that awaits us in eternity. My aunt raised me in southern Georgia after my mother passed on when I was two years old. I remember walking three miles to church when I was eleven years old. While walking, my aunt would sing along the way. One song I remember went, "Run on, you've got a race to run, all of God's children got a race to run." It was music to the ear. I did not understand her worship experience, but I knew it was not fake. Sometimes, she almost shouted! Before arriving at church, she was preparing because her soul was happy. That was in the African American tradition. Worship had reverence, spirit, and joy. When we arrived at church, the deacons had the fire blazing, accompanied by singing, testifying, and praying. As I grew older, I sensed a holy cadence of music glorifying God. In worship, Jesus was the Lamb that was slain from the foundation of the world. As a result of being raised in a Christian home, I was baptized at the age of eleven. I can vividly remember that day. Oh, how excited I was, running down the dusty road from the creek to the house!

THE BREAKTHROUGH OF WORSHIP

As the clouds thicken in the atmosphere, the sun's rising breaks through to give birth to another day. The same holds for worship. Worship is a passionate pursuit to connect with God through the hearts and souls of believers. After the breakthrough, reflecting on personal plights, God wants you to reach him with pure and authentic worship. Every time you worship, it is the birth of a new moment, marked by a unique experience. Starting a new day is a new experience, and then comes a satanic confrontation. Satan does not want you to experience a breakthrough. The evil one does not have the power to prevent the breakthrough, but only false promises that cause harmful distraction. A breakthrough for worship is necessary for spiritual growth. Worship must have meaning and purpose to connect with God. The breakthrough of worship is God's work through the Holy Spirit. You will never experience the whole meaning of worship until you get a breakthrough. My breakthrough came when I was discharged from the army in 1966, during the Vietnam conflict. I was deployed in Korea during that era. I worshiped God through consistent prayer and the study of the word. Soon after being discharged, I accepted the call to the gospel ministry. Worship became more passionate and sacred for me.

When in worship, we need to listen to God speaking to us. Make no mistake; there will be good news from the Almighty and comfort from the Holy Spirit while Jesus intercedes on our behalf. Suppose you are depressed, lonely, broke, dejected, abused, homeless, paranoid, or experiencing anxiety and anger. Don't give up; remember an example of God's promise to Israel to deliver them. The promise was to deliver them and keep them safe from the water. No fire would burn them. He made a declarative promise to redeem them from the enemy (Isa 43:1–30). Through this promise, Israel was set to worship. His favor was on them. Just like Israel, God is waiting for you to worship him. After your breakthrough, you will praise him for the results of deliverance and the joy that comes with it. Your breakthrough is coming with Jesus' interceding on your behalf for any unavoidable circumstances.

REFLECTIVE SUMMARIZATION AND RESPONSES TO ACTION

The believer's goal is to spend more time in the presence of God. Worship gives birth to strength for a lifetime journey. When you think about how God feels about you, you will think about the moments when God rescued you from your depression, disappointments, and anxiety. God is more than worthy to be praised. As you read these nuggets and vignettes, worship flashes through your mind and warms your heart for the opportunity to share space with the Almighty. Be prepared to face Satan when accosted to derail your path of worship with God. Make every day a day of persistence in developing sacred time with God and honoring his holy name.

The Point of Emphasis

God is attracted to dedicated worship.

The Relevant Question

How much discipline do you have for your worship?

A Prayer of Worship

In the name of Jesus, please help me continue to build my worship experience with the Father. Lord, I desire to feel the power of the breakthrough and give God glory for intimacy in worship. Lord, keep me day by day to practice and apply moments with you daily. Amen.

DAY 32

The Pearl of Discipleship Is the Apple of God's Eye

And Jesus came and said to them, "All authority in heaven and on earth has been given to me. Go therefore and make disciples of all nations, baptizing them in the name of the Father and of the Son and of the Holy Spirit, teaching them to observe all that I have commanded you. And behold, I am with you always, to the end of the age.

—Matthew 28:18–20 ESV

The very process of facing and dealing with life's challenges is how we become strong people. You can't develop strength without pressure and without a degree of stress (and sometimes even pain). The hard times can make us strong. Smooth seas do not make skillful sailors.

—African Proverb

Discipleship requires dedication and commitment. God is waiting, monitoring, and assessing the activity of believers and the church. The modern-day beatitude is: blessed are the ones who disciple others. The Pearl of Discipleship is essential and matters because it is the apple of

God's eye, and it is the mandate to follow Christ and make disciples. The apostle Paul shares a teaching proclamation: he says, "Him we proclaim, warning everyone and teaching everyone with all wisdom, that we may present everyone mature in Christ. For this I toil, struggling with all the energy that he powerfully works within me" (Col 1:28–29 ESV).

It takes a strong constitution and courage to warn those who are flirting with inadequate spiritual growth. It is not an option to pursue another activity. The Bible says, "Like newborn babies, crave pure spiritual milk, so that by it you may grow up in your salvation" (1 Pet 2:2). You must keep pursuing the benefits of the Great Commission. When you follow the mandate, you will experience the benefits of growth, witnessing, training, and teaching. The Great Commission is at heart, and as you start this day, start it with the passion to follow the mandate in detail, by baptizing, teaching, and obeying. Jesus urged his disciples to honor this Wisdom Pearl as genuine followers. Following the mandate takes faith, courage, and determination to partner with other believers in implementing the oracles of God. Despite the enticing allure of sin, as a follower of Christ, you must apply and implement this passage in your witnessing agenda to show others that discipleship matters and let them know. Don't allow the lusty lures of sin to deter you.

The book of Jude places a strong emphasis on discipleship, encouraging believers to contend for the faith amid false teachers and to shun ungodly living (Jude 1:1–4). Many believers overlook the message of the Great Commission and the purpose of discipleship, often hindered by numerous distractions. The theological emphasis of this Pearl is that Christ provides the blueprint, leads the way, and is "the truth, the way, and the life" (John 14:6). He speaks truth to the situation at hand, stating what is present and what lies ahead.

Jesus taught his disciples to be committed servants, serving with compassion. He emphasizes that authority has been given to him by God and charges believers to make disciples. Christ has guaranteed that he will be with us until the end of the age (Matt 28:18). What a marvelous blessing of encouragement to know that we have safety when making disciples, baptizing them, and teaching the word. Discipleship is an expression of God's love in responsible action. That is the work that is the apple of God's eye. God has poured himself into believers to use the gifts of service to reach others. This chapter urges you to examine yourself because God has instilled in your spirit a driving passion for the discipleship-driven life. Life is valuable and rich when we move beyond the superficial and discover the purpose of authentic discipleship. It is pressing to cling to the spiritual passion and fire to possess the essentials for executing and adhering to the Great Commission. This day serves as a reminder to answer the call to be a devoted disciple, honoring both horizontal and vertical living through discipleship. It is reaching up to God to reach out to humanity.

A genuine disciple will value the words of the Great Commission in Matt 11:28: "Go into all the world and preach the gospel, baptizing and teaching." Discipleship is a Pearl that brings happiness, honor, and respect to God's mandate. It is to live both horizontally and vertically. This living emphasizes spiritual living as a duty call to God's service. Living vertically is to answer to God, and living horizontally is to serve humanity through ministering. Serving humanity horizontally is sharing spiritual ingredients such as love, joy, comfort, and mercy. The Creator expects compassion and valuable service for the kingdom.

GOD IS CONCERNED ABOUT DISCIPLESHIP

Today reminds believers to be spiritually vigilant about the cost of discipleship. The next thought is a lifter of hope and the eyebrows. As a believer, think about the prevailing thought: God is concerned about discipleship because "the church must merge to motivate and inspire others to break out of their comfort zones and effectively disciple others."[1] What is your response to such a statement? Does God's concern for discipleship grab you? God's concern is an urgent appeal for servants to act with passion. Therefore, we must be ready to live each day, clinging to the driving force of the Holy Spirit, to remain obedient to the cause of discipleship. God wants us to be more than usual individuals; that is why the Pearl of Discipleship is the apple of God's eye. The phrase attests that the Almighty keeps watch on every believer to manifest the need for discipleship. Oh God, you speak through your Son: "This is to my Father's glory, that you bear much fruit, showing yourselves to be my disciples" (John 15:8). This verse teaches us the ministry of union. Jesus and the Father are one to make a statement for believers to the heart and bear fruit. Therefore, authentic discipleship

1. Turner, *Biblical Theology of Christian Discipleship*, 22.

is evident in bearing fruit. How glorious are these words of hope in an imperfect world. It is encouraging to know that discipleship is sparkling with opportunities to reach out and share a word of hope through teaching and training. He expects us to implement the ministry of discipleship as the ideal principle of his mandate.

ABIDING IN CHRIST

Abiding in Christ is a testimony that you are spiritually capable and prepared to make disciples. It is a responsible duty to do this ministry. Well, God trusts you and expects you to carry out this ministry from the Great Commission to reach those broken and fragile communities. Jesus fully represents the Father in these words: "Abide in Me, and I in you. As the branch cannot bear fruit of itself, unless it abides in the vine, neither can you, unless you abide in Me" (John 15:4 NKJV). *Abide* means total collectedness for guidance, inspiration, and the anointing of the Holy Spirit to bring hope to a lost harvest. Abide ultimately means to attend to the harvest, because the Savior says, "The harvest is plentiful, but the laborers are few; therefore pray earnestly to the Lord of the harvest to send out laborers into his harvest" (Matt 9:37–38 ESV). It is a divine honor that God chose you to be the apple of his eye in making disciples. Gracious Father, I recognize the opportunity to help the harvest recover and experience redemption. As you respond to the harvest, remember these encouraging words of confirmation that God is with you: "Now to Him who can do exceedingly abundantly above all that we ask or think, according to the power that works in us" (Eph 3:20 KJV). The trust stated in this verse brings hope to a hopeless situation. It is faith for believers to trust the God of grace and mercy to go beyond the ordinary and seal the memory of release. Forget those past things that impede your progress and just press toward the mark for the prize of a higher calling and a dedicated servant (Phil 3:13–14). Praise his holy name for choosing you to be an asset for his kingdom-building enterprise.

REFLECTIVE SUMMARIZATION AND RESPONSES TO ACTION

Thinking about discipleship is a monumental thought that responds to the destitute harvest. People need help most solemnly. Since God is concerned about discipleship, it reminds me to consider the importance of being concerned about others. The response should be to live a balanced lifestyle, both horizontally and vertically, to make a difference in helping to attend to the harvest. This spiritual growth journey is a wake-up call for believers to heed the call of the Great Commission.

The Point of Emphasis

Don't allow the lusty lures of sin to deter you.

The Relevant Question

Does God's concern for discipleship grab you?

A Prayer of Discipleship

Merciful God, thank you for giving me the strength and fortitude to read this day on discipleship. Please endow me with patience to abide in Christ as one of your living branches to bear fruit of disciple-making for your glory. I press toward the mark for a higher calling of discipling others. Keep me under the shadow of your wings. In your name. Amen.

DAY 33

The Pearl of Stewardship Is Accountability

Each of you should use whatever gift you have received to serve others, as faithful stewards of God's grace in its various forms.

—1 Peter 4:10

Every good gift and every perfect gift is from above, coming down from the Father of lights, with whom there is no variation or shadow due to change.

—James 1:17 ESV

You were created to be held accountable, not to be lackadaisical, but to be useful. God carved you out and designed and shaped you for a purpose. Your design is that of an accountable steward. The question is, What are you doing with your gift? Your gift must be used as a ministry asset in the body of Christ. Moreover, God is watching and waiting for your faithful service to take shape for kingdom work. Stewardship is the Pearl that tests your obedience. Because of your stewardship, it serves as a reminder to love the Lord with your whole heart, soul, and mind. It is necessary for obedience (Deut 6:5). In addition, part of your obedience is to serve others using your spiritual gifts (1 Pet 4:10). The objective of stewardship is to prepare you for being a faithful and accountable steward. How marvelous that the Bible lays out the succinct fundamentals of stewardship. Most importantly, the Pearl of Stewardship encourages disciples to refocus, refresh, and renew their spiritual walk through Bible teachings and prayer. Every believer must use the spiritual gift that God has given to serve others faithfully with God's abundant grace (1 Pet 4:10). Stewardship requires the use of your spiritual gift to fulfill stewardship accountability. The accountability began in the garden with Adam. God spoke to Adam and Eve in the garden with clear directions. "The Lord God placed the man in the Garden of Eden to tend and watch over it" (Gen 2:15 NLT). Adam being the first steward, God assigned him to the garden, as the verse says, "to tend and watch over it." This accountability was a great responsibility to manage. God trusted Adam to oversee the garden carefully. He was in the position of implementing a continuous watch care of God's creation.

FOCUS ON USING YOUR GIFT

Once you realize how important it is to focus on your gift, you will realize that you are stepping into God's will as an authentic steward. If we could link Adam's accountability to the New Testament teaching of using a gift, he would be suited to the gift of administration to work in the garden. God in his wise providence, looked into the future of the New Testament, equipped Adam with the gift of administration. "If your gift is to encourage others, be encouraging. If it is giving, give generously. If God has given you leadership ability, take the responsibility seriously. And if you have a gift for showing kindness to others, do it gladly" (Rom 12:8 NLT). In the garden, he had to be obedient and have compassion. In considering Adam's stewardship, let us pray, meditate, and prepare ourselves to be stewards of what God has entrusted to us to care for. Whatever it is, or how small, treat it with care. Keep focusing on your goal, and remember "the purpose of your life should be the basis and motivating force behind your giving."[1] You must organize and stay focused to manage your ministry. Whatever your gift is, use it for the glory of God. Notice the lesson on how Jesus explains his requirement concerning the servants and the use of talents.

1. Sutherland and Nowery, *33 Laws of Stewardship*, 81.

Christ clearly requests faithful and sincere accountability. Here is the point he stressed: "His master said to him, 'Well done, good and faithful servant; you have been faithful over a little, I will set you over much; enter into the joy of your master" (Matt 25:21 RSV). The master was pleased that one of the servants gained five additional talents. Obedience and trust were significant factors for accountability. The trust was repeated with another servant with two talents (v. 22). After his obedience: "His master said to him, 'Well done, good and faithful servant; you have been faithful over a little, I will set you over much; enter into the joy of your master" (Matt 25:23 RSV). The obedient servants learned a valuable lesson of authentic accountability. The servant with one talent missed the opportunity to add value to accountability. That servant exercised no faith in trusting Jesus. He hid his talent, thinking it was the safest and best option (Matt 25:24–25). This servant was a bad example for believers today because he sat down on the master's money, was afraid and lacked faith. Jesus wasted no time in passing sentence for disobedience. He said, "But his master answered him, 'You wicked and slothful servant! You knew that I reap where I have not sowed and gather where I have not winnowed" (Matt 25:26 RSV). Action speaks, and this action points to obedience. The obedient servants prayerfully thought and used their time wisely. They heard and responded accordingly. That was practical theology at its best.

THE ABUNDANT LIFE

When believers model themselves after the obedient servants in this parabolic pericope, their lives will be enriched, allowing them to live the abundant life. The abundant life attests that one will testify of changes in life's commitment and dedication. To live the abundant life is to utilize the spiritual gift that has been given for abundant and victorious living. The abundant life has a positive message to vile opposition. The Holy Spirit is the only agent capable of conquering all acts of spiritual interference. Believers must strive to experience confidence by utilizing their gift with victorious living. Victorious living is not possible without abiding in Christ. Beloved brothers and sisters, make sure to live with his teachings. God guarantees to grant your wishes. Our Christ says, "If you remain in me and my words remain in you, ask whatever you wish, and it will be done for you" (John 15:7 KJV).

This kind of living brings joy and peace, fostering a purposeful life. When believers model themselves after the obedient servants in this parabolic pericope, their lives will be enriched, allowing them to live a victorious life. The victorious life attests that one experiences confidence when they use their gift through victorious living. Victorious living is living that meets God's standards. While remaining in Christ and continuing in his teachings, he brings abundant blessings. These are blessings that you will never forget. The abundant life is the life that brings joy, happiness and peace.

REFLECTIVE SUMMARIZATION AND RESPONSES TO ACTION

This guide is a test of your faithfulness, obedience, and faith. Accountability is the faithful act that believers must perform to demonstrate obedience. The central factor of this reflection is the importance of continuing in Jesus' teachings. His teachings shape one for the abundant life and victorious living. As a believer, your responsibility is to be a faithful servant. Stewardship is the accountable action of being an obedient servant. A deeper obedient response is to utilize your spiritual gift for the glory of God. In retrospect, just as God assigned Adam and Eve in the garden to tend to it, you have a responsibility to tend to the things that God has assigned you as a steward and the effective use of your gift.

The Point of Emphasis

The abundant life is the caveat to vile oppositions.

The Relevant Question

What are you doing with your gift?

A Prayer for Stewardship

Eternal God, keep me rooted in your power and presence, that I may remain a faithful and accountable steward. Help me to live an abundant life and encourage others to take stewardship more seriously. Thank you for your blessing and allowing me to be a disciple for your glory. Stewardship is the accountable action that you require authentic living. In your holy name. Amen.

DAY 34

The Pearl of Evangelism Is a Passionate Endeavor

For I am not ashamed of the gospel, because it is the power of God that brings salvation to everyone who believes: first to the Jew, then to the Gentile. For in the gospel the righteousness of God is revealed—a righteousness that is by faith from first to last, just as it is written: The righteous will live by faith.
—ROMANS 1:16–17

Could a mariner sit idle if he heard the drowning cry? Could a doctor sit in comfort and just let his patients die? Could a fireman sit idle, let men burn and give no hand? Can you sit at ease in Zion with the world around you damned?
—LEONARD RAVENHILL

It takes a passionate person to boldly ask another person or a stranger if they would die today, would they go to heaven. Most would answer "I hope so." Some would say "Yes," and others would say "I don't know." Despite these answers, the person asking must have the spirit of the apostle Paul: "I am not ashamed of the gospel, because it is the power of God that brings salvation to everyone who believes: first to the Jew, then to the Gentile" (Rom 1:16). The objective of the believer is to present the gospel with care, courage, and confidence. To share the gospel is no put-down; it is a power lifter of faith. As a believer, don't be ashamed, because you must have the theology of passion, and the passion of Christ for the unrighteous. Act and witness with the boldness of the persuasive holy writ. The assurance is that the power of God opens hearts, ultimately leading to salvation. This passion is a blessing for beloved brothers and sisters because Paul makes a confident statement about his faith, and has a *robust passion for evangelism*. The Pearl of Evangelism is a theological Pearl that points to eternal salvation. Jesus gave the plan of evangelism to his disciples to go into all the world by implementing the Great Commission (Matt 28:18-20). Evangelism and discipleship are closely intertwined. Overall, the Great Commission is about discipleship.

Evangelism is a crucial component of discipleship. These verses support the title of this book, *The Purpose Driven Disciple*. It is time to ask Christ to intercede on your behalf, gaining the courage and confidence to discuss your eternal destiny with someone. As a believer, you must be passionate about leading others to the threshold of redemption. If you know of someone who is lost, they have no clue what it means to be saved. Leading them to Christ does two things: they will experience a new life filled with hope and love, and second you will experience the blessing of sharing the gospel. The aim of this Pearl is twofold: to make you think about salvation, and to encourage you to take action to go to the harvest and help pull out those who are in the quicksand of sin and sinking to damnation. Again, ask Christ to give you the power of the Holy Spirit. Have the will to witness to someone that will impact and change their destiny forever. The book of Romans is one of the books in the New Testament that anchors deeply with the major theme that the righteousness of God is paramount and available to everyone. God speaks through the apostle Paul regarding the righteousness of God. The focus for today is critical because evangelism falls under the doctrine of salvation, and it is essential to understand the concept of God's *righteousness*. It will help you develop into a greater asset to the kingdom. Pray and meditate as you read this daily synopsis.

Righteous living has eternal benefits. There are numerous benefits for the righteous as found in Proverbs 11. One benefit is to reap a sure reward (Prov 11:18). The sure reward is salvation from sowing righteousness. Proverbs 11 serves as confirmation of eternal security, which is the goal of evangelism. The righteousness of God is his action and passion to save unbelievers. The Greek word for "righteousness" is *dikaiosune*, which means right or just,[1] and *theos* is the Greek word for "God."[2] Paul makes a critical observation regarding God's righteousness. The gospel declares that the righteousness of God has been revealed, and because of it, the righteous will live by faith (Rom 1:17). As a believer, you are among the righteous and must know the significance of living righteously. There is a difference between the righteousness of God and the righteous living by faith for the believer. According to Strong's Lexicon, the Greek word for "righteous" in v. 17 is *dikaios*, which means righteous, just, or upright.[3] In this context, righteousness is for the believer, not God. Upright here is not for God, only right or just, as in *dikaiosune*. To live righteously is to walk by faith, trust God, and believe that God is genuinely just and right.

HOPE FOR THE UNSAVED

The voice of the Lord spoke loudly in the Old Testament. Evangelism in the Old Testament is not often discussed, but the need was present. The Lord Jehovah showed passion for those who were unsaved before Jesus was born. The scene was revealed when Ezekiel saw in a vision a battle with Gog, chief prince of Meshek and Tubal (Ezek 38:1–3). The evangelistic thrust is identified. God said, "So I will show my greatness and my holiness and make myself known in the eyes of many nations. Then they will know that I am the Lord" (Ezek 38:23). God used Ezekiel to bring the nations to the forefront. The message of evangelism was stated in the phrase "I will show my greatness and my holiness." This message was an invitation to salvation before Christ's time. You must thank God for the grace given to know that door was opened for eternity. What a blessing to praise the Almighty who left the door open for New Testament unbelievers to be saved.

---

1. Vine, *Expository Dictionary*, 298.
2. Vine, *Expository Dictionary*, 148.
3. Bible Hub, "Dikaios."

THIS OLD TESTAMENT PERICOPE HAS HOPE FOR FUTURE BELIEVERS

Hope for the unsaved is the clarion call for salvation. Scripture also teaches us that Jesus unequivocally alerted his disciples that the harvest is overflowing with unsaved souls but lacks workers. The demand for this ministry is overdue. It is urgent to pray and meditate on this worthy cause. Jesus was passionate, reaching out to harvest. He issued an urgent call for workers to harvest the crops. Pray to the Lord to send workers to work the harvest (Matt 9:37-38). In your daily meditation, think about someone you may know who is burdened in the community, such as a family member, coworker, someone you follow on social media, or a member of your fraternity, sorority, or club. It is wise for believers to heed the biblical mandate to ask the Lord to send out workers (v. 38). Many believers may be intimidated by nonbelievers into not evangelizing. Sharing the gospel should be done without entering the conversation with a negative tone or superiority complex. Remember, you intention must be positive and uplifting. Assure the unbeliever that eternal life in Christ guarantees a new direction. Encouraging words from Paul: "Therefore, if anyone is in Christ, he is a new creation. The old has passed away; behold, the new has come" (1 Cor 5:17 ESV). These words were meant to be a source of confidence for the church at Corinth, assuring them that once saved, the old life no longer has controlling power and influence over them. The new creation means new thoughts, ideas, and perspectives.

Your relationship with Christ should urge you to reach out with passion so others can be released from the rigors of a worldly lifestyle. The question arises, Why must believers engage in evangelism? The answer is because evangelism was at the heart of Jesus' ministry. He connected to people and demonstrated love. Another pericope gives credence to the passion for evangelism. Jesus taught his disciples about the significance of love and keeping his commandment. As disciples, we must love and obey Jesus' teaching, and we will be granted salvation (John 14:20-23). My colleagues in Christ, let nothing discourage you from seeking out those who are living in the trenches of pain, defeat, depression, derailment, disillusionment, and in some cases poverty. A word of hope will be appreciated, and they will say "Hallelujah!" after receiving Christ!

REFLECTIVE SUMMARIZATION AND RESPONSES TO ACTION

The Pearl of Evangelism is an encouraging clarion call to responsibility. The main takeaway question is why believers must participate in evangelism. The purpose of this Pearl is to alert you to act upon your salvation and move with haste and work the harvest to help release the captives. Don't waste time procrastinating; utilize your skills and passion to make a difference in the lives of those who are unsaved, helping them establish a new relationship with God. If God worked through Ezekiel before Christ was born, he can do wonders now. Remember, there is hope for the hopeless in these times we live in.

The Point of Emphasis

Righteous living has eternal blessings.

The Relevant Question

Have you ever led someone to Christ?

A Prayer for Evangelism

Gracious God, thank you for this day, and for meditating on this Evangelistic Pearl. In these critical times in which we live, bless me with the passion to share these thoughts and nuggets with others and help them see the big picture of salvation. Thank you for opening my eyes to gain greater insights that will help release captives and be a greater asset to the building of your kingdom. In your holy name. Amen.

DAY 35

The Pearl of Missions Cares About the Unredeemed

But you will receive power when the Holy Spirit has come upon you, and you will be my witnesses in Jerusalem and in all Judea and Samaria, and to the end of the earth.

—Acts 1:8 ESV

It is the whole business of the whole church to preach the whole gospel to the whole world.

—Charles H. Spurgeon

The Pearl of Missions is a vital outreach to improve the lives of the unredeemed. God expects believers to take immediate action to help. Therefore, the time is critical to utilize your willingness to make others feel happy, worthy, and loved. The Bible says, "His greatness will reach to the ends of the earth" (Mic 5:4). The cares of the unredeemed are intended for those who are hungry, homeless, helpless, and unredeemed. People are craving compassion and the love that comes with hearing the proclamation of the gospel. Our Lord and Savior Jesus drew near to the masses and was concerned about the unredeemed. He took the time to visit villages and surrounding regions to share the gospel and connect with people in the marketplaces (Mark 6:56). Time was not wasted in those regions and villages. I'm reminded of the encouraging words the apostle Paul said to the Ephesians: "Making the best use of the time, because the days are evil" (Eph 5:16 ESV). Christ knew that people were living in desperate situations and a negative state of mind. Time to change was of the essence. Actions speak louder than words. The redeemer actions were straightforward, optimistic, passionate, and genuine. The Father used the Son to initiate the mission agenda to reach people. Moreover, God was at work for this cause. Christ's example paved the way for believers today.

THE HEART OF MISSION WORK

The heart of mission activity is yearning for outreach and help. The reason why the heart of mission work is essential is that Jesus died for your salvation, as he purchased it with his blood on Calvary. The Scripture says, "In him we have redemption through his blood, the forgiveness of sins, following the riches of God's grace" (Eph 1:7). This verse should send you into a moment of worship and shouting! After thanking Jehovah for sending his Son, you should have the heart for a mission to share with those who have no clue about the power of the blood. Here are three main strategies for working the mission field: (1) observe the location where people congregate; after meeting them, (2) hear them out, and (3) assess their circumstances. Through these strategies, you will have the opportunity to approach them in a comforting manner, thereby gaining their trust. Help is needed and help is on the way through you. The question is, Are you available to go to the mission field, whether home or abroad? The next question is, Are you willing to be part of the incredible release of the redeemed? Henry Blackaby emphasizes that "God takes the initiative to invite you to join him in his work. God's revelation of his activity is an invitation for you to join him."[1] Since God takes the initiative, it is a privilege and honor to acknowledge the Creator on ministry projects that he orchestrates. Wise actions urge you to take God at his word and go into the villages and hamlets of your communities, connecting and

---

1. Blackaby et al., *Experiencing God*, 38–39.

building relationships. It will help you to sit in silence, meditate, and pray for the Creator's directives. "It is amazing what God is doing when we are least looking for his activity."[2] Since God is sovereign, there is no limit to his presence, power, and activity. As a believer, I'm proud to say that I serve and worship a God with mighty strength. He is beyond running out of words to say and activities to engage. It is time for you to seriously think about responding to God's invitation to engage in mission work to redeem the lost. There is an urgent call to respond to God's voice. Heeding the power of the Holy Spirit prepares you to be effective and authentic for mission activities. You must utilize every opportunity to respond to the needs of people from every walk of life.

THE COST OF MISSION

Undertaking the sacred call of mission work is to step into a journey that requires faith and patience. It is a labor of love and compassion. The cost extends beyond finances to you pouring out your soul and heart in unfamiliar territory. It is costly to sacrifice and undertake such a task. It costs you time, finances, and dedication. The cost could be $6,000 for six months for a five-hundred-mile radius from your home. As a member of the body of Christ, "the Evangelical church's need is never to devalue salvation but initiate the method of what I call know and show."[3] An example of know and show is witnessing the mission field and interacting with the individuals. You must be dedicated and committed to following through with this ministry.

Those who embark on this journey will find it to be holistic, encompassing mind, body, and strength, experiencing the richness of profound encounters. Catch Jesus' passion for the mission field and be an asset for redemption. You must have the passion to know the high significance of the mission. Jesus' commitment to the Father is evident in his words: "As you sent me into the world, so I have sent them into the world" (John 17:18). When Jesus sends you into the mission field, he will provide everything you need, regardless of the cost. Irrespective of your circumstances, God will abundantly supply and deliver your needs (Phil 4:19). Be assured that the Creator provides for you promptly. Through mission ministry, you can connect with individuals

---

2. Humphreys and Humphreys, *Show and Then Tell*, 37.
3. Turner, *Biblical Theology of Christian Discipleship*, 54.

and address their needs, whether physical, emotional, or spiritual. It is honorable to serve others and give them hope for a more fulfilling and changed life so they can discover their purpose and restore hope.

THE REWARDS OF MISSIONARY WORK

After you heed the missionary call to help others, despite the costs, there are rewards for your dedication and commitment. While engaging in mission work, you connect with others and begin to build meaningful relationships. Maintaining a vibrant and sacred prayer life authenticates credible witness. Be loyal to the Creator for blessings. Building relationships with others is a lifelong endeavor. God is waiting to see what you will do. The rewards are sure to come when you, whether clergy or laity, have compassion for those who are destitute. We are living in the end times, and God is looking for you to be a spiritual and social agent, reaching others for the kingdom. Jesus' words: "And this gospel of the kingdom will be proclaimed throughout the whole world as a testimony to all nations, and then the end will come" (Matt 24:14). There are opportunities to share the gospel and/or minister to the needs of others. There are *rewards for mission ministry*. Here are some rewards to consider:

- Sharing your beliefs in another setting can be valuable.
- Divine interventions can bring blessings into your life as you cultivate a deeper relationship with God.
- Discover the strength of your convictions and faith.
- You must value opportunities to share the gospel in other cultures, as they can be fulfilling.

These rewards will make a difference in your life as you engage in the serious work of missions. Valuing these rewards will pave the way for personal growth and a more meaningful life. Make good use of the opportunities that become available. No matter the difficulty, press toward your goal and pray that you reach the masses God assigned to you. Reflect on the rewards. If you feel like a believer as well as a nonbeliever, remember God will use the Pearl of Mission to come your way. No worries, because no one should feel hopeless, especially when they are an outcast in society. The Bible assures all hope and deliverance for brighter days to come, and you can "cast all your anxieties on him, for he cares about you" (1 Pet 5:7 RSV). Whatever you do to grow stronger and help others, be genuine, Christ-centered, and Christ-focused.

REFLECTIVE SUMMARIZATION AND RESPONSES TO ACTION

The fields, corners, streets, mountains, and valleys will test your missionary attempt to rescue souls for eternity. As a believer, act and implement the strategies relevant to the situation. The purpose of this chapter is to test your vision for mission work. There are many from all walks of life headed in the wrong direction. Some are probably hopeless and depressed, and feel they are outcasts in society. This Pearl is a challenge for you to spend time with Christ, as he pleaded on your behalf so that you can minister in the power of the Holy Spirit for the glory of God. Your rewards are waiting for you, and the unredeemed, whether family, friend, or enemy. It is up to you to act with love, patience, and care.

The Point of Emphasis

A sacred prayer life authenticates a credible witness.

The Relevant Question

Are you willing to be part of the incredible release of the unredeemed?

A Prayer for Mission

May the grace of God rest on me as I prepare for the needed work of mission. Help me to catch the vision and seek those who are living outside the safety of eternity. Give me the courage and faith to emulate Jesus' example by mingling among those in the community and serving their holistic needs. Instill in me the passion and heart for the ministry of missions, and guide with your Holy Spirit to the unredeemed to the eternal family of God. In your name. Amen.

DAY 36

The Pearl of Praise Touches God

You, God, are my God, earnestly I seek you; I thirst for you, my whole being longs for you, in a dry and parched land where there is no water. I have seen you in the sanctuary and beheld your power and your glory. Because your love is better than life, my lips will glorify you. I will praise you as long as I live, and in your name, I will lift up my hands.

—Psalm 63:1–4

Genuine praise touches God and it is a personal expression of awe that extends to God for appreciation, admiration, and trust. Praise bursts with flames of joy and exaltation, yet it is a humble communication. The psalmist passionately seeks to praise God. The action of the psalmist is a statement of wanting close intimacy. We should have the same passion and desire to thirst for God. Desiring to praise God is a thankful act. It is a thankful act because the center of your life and relationship expresses love for God through praise. Therefore, let us further define what praise is. Praise is to seek God's presence to express adoration for what God has done through bowing heads, lifting hands, and singing with joy and thankfulness. "Praise takes first place in the vocabulary of worship, as God comes first in the life and thoughts of believers."[1] The Pearl of Praise undergirds one's testimony of building a real relationship with God and sets the tone for a loving and meaningful relationship. The name for God in Pss 63–64 is Elohim, meaning "the strong one" and the Creator God.

The pertinent meaning of the above verses points to the essence of devotion. The above verses are a quintessential identification of a personal praise relationship. It is worth noting that the Bible is filled with Scripture references about praise (see, for example, Isa 25:1; Ps 18:3; 89:5; 103:20; 150:6; and Acts 16:25). Every believer must earnestly seek God's (Elohim's) presence and engage in thirsting for divine shelter with the strong one. In this psalm, David reaches out to God with the determination that a dry lifestyle requires water for spiritual refreshment. Thirsting for God is the epitome of upgrading from a parched place to a place of satisfaction. The purpose and foundation of praise is an act of appreciation to God for miracles, favor, grace, and mercy.

The psalmist has seen God in the sanctuary and has beheld the power and glory of God. That recognition connects the psalmist's experiences to an authentic experience in the sanctuary. The refuge is the personal presence of Elohim. The meaning of the word *beheld* in Hebrew is "I have appeared before thee, i.e., come to see thee."[2] The moment is the full expression of being in a state of praise. The focus of these verses drives one to seek a spiritually driven life. However, praise is rooted in God's presence and is about who God is, not us. Praise is empty and without "worship." A startling expression of praise is described in Paul's understanding of praise: "About midnight, Paul and Silas were praying and singing hymns to God, and the prisoners were listening to them, and suddenly there was a great earthquake, so that the foundations of the prison were shaken. And immediately all the doors were opened, and everyone's bonds were unfastened" (Acts 16:25–26).

THE NATURE OF TRUE PRAISE

Quality time is an honor to embrace the presence of God. Therefore, God seeks our intention to praise him. He has already chosen us to serve and worship him. That is clear and final. Many people are clueless

---

1. Richards, *Expository Dictionary*, 494.
2. Butterick, *Psalms*, 330.

about the true nature of praise. Praise is a significant response to our encounters with God's loving presence and work in our lives. Therefore, praise never is exhausted; you start in the morning and end at night, "from the rising of the sun unto the going down of the same the Lord's name is to be praised" (Ps 113:3 KJV). Praising God is a lifelong commitment that honors Jehovah's presence and power (Ps 145:1–20). Let me be clear: praise is a priceless moment in the presence of the Creator. It is showing and appreciating the opportunity to address God properly.

A PRAISE RELATIONSHIP WITH GOD

Developing a praise relationship with the Creator is a spiritual transformation. This relationship is spiritual growth and encourages additional praise. It floods your soul to praise more. When you praise, pray, and meditate, the terms of praise are powerful to express. There are over fifty Hebrew words for praise in the Old Testament and five Greek words for praise, with one Greek word for "hymned" which means to sing hymns, sing praises.[3] The Greek word for hymned relates to the Hebrew word *hallel*, which means "to sing praise." The essence of praising God is rooted in seven basic Hebrew words that express holy significance on the nature of genuine praise. Those Hebrew words are the foundation for the conceptual expression of praise. All Hebrew words are actual words of praise. The following words are taken from Strong's *Concordance*: (1) *halal* is the transliteration of the Hebrew word *hallel*: to give thanks, to cheer, extol (Ps 150:2);[4] (2) *yadah*: to extol, give thanks, to raise hands upward to confess (Isa 25:1).[5] "And David danced before the Lord with all his might, and David was girded with a linen ephod" (2 Sam 6:14). When David danced before the Lord God, all his moves were moves of praises to God. His moves were praising expression as he worshipped God through dancing. You can dance before the Lord like David. The Hebrew word for "dance" in 2 Sam 6:14 is *karar*, which means a spinning and whirling of joy and worship.[6] David danced with all his might.

3. Strong, *Strongest*, 2070.
4. Strong, *Strongest*, 2008.
5. Strong, *Strongest*, 1874.
6. Bible Hub, "Karar."

TOWDAH

The Hebrew word *towdah* is one of the most potent words that exuberates the moment of praise to God. It means to praise the excellence of God.[7] The following scriptures merge to concur with the meaning of *towdah*: for example, Ps 100:4 says, "Enter into his gates with thanksgiving, and into his courts with praise. Be thankful unto him and bless his name." This verse is a praise-loaded verse with thanksgiving, courts, and blessings. *Bless* is another word for praise. Jeremiah 33:11 says, "The voice of joy and the voice of gladness, the voice of the bridegroom and the voice of the bride, the voice of them that shall say: 'Praise the Lord of hosts, for the Lord is good, for his mercy endures forever'—and of them that shall bring the sacrifice of praise' into the house of the Lord" (NKJV).

Shabach is another Hebrew word which is exuberant praise. A loud, shout of celebration of joy. Strong states that it "can cause stillness"[8] (Ps 145:4). This word impacts the soul and heart of the worshipper during the praise moment. *Shabach* takes one to a higher level of praise and anointing. The praise is so powerful that it causes one to be still and focus on the power and presence of God. This element of praise brings a peaceful calm (Ps 46:10).

Zamar: The praise that focuses on the instruments and voice to glorify God (Ps 98:4).[9] The psalmist emphasizes a different mode of praise to glorify God through playing an instrument with a passion of love from the heart. The focus must stay on utilizing the instrument. God hears the sounds from instruments that have been dedicated, as well as the player, to show praise to Jehovah. Your praise magnifies the Lord.

Barak: To kneel in reverence and submission.[10] Moreover, kneeling is a posture that embodies the spiritual ambiance of the powerful presence of the Eternal Spirit. When one kneels, one shows adoration and honor to Jehovah as almighty and divine. Kneeling is a powerful, personal, and pivotal expression of turning from self to the omnipotent. When we kneel, it is both an external (physical) and an internal (inward) gesture to convey a spirit of deep passion and intimacy. This moment is a time for authentic devotion regardless of circumstances

---

7. Strong, *Strongest*, 1976.
8. Strong, *Strongest*, 1961.
9. Bible Hub, "Zamar."
10. Bible Study Tools, "Barak."

TEHILLAH

The word *tehillah* is a strong Hebrew word that focuses on praising God through song.[11] This word originates from *halal* and means to sing loudly. When one praises God, a song will emerge because passion ignites the soul and heart to address God with respect, adoration, and love. There are several scriptures where *tehillah* is the expression of praise. David writes from experience, "Sing joyfully to the Lord, you righteous; it is fitting for the upright to praise [*tehillah*] him" (Ps 33:1). David also uses *tehillah* in Ps 22:3: "Yet you are enthroned as the Holy One; you are the one Israel praises." Psalm 22 is written to the choir director with a portion that emphasizes God's name Elohim, "the strong one," and in later verses as Yahweh (vv. 8, 19, 23–28). Elohim is enthroned in majesty, divine presence, and rules in his providence. When we approach God, we must do it with a praise passion rooted in prayer and exuberant expression as we passionately worship in the sacred moment.

Genuine praise is about letting go of self-expression and worshiping God through praise. Your spiritual DNA includes studying the word, prayer, praise, meditation, and obedience. Each spiritual DNA offers a distinctive praise to God. How important is your spiritual DNA? Your spiritual DNA moves your heart to keep in step with being a purpose driven disciple. All glory is for the Almighty. The Bible says, "Praise be to the God and Father of our Lord Jesus Christ, the Father of compassion and the God of all comfort" (1 Cor 1:3–4). The least we can do is show our praise in high exaltation. The Pearl of Praise is the personal moment of being with the Holy. It is a time to treasure the moments of thankfulness that never end. Praise never ends because it is impossible to exhaust God's power within the time it takes to fully embrace his sovereignty and grace. God's sanctuary is the abiding omnipotent presence and power of God.

---

11. Bible Hub, "Tehillah."

REFLECTIVE SUMMARIZATION AND RESPONSES TO ACTION

Once we experience the presence of God, we will never be the same. Thinking about praise is a healthy thought, as well as appreciating what it is like to praise the Creator. Praise encourages us to extol God in adoration and lift our hands with a shout of praise. It is essential to focus on the Hebrew word *towdah* for praise. It is letting go to glorify God in the highest spiritual ambiance, giving honor. Genuine praise reminds us of what it means to be in the presence of the Holy Spirit. This spiritual ambiance sets us apart from the hustle and bustle of worldly actions.

The Point of Emphasis

Praise is never exhausted; it starts in the morning and continues through the night.

The Relevant Question

How important is your spiritual DNA?

A Prayer of Praise

Oh, Eternal God of grace and mercy. Thank you for the moments you have allowed me to experience and express my gratitude for the time we spent together. I echo the psalmist: my lips will glorify you. Oh God, grant me the passion to have a heart full of praise. Thank you, God, for the strength to praise your holy name. Amen.

DAY 37

The Pearl of Respect Creates a Loving Environment

Show yourself in all respects to be a model of good works, and in your teaching show integrity, dignity, and sound speech that cannot be condemned, so that an opponent may be put to shame, having nothing evil to say about us.

—Titus 2:7–8 ESV

In the stillness of the quiet, if we listen, we can hear the whisper of the heart giving strength to weakness, courage to fear, hope to despair.

—Howard Thurman

A peaceful loving environment is God's will for individuals to implement. The proper interaction among individuals determines the outcome of courage and fortitude. Respect is the key for healthy and godly living. The Scripture says, "So I will turn toward you and make you fruitful and multiply you, and I will confirm My covenant with you" (Lev 26:9 NASB). This verse expresses one of God's attributes, the attribute of goodness. Since God was good to Israel as promised, respecting them by establishing his covenant, respect is a Pearl that believers must adopt. Respect is a common trait that is often demonstrated through peaceful conversation. It is in your DNA, and if you value others, you can't help but show respect.

This Pearl creates a loving environment because you are the model of "good works" (Titus 2:7 ESV). In a calm spirit, one can experience the warm love to comfort others during conversation. This action aligns with what God requires in your walk, talk, and actions as a follower of Christ. It is honorable to respect God in all that you do. The question is, How do you respect God? You respect God by listening, obeying his will, and paying attention to God's direction. Respecting God teaches you to take care of your body (1 Thess 4:11). When you take care of your body and strive to live a life that is pure in God's sight, then you can be successful in respecting others. Having a plan of action makes one feel worthy when you smile and listen to them. To fully live out respect, the above passage of Scripture is the foundation and tone.

WHY SHOULD YOU RESPECT OTHERS?

Respecting others shows the authenticity of a true believer and a person with spiritual and social value. To put it bluntly, many people lack social graces. They live under the shield of a smoke screen and avoid positive interaction. You should respect others because it builds strong relationships. Respect prevents arguments that can get out of hand. Titus emphasizes the necessity of teaching, integrity, dignity, and sound speech that puts all evil to rest (Titus 2:7–8). Believers must seize the moment to embody the Holy Scriptures and act on the importance of respect. The greatest strength in the world is respect. The greatest joy is knowing that respect is received. Integrity, dignity, and mercy are all intertwined by respect. Disregard is the opposite of respect, but "the Lord is gracious and righteous; our God is full of compassion" (Ps 116:5). Those whose hearts are filled with integrity will honor others by respecting the highest. It takes God's divine love to radiate in your heart to show it to others genuinely. There is much disrespect in the world, and believers must encourage those living in disbelief and hate. The torment of others can transform their brokenness and fragility into giant steps for significant change. These readings stress the purpose of practicing the honor of treating others with compassion.

When disrespectfulness is on the prowl, it keeps coming from those who don't care. In that case, you need the comforting arms of Jesus to see you through. God does not want you to succumb to the dictates of disrespectful tones. Don't let others bring you down to their level. Remember, your life is unfulfilled when you avoid the Pearl of Respect toward God and others. All people must remember that God created us to show proper respect. You should not have an agenda that negates human value. The word "respect" is the same as "honor," and the Greek word is *timao*, which means valuing Christ at a price, and honoring a person.[1] This high price placed on something lingers in the consciousness of the believer. The power of respect awakens curious minds for communication.

THE PASSION FOR BEING RESPECTFUL

Human dignity is the core of interacting with others with passion and compassion. When you respect others, you respect God. Walking in the spirit of honor and ultimately respecting all is wise. Do good and show mercy. What is your passion for respecting others? It is all about your feelings. A word of caution: be careful, think soberly, and never fall prey to antagonistic behavior. It will damage your walk with God, and others will avoid your presence. Therefore, "do nothing out of selfish ambition or vain conceit. Rather, in humility value others above yourselves" (Phil 4:3). A selfish ambition tears down character. It means no good. The Bible further teaches the authentic principle of Jesus' stance on social and spiritual reciprocity: "So in everything, do to others what you would have them do to you, for this sums up the Law and the Prophets" (Matt 7:12). This biblical principle of the Law and the Prophets sets the standard for your guide and guidance. It comes from the heart of Jesus as he sums up the Law. An astonishing question: What does it mean to live a respectable life? This question should capture your attention and prompt you to think critically, sharing your thoughts to facilitate valuable conversation and action. I pray that we all check our state of mind and act accordingly. The state of mind is the image of God working through us because respect tests the integrity of pursuing a loving environment.

---

1. Vine, *Expository Dictionary*, 231.

Recognizing the body of Christ, meaning every local church, is critical. Eugene H. Merrill sums up the doctrine of the image of God. He says, "To be in God's image is indeed to be godlike though obviously in a highly nuanced and restricted sense."[2] Since everyone was created in the image of God, we must be respectful (Gen 1:27). Since we were made in the image of God, all need to be respectful. I'm reminded of when Adam and Eve walked in the garden of Eden. God's voice was relevant, powerful, and urgent. When he spoke, it was the voice of finality (Gen 3:2–10). The message lingers in the core of the conscious for direct response. Your image of God alerts you to the importance of knowing the magnitude of your relationship.

Hear these words: "Be devoted to one another in love. Honor one another above yourselves" (Rom 12:10). It may seem complicated to be devoted to one another. Still, the prophecy in Revelation authenticates genuine respect. God is worthy to be praised. It is incredible how the twenty-four elders worshiped God. "The twenty-four elders fall down before him who is seated on the Throne and worship him who lives forever and ever. They cast their crowns before the Throne, saying, 'Worthy are you, our Lord and God, to receive glory and honor and power, for you created all things, and by your will they existed and were created'" (Rev 4:10–11 ESV). It is your duty and responsibility to honor God. Honoring God is to worship him on the throne. Honor is the highest respect you can show to Jehovah. Just visualize what it feels like to bow and worship Jehovah on the throne as the elders did. Many scholars differ on who the twenty-four elders are. Some say the tribes and the apostles or the heavenly council. They could be an angelic host to show respect for God's sovereignty. It adds significance to your worship and praise. The above text genuinely teaches that respect is not authenticated. While we live on the periphery of end times, let us keep God in view as the goal of implementing respect, making the world a loving, healthy, and spiritual place.

REFLECTIVE SUMMARIZATION AND RESPONSES TO ACTION

Respect urges us all to consider what must be done rightfully. It is critical to sit in quietness to be able to hear the glorious voice of Jehovah.

---

2. Merrill, *Everlasting Dominion*, 169.

His voice is like many waters roaring on the sea of life. It is essential to take the time to reflect on the significance of living, worshiping, and honoring God. The wise response is to practice praising God and others. Also, it is wise to walk away from foolishness and strife and seek to live with dignity. God's will is for you to realize the divine nature of the sovereign God almighty.

The Point of Emphasis

The power of respect awakes curious minds for communication.

The Relevant Question

What is your passion for respecting others?

A Prayer of Respect

On this day, eternal God, give me the heart to follow the Law and the Prophets that Jesus referred to in the Gospel of Matthew. Life would not have significant meaning without respect, dignity, and honor. Thank you for the strength to walk in your presence and be used for the merit and purpose of honoring others. I take seriously the responsibility to show respect to the highest. Guide me, oh thou great Jehovah, to be devoted to you and committed to serving your people. Amen.

DAY 38

The Pearl of Sacrifice Is the Excellent Way

I beseech you therefore, brethren, by the mercies of God, that ye present your bodies a living sacrifice, holy, acceptable unto God, which is your reasonable service. And be not conformed to this world: but be ye transformed by the renewing of your mind, that ye may prove what is that good, and acceptable, and perfect, will of God.

—Romans 12:1–2 KJV

It is your responsibility to surrender your life to God humbly. Sacrificial living is highly essential, as the apostle Paul placed much emphasis on encouraging the Roman Christians to live this way. The above passage is made possible by Christ's blood. Living in a particular manner reveals a *theology of sacrifice*. A theology of sacrifice depicts the seriousness of your presentation and/or requests to God. You must approach God with humble adoration and reverence. Therefore, the sacrificial life is a life that the blood sacrifice of Christ has impacted. Our Lord sacrificed his blood on Calvary for our sins because the blood of animals would not suffice, only a temporary covering. Jesus was the acceptable source (Heb 10:4–10). His living was satisfactory to the Father on our behalf. He sacrificed vicariously to provide the eternal arrangement. As a response to his sacrifice, we are indebted to sacrifice our lives through our walk in appreciation because of his atonement. This reading is a Wisdom Pearl, because the right thing to do is to present your life wholly to God. It pleases God and warms his heart when we present our bodies in a sacred way. Sacrifice is time sensitive, and I implore all believers to make this day and the rest of your life a demonstration of your bodies to him. After acceptance, you have a new menu to feast on, a brighter and more prosperous path to travel under God's providential care. Early instances of sacrifice in the Old Testament emphasized its magnitude. The story of Cain and Abel provides evidence of two distinct forms of sacrifice. God accepted Abel's offering because it represented the firstborn of the flock (Gen 4:4) and rejected Cain because it represented the fruit of the land (Gen 4:4–5).

Because of your sacrifice, God will mend your contrite and broken spirit (Ps 51:17). While I am completing this project, I hear the Master saying, "Make every effort to live in peace with everyone and to be holy; without holiness no one will see the Lord" (Heb 12:1). Having said that, let's examine the Greek word for "sacrifice" in the above verse for the benefit of contextual explanation. The Greek word is *thusia*, which is a noun meaning "to present or offer."[1] Sacrifice is to abdicate the life that has been torn and worn by sin. The Hebrew word for sacrifice is *qorban*, which means "drawing near."[2] *Near* here means closer to God. This Pearl is vital because the essence of this Pearl glitters with radiance and a spark of humbleness. It is a bold step of faith to embrace and walk with the Holy. Walking with the Holy helps you grow deeper and broader in all spiritual encounters with the Holy. Here are three significant stages of sacrifice:

- You must communicate with the Holy,
- listen to the Holy,
- and do the will of the Holy.

The above stages enable you to acknowledge the Holy in a spiritual encounter, thereby proving your self-worth and implementing sacrifice. Living sacrificially prepares one to avoid a spiritually deficient

---

1. Strong, *Strongest*, 2373.
2. Bible Hub, "Qorban."

life. A spiritual deficit life will erode your heart, soul, and conscience, and leave you lifeless. The good of leaning on God's mercy is that you are waiting on him to accept your worship. Ernst Käsemann explains worship this way: "True worship means agreement with God's will to his praise and thought, will, and act."[3] Keep your spiritual tracking intact. Pray, meditate, and study the Scriptures. To go further, sacrifice is pushing through life struggles and disappointments to experience the benefits of a better way. The excellent way of life is genuine and honest, and it is real because God expects you to dedicate your life to him faithfully. It has been said repeatedly that obedience is better than sacrifice. Let's examine this statement from the biblical perspective. The prophet Samuel shares with King Saul that God is pleased with burnt offerings and sacrifices, but obedience is more important (1 Sam 15:22). It does not mean that sacrifice is nonessential. Still, obedience requires sacrifice to please God, and sacrifice necessitates obedience to achieve total accountability. What is your state of mind regarding living sacrificially? Jehovah is waiting for your response, and only you can answer. Case in point, to offer sacrifices, there must be obedience. The primary objective of this spiritual journey is to present yourself as a living testimony to Jehovah. All in all, it is about giving up self-centered living to adopt a God-centered life. God-centered living validates a living servant. Moreover, the essence of sacrifice is trusting God through tough times as well. There are times when you will be hard-pressed to step out in faith and act in obedience, trusting God in ways that are beyond normal. Because Jesus is the excellent way, the sacrificial message is ideal to praise God for his authentic trustworthiness. The Pearl of Sacrifice is a biblical directive to experience God marvelously. Experiencing God is a relationship that one will enjoy spiritually on the journey. The objective is to please God, and pleasing God is a wise action.

FOCUS ON SATISFYING GOD FOR HIS EXPECTATIONS

The biblical context of *sacrifice* is far more than what you think about the word itself. It is a term that engages our consciousness and keeps us guessing what we should do. The guiding question for this devotion is, What does God want from your sacrifice? This question is an

---

3. Käsemann, *Commentary on Romans*, 219.

attention-getter because it promulgates the reason for sacrifice. The prophet Micah says, when you realize what God wants, you will see the need and understand why it is essential to meet his expectations (Mic 6:8). Abraham met God's expectations when he was directed to sacrifice his only son as a burnt offering on Mount Moriah. As he approached the mountain, Isaac asked, "Where is the lamb for the sacrifice?" Abraham said, "God will provide." When he had prepared the fire and the wood, the angel directed him not to touch his son (Gen 22). Because of his faith and obedience, God's grace and mercy rewarded Abraham. Satisfying God is a keen sense of focus. The word *sacrifice* has a profound meaning. The sovereignty of God governs expectations. It is a theological word that tests our eagerness and willingness to emulate the words of the psalmist: "He says, 'Be still, and know that I am God; I will be exalted among the nations, I will be exalted in the earth'" (Ps 46:10). The question is, What is God saying to us about sacrifice? He is saying that being still is the time to experience intimacy as you listen to his voice.

God's expectation for sacrifice is vital. It is essential because emphasis is placed on sacrificing yourself rather than things or situations. Paul gives a direct imperative to practice: "And walk in love, as Christ loved us and gave himself up for us, a fragrant offering and sacrifice to God" (Eph 5:2). Christ's sacrificial offering to God is on your behalf. Focus on walking in love to show God that you are willing to give up all and "present your body as a living sacrifice" (Rom 12:1). What does Paul mean by making this sacrificial commandment? This question inspires your spirit to act with love and joy in the presence of God. Believe that your life is impacting you in a way that you know pleases God. The impact is that a new agenda has emerged, and its focus is on living up to expectations. God looks for your service, holiness, and a renewed mind. The key to sacrifice is transformation. As a believer, you are transformed from the inside out. You have new thoughts that get God's attention; thoughts with purpose and meaning.

PRACTICE THE SACRIFICIAL LIFE FOR SPIRITUAL MATURITY

Remember that the Creator can detect the status of your life. Are you willing to offer your life to God daily? Practicing the spiritual life begins with the heart, and then the heart encourages the mouth to respond. King David's example is a robust biblical reference to the significance of the spiritual life. He humbly requests mercy that his worship be accepted: "Let the words of my mouth and the meditation of my heart be acceptable in your sight, O Lord, my rock and my redeemer" (Ps 19:14 ESV). Every day goes higher and higher when you capitalize on improving your relationship with Christ. Adhering to the Romans passage means one is willing to go all the way and live a genuine, purposeful life. This life authenticates the practice of being a purpose driven disciple. The primary goal is to emulate Jesus.

Sacrifice helps one to understand the mold and shape of the image of Jesus. John Mark Comer says, "Formation in the image of Jesus isn't something we do as much as it's something done to us, by God himself as we yield to the work of transforming grace."[4] Make every effort to make every moment count by offering every spiritual fiber to the God of glory. This action can be done by listening to God. There is no other way to show the Creator that you care about your sacrifice. Remember, your reasonable service is part of your spiritual growth. Your maturity is God's mercy. Continue to pursue a closer walk and a more profound commitment to a living sacrifice and a testimony of spiritual growth.

REFLECTIVE SUMMARIZATION AND RESPONSES TO ACTION

When you come to sacrifice, it is a spiritual test for your willingness to cling to presenting self to God. Jehovah wants all your attention, so that you can properly praise and worship the Creator. Time spent listening to the Holy Spirit is valuable time spent getting closer to God, the Father, the Son, and the Holy Spirit. While on this journey, keep your spiritual log of walking with God in your heart because he knows every spiritual act.

The Point of Emphasis

Sacrifice prepares one to avoid a spiritual deficit.

---

4. Comer, *Practicing the Way*, 70.

The Relevant Question

What is your state of mind regarding living sacrificially?

A Prayer of Sacrifice

Oh God, this day has touched my heart, mind, and soul about the essence of presenting my body as holy for your service. Strengthen me and guide me daily to meet your standards as a believing and practicing disciple. Help me to stay on the path of righteousness as I grow into spiritual maturity. I need you every moment as I hear your comforting, robust voice that moves and awakens my conscience to walk by faith in your name. Amen.

DAY 39

The Pearl of Resilience

Trials, Testing, and Tribulation

Therefore, since we are surrounded by so great a cloud of witnesses, let us also lay aside every weight, and sin which clings so closely, and let us run with endurance the race that is set before us, looking to Jesus, the founder and perfecter of our faith, who for the joy that was set before him endured the cross, despising the shame, and is seated at the right hand of the throne of God. Consider him who endured from sinners such hostility against himself, so that you may not grow weary or fainthearted.

—Hebrews 12:1–3 ESV

Do not judge me by my success, judge me by how many times I fell down and got back up again.

—Nelson Mandela

Resilience is a Pearl that shows impeccable strength amid extremities. Therefore, the power of resilience is a testament to the strength of determination. As you begin this day, ask God to grant you the strength and stamina for the challenges ahead. The book of Hebrews reminds us of the history and heritage of faith, meaning that faith never dies

(Heb 11:6). Faith is connected to resilience, giving you the strength and power to rise above any attempted defeat. The writer of Hebrews reminds us of the spiritual resilience God provides through faith. The goal of resilience is to recover and resume normal activities.

We are blessed to have the cloud of witnesses who have died as faith warriors, who encourage us to stay the course (v. 1). None of us can run the race weighed down with fears, anxieties, and sins that prevent spiritual success. The purpose is to eliminate them immediately. God provides what is needed for combative confrontations in the darkest moments. The Scripture says, "I cannot carry all these people by myself; the burden is too heavy for me. If this is how you are going to treat me, please go ahead and kill me—if I have found favor in your eyes—and do not let me face my ruin" (Num 11:14-16). Moses had dark moments and wanted to give up because his load was heavy because of the people. He wanted God to kill him, but instead, God gave him seventy elders to be with him in the tabernacle. This pericope describes the burden of Moses because all the people were hungry. Moses was so burdened about the people until he requested that the Lord kill him. His example shows that God will protect through trials. Confrontations are moments that alert us that the devil is real and confrontational. When this happens, it is critical to depend on God.

You cannot follow Satan and rely on God at the same time. It is one or the other. Paul affirms the power of resilience: "Therefore, my dear brothers and sisters, stand firm. Let nothing move you. Always give yourselves fully to the work of the Lord, because you know that your labor in the Lord is not in vain" (1 Cor 15:58). I urge all believers to hunker down and recover from any setbacks. The quality of your faith is the foundation for going forward. We will explore three main elements that challenge believers on the path of resilience through trials, testing, and tribulation. Resilience is often tested through personal trials to witness what God does through them. It does not matter how frequently you fall; get up with pride, ask God to give you the strength and faith to shake off fear and frustration, and reset for the present and the future.

TRIALS

Trials are an intricate part of life. There are two types of trials: trials from the world and trials from God. Worldly trials are devious and sadistic. Devious and evil trials are in your path (Eph 6:16). It is impossible to live a trial-free life. God's trials are to strengthen for spiritual growth. The Bible provides the big picture of the goals of trials: "Blessed is the man who remains steadfast under trial, for when he has stood the test he will receive the crown of life, which God has promised to those who love him" (Jas 1:2 ESV). The purpose of trials is to determine the status of our faith and whether we have the stamina to endure.

Therefore, trials are designed to strengthen and purify our faith. James emphasizes the importance of clinging to a strong faith theology to find hope and resilience in the face of trials. The goal is never to give up. As we read and meditate on Heb 12:1–3, we must not focus on those matters that hold us back from moving forward. Trials are designed to shape and prepare disciples for witnessing. The context of Jas 1:2 is assurance in the face of duress and confrontation. You must keep pushing through the rubbish of hostile life. As you strive for the light at the end of the tunnel, look with anticipation of seeing the results of the work of resilience. There will be a time of celebration. James encourages the church to reflect on the promise of counting their joy when they meet testing and remain on a firm footing so that they can find their way. Use wisdom and walk by faith through strong winds of time (Jas 1:2–8). This passage from James is about the theology of faith: when you resort to joy amid robust trials, you develop spiritual resilience. Praise God for a conquering foresight in Christ.

Paul says, "As it is written: 'For your sake, we face death all day long; we are considered as sheep to be slaughtered.' No, in all these things we are more than conquerors through him who loved us" (Rom 8:36–37). As you begin your day with eager confidence, you are subject to evil confrontations, fatal attacks, and physical, mental, and emotional encounters; remember, you are covered. You surrendered to Christ, seeking spiritual guidance found in these verses. Rest assured, whether you are a novice believer or a veteran believer, you can always be prepared to experience enjoyment in Christ. When conquering trials, tests keep coming your way.

TESTING

The Pearl of Resilience has its purpose during your journey. The testing moments are part of your trials. They are woven to share the same thing. Tests show the difficulty of how you handle the outcome. It is about the quality of your endurance. Trials are the challenges that test your faith. Therefore, when one phase is complete, another round begins. You encounter evil on your spiritual journey. God allows the believer to experience tests for spiritual growth. As you read while on this forty-day journey, you may be experiencing a test; if so, hear what Solomon says: "Fire tests the purity of silver and gold, but the Lord tests the heart" (Prov 17:3 NLT). This verse serves as a reminder of the true test of the heart. Whatever you experience as a believer confronting opposition, can you do it yourself? The answer to this question is, "For we do not have a high priest who is unable to empathize with our weaknesses, but we have one who has been tempted in every way, just as we are—yet he did not sin. Let us approach God's throne of grace with confidence so that we may receive mercy and find grace to help us in our time of need" (Heb 4:15–16). Looking forward to God extending mercy is not limited to Heb 4. There is more to come. Regardless of how weak we may become, there is hope. The Scripture affirms, "But he said to me, 'My grace is sufficient for you, for my power is made perfect in weakness.' Therefore, I will boast all the more gladly about my weakness so Christ's power may rest on me" (2 Cor 12:9). The reason to boast is the testimony of deliverance-from-being-bound testing encounters. Thank God for what he has done. When you have given Christ your all to follow him, you can and will be able to conquer the trials and the tests. After trials and tests, tribulation awaits its turn.

TRIBULATION

We have been living in the last few days. The word "tribulation" refers to an intense experience that includes trials and testing. The Greek word for "tribulations" is *thlipsis*, meaning affliction, distress, and persecution. Thayer goes deeper to say it is a "pressing together, pressure."[1] This word draws attention to devious confrontations designed to crush your spirit and is found forty-five times in the New Testament.

---

1. Bible Hub, "Thlipsis."

As you meditate, pray, and read this book, the Scriptures give assurance through the Pearl of Resilience to conquer these encounters of severe affliction, distress, and oppression. What does your resilience look like? It should resemble a spiritual embrace through prayer, faith, Christian doctrine, and the study of the word.

Therefore, the aim is to embrace self with faith and hope to prepare for any pending distress. The Old Testament points to the seven-year future of events leading up to the end times (Dan 7:25). Thank God for other scriptures that assure us of the meaning of immediate preparation for the end. God speaks with power to the church at Thessalonica: "For you yourselves are fully aware that the day of the Lord will come like a 'thief in the night'" (1 Thess 5:2 ESV). The day of the Lord is judgment, and it will be a time to pray and meditate on the coming of the Lord. Therefore, the Pearl of Resilience prepares you for the day of the Lord. The day of the Lord represents bits and pieces of the last day sufferings and intense attacks. Staying resilient is the will to conquer confrontations. The end is near, and it is past time for personal assessment. Jesus is the ultimate answer for inadequacies. Samuel Whitefield wonderfully says, "Knowing the revelation of Jesus is the central purpose of the end of the age will give the church strength to endure the most difficult hour of history."[2] This quote should inspire you to keep focusing on your resilience. Your primary goal is to maintain a strong theology of faith during your spiritual growth. Be determined to keep your connection. Paul says, "Who shall separate us from the love of Christ? Shall tribulation, or distress, or persecution, or famine, or nakedness, or peril, or sword?" (Rom 8:35). Make this your day to survive. Read the Psalms deeper and gain the psalmist's keen insights to survive the pressures from the enemies' attacks (Ps 59:9–15). Remember, your resilience is nestled in the following verses to conquer your trials, tests, and tribulations: "Trust in the Lord with all your heart and lean not on your understanding; in all your ways submit to him, and he will make your paths straight" (Prov 3:5–6). The fulfillment of God's promise is to pray without ceasing and remember that the prayers of the righteous weigh heavily on God's heart (Jas 5:16). By using your faith and perseverance, you will maintain the power of resilience.

---

2. Whitefield, *Gospel of Daniel 7*, 70.

THE CONDITION OF WEAK BELIEVERS

There is an opposite contrast in Romans. Those who are weak in the faith and need rededication from a deranged lifestyle are among those who are weak. Paul identified the weak and the strong in Rome (Rom 14:1—15:13). His message was an appeal for spiritual adjustment. This forty-day spiritual guide is an eye-opener for believers; those strong in faith must help the weaker become strong. This Pearl is an encouragement to make a difference. Have you thought about your spiritual condition and state of mind?

REFLECTIVE SUMMARIZATION AND RESPONSES TO ACTION

There is incredible power, persistence, and perseverance in the word *resilience*. The writer of Hebrews serves as a reminder to reflect on the great cloud of witnesses before us, for they have charted the course, giving us hope to keep moving forward. Resilience conquers heavyweights and burdens that stifle and interfere with the spiritual journey. Responses to action are to pray, walk by faith, and remember that Jehovah Jireh will provide. This reading experience encourages dedication and a strong commitment to persevere through the trials, testing, and tribulations of these times, preparing for the future.

The Point of Emphasis

Getting up is the will to conquer confrontations.

The Relevant Question

What does your resilience look like?

A Prayer for Resilience

Thank God for another day to experience the strength to conquer all devious and pressing oppressions. You are Jehovah Jireh, the Lord will provide. I need daily resilience to please you adequately. Endow me with the faith required to defeat all evil encounters in this day and the days to come. I remember these encouraging words of the psalmist: "Surely God is good to Israel, to those who are pure in heart. But as for me, my feet had almost slipped; I had nearly lost my foothold" (Ps 73:1–2 ESV). Thank you for your comfort through the Holy Spirit in your most holy name. Keep me deeply rooted in your power and presence as a purpose driven disciple. Amen.

DAY 40

The Pearl of Meekness Embraces Serenity

Seek the Lord, all you humble of the land, you who do what he commands. Seek righteousness, seek humility; perhaps you will be sheltered on the day of the Lord's anger.

—Zephaniah 2:3

Therefore we ourselves boast about you in the churches of God for your steadfastness and faith in all your persecutions and in the afflictions that you are enduring.

—2 Thessalonians 1:4 ESV

I commenced this forty-day writing endeavor with an attitude of love on the initial day, and now, as I reach its conclusion on the fortieth day, I do so with meekness. As a believer, one's principal objective should be to cultivate serenity by embodying calmness and peace, conscientiously refraining from engaging in strife. Meekness becomes the spiritual air you breathe. It is the will to avoid conflicts. Meekness is the strength of discipline as it inherently fosters serenity, as both qualities resonate in harmony with the mercy and love of God. Oh, how close they are to the heart and pulse of God. I hear David's plea for his pain and sorrow, and I hope you do as well. He prays, "Give ear to my words, O Lord; consider my groaning. Give attention to the sound of my cry, my King and my God, for to you do I pray. O Lord, in the morning you hear my voice; in the morning I prepare a sacrifice for you and watch" (Ps 5:1–3 ESV). As he cried for help in the most depressing time, his request was in the Creator's hands.

The Epistle of James directs our attention to the theological assurance afforded to those who walk humbly. He says, "Humble yourselves before the Lord, and he will lift you up" (Jas 4:10). When one adopts humility, the spirit of meekness naturally becomes the atmosphere in which one thrives; it is the guiding will that inclines the heart away from conflict. Indeed, no day can be considered honestly well spent unless the spirit of meekness is consciously guiding while being integrated into our daily conduct. Such virtues are intimately connected to the heart and pulse of God.

ENGAGING IN THE SPIRITUAL WALK

Embracing this study presents a true challenge for your spiritual journey. At times, confrontations will emerge in your personal space, and it becomes essential to discern how to respond in a way that preserves your integrity. Meekness should not be mistaken for weakness; rather, it is an invitation to pause, reflect, and carefully consider how to react or when to remain silent.

Your spiritual walk stands as the truest measure of your character and behavior. The beatitudes, therefore, offer a powerful lesson for believers, encouraging the pursuit of righteousness. As Scripture says, "Blessed are the meek, for they shall inherit the earth" (Matt 5:5 ESV). Let this be a word of encouragement along your journey—how blessed it is for the meek to inherit the earth.

Meekness means demonstrating strength amid profound difficulties. It is living by faith and relying on the guidance of the Holy Spirit to exercise self-control, even in the face of devious, cunning, rude, or disrespectful actions. In a world gripped by chaotic stress and longing for deliverance—where political systems slide dangerously toward social and political disorder that leads to derailment. The call to meekness and integrity becomes more vital in a sadistic society.

WHAT IS YOUR GOAL FOR MEEKNESS?

This is the question of *submissiveness*. How will you respond to others as you seek to control your attitude under chaotic pressure? The heavy load of responsibility will challenge you to press toward your goal. Meekness enables you to maintain control over your strength during devious adversity. It is crucial to know the strength of meekness. The strength of meekness is when you graciously submit to God. The Greek word for "meekness" is *praus*. It means gentile, mild, or meek.[1] Your goals should be to *stay positive, keep temper under control*, and *avoid selfishness* that drives the stake of being vain. Those three goals are the main foundation for other descriptions.

The spirit of meekness can and will withstand all odds of attacks. Being meek is showing submissiveness to God's will and recognizing Jesus as your Lord and Savior. In short, the meek accepts the lordship of Jesus because God sent Christ so that we can live through him. Living through him means trusting, loving, and showing obedience (1 John 4:9). When you focus on staying on the lordship track, your life has significance, and you will always be fulfilled. Paul wrote to the churches in Galatia regarding the fruit of the Spirit. There are nine characteristics of the fruit of the Spirit. Among the nine, meekness or gentleness is the humble way one is submissive to God. Because of your submissiveness and love for the Trinitarian Godhead (Acts 17:29; Rom 5:5; Col 2:9), God grants favor for you to experience the power to live under the controlling spirit of the Holy Spirit. That is a blessing to reflect on during daily interactions. Questions for serious thought and evaluation: Do you struggle with uncontrolled anger? Does rage incite vehement actions that cause emotional explosions? If so, then position yourself to ask Jesus to intercede on your behalf for a major change. Meekness is the supernatural power that God designed to conquer vile behavior. It is essential to note that God is aware of your sin history, and help is needed.

The Bible says, "For all have sinned, and come short of the glory of God" (Rom 3:23 KJV). We all share a commonality regarding the issue

---

1. Vine. *Vines Expository Dictionary*, 55.

of sin. We have disappointed Jehovah with our polluted nature. Having accepted Christ as our personal Savior, he blesses us with meekness. The test is the challenge of spiritual warfare. It challenges us when we have been submissive to God. The fighting continues; Paul says, "I find then a law, that, when I would do good, evil is present" (Rom 7:21 KJV). All the above tags on the Pearl of Meekness. The good news is that once Christ is in your life, you are endowed with meekness to battle the forces against meekness.

Remember, the Spirit of meekness does not allow you to fight because you have an intercessor who fully represents you in the eternal chambers of glory. I strongly believe there is no challenge too big for the Creator to handle. Paul gave Timothy an encouraging lift: "But as for you, O man of God, flee these things. Pursue righteousness, godliness, faith, love, steadfastness, gentleness (1 Tim 6:11 ESV).

Meekness will carry you a great distance with open doors waiting on you.

MEEKNESS THAT PLEASES GOD

Meekness that pleases God is when one has submitted to God. The character of meekness is the opposite of the world. This lifestyle is characterized by gentleness, calmness, and faithfulness. The character of a meek person stands out, and Moses exemplified meekness with serenity. The Bible states, "Now the man Moses was very meek, more than all people who were on the face of the earth" (Num 12:3 ESV). You must show meekness when experiencing tensions. It must be highly noticeable because others will detect how being humble shows souls are at rest with God, being obedient, caring, and loving. The ultimate perfect example of perfect meekness is further exemplified through the teaching of Jesus. Jesus says, "Take my yoke upon you. Let me teach you, because I am humble and gentle at heart, and you will find rest for your souls" (Matt 11:29 NLT). Christ taught in many towns and was mild and gentle from Bethlehem to Calvary and from Calvary to his ascension. He pleased his Father with the life he lived. Other biblical characters were poised and reserved, such as Joseph, who was mild and meek. His brothers plotted and launched a strategy to murder him. Fortunately, it failed (Gen 37:18–37). His meekness did not allow retaliation because it embodies serenity. Not only Joseph but also Moses was another example of profound meekness. We find in Num 12 that his siblings expressed personal attacks against him, but he was gentle. Reflect on these examples of meekness from leaders who persevered among sadistic attacks.

Ask yourself a question: Is God pleased with my meekness? The question should lead to a profound awakening of your consciousness. You can see the need to include more meekness in your life. You cannot reach the goal of genuine meekness alone; you need God to accomplish such status. You must stay in his presence. The profound writer John Piper says it best: "The deepest longing of the human heart is to know and enjoy the glory of God."[2] The real emphasis is to embark daily to receive and utilize the spirit of gentleness as you interact and impact the body of Christ and the world. When you dig deeper to experience God, you will find the precious gems of life that will make you happy and pleased to be a kingdom believer. Take the time to assess your life and what drives you toward being a purpose driven disciple.

REFLECTIVE SUMMARIZATION AND RESPONSES TO ACTION

The essence of this chapter is continuous steadfastness to maintain peace and harmony. There is no need for verbal atrocities and retribution. The heart of genuine believers maintains the character of Christ. I strive to follow Jesus in all my interactions. Those who abuse and seek to belittle you just leave the vindication to God. When you bow in prayer, let your devotion center on pleasing him and him alone. Keep the spirit of serenity in focus. Those who hear the voice of the Creator will receive the power of anointing and blessings to live in meekness.

The Point of Emphasis

The spirit of meekness is the supernatural power of God designed to conquer a vile behavior.

---

2. Piper, *Seeing and Savoring Jesus Christ*, 14.

The Relevant Question

Does rage incite vehement actions that cause emotional explosions?

A Prayer for Meekness

Everlasting God of hope, thank you for these encouraging words, phrases, and scriptures for guidance and encouragement. I bow today in your presence to experience the anointing of the Holy Spirit to demonstrate meekness. I came to know and accept this Pearl of Meekness, an eye-opener for me, allowing me to see the big picture of taking control of my emotions during emotional encounters. I pray for strength to stay in my lane of righteousness and meekness for your glory. In your name. Amen.

Epilogue

Let me share with each reader the magnitude of sharing seeds of thoughts in these Pearls of Wisdom. The thoughts of this book took root while I was still pastoring and working in New York. One day, out of the blue, I thought about writing about Pearls. I started by outlining the book with a forty-day spiritual growth journey. I had a few thoughts that had not been developed but lingered in my spirit for years. I even wrote two other books while the thoughts of this book took shape. Much of the shaping of this book occurred during the COVID-19 pandemic, and the rest came after it. During the loss of so many friends, pastors, and laypersons, I heard from God. Through these experiences, God gave me insights, especially those not included in the first revelation of thoughts. Sometimes I tried to write, but I couldn't because God had something else in mind. I wanted to finish the book long ago, but I realized that I didn't have enough time. God was still revealing the content and context of each Pearl. Here is what he was doing: he was growing and shaping the Pearls to be birthed out of my consciousness, experience, and maturity to share with the body of Christ. This book would not have had a spiritual impact without prayer and meditation. This assignment given by the Holy Spirit took time as I developed a more profound, intimate relationship with God, Christ, and the guidance of the Holy Spirit. The most significant impact of this engaging epic was my shaping of thoughts as I ministered to the churches through preaching and teaching. I submitted to the voice of God while praying for insights to share on these pages. I pray that the body of Christ would find spiritual value and maturity while incorporating each Pearl into a particular ministry. The use of spiritual gifts for each Pearl pleases God.

This book's message encourages believers to grow in responsibility and maturity. The initial Pearl of Love to the concluding Pearl of Meekness bridges the gap of all Pearls to realize that love is needed to be efficient and effective, and to have the meekness to cultivate serenity, conscientiously refraining from engaging in strife. The Pearls in this book serve as spiritual markers that remind believers to push through the entanglement of danger and strive to make spiritual growth a meaningful encounter with God, grow in grace and knowledge, and appreciate Jesus as your intercessor.

Appendix 1

Wisdom Pearls Evaluation

Evaluate yourself for each Wisdom Pearl on a scale from 1 to 10, 1 being the lowest and 10 the highest. *Note: Respond honestly to the way it is, not what you want it to be.*

1. Love is a priority practice toward God and others in my ministry.

    1   2   3   4   5   6   7   8   9   10

2. Regardless of what I face, I spend much time with God in prayer.

    1   2   3   4   5   6   7   8   9   10

3. I am strong on forgiving others.

    1   2   3   4   5   6   7   8   9   10

4. I walk by faith more than I walk by fear.

    1   2   3   4   5   6   7   8   9   10

5. Commitment is a top priority for my ministry.

    1   2   3   4   5   6   7   8   9   10

6. I have mercy for others, no matter how they treat me.

    1   2   3   4   5   6   7   8   9   10

7. I have the patience to wait on God while he works the process in my life.

   1   2   3   4   5   6   7   8   9   10

8. My hope in God is at a high level of anticipation.

   1   2   3   4   5   6   7   8   9   10

9. I follow God's guidance for justice, showing honesty and integrity to others.

   1   2   3   4   5   6   7   8   9   10

10. I am eager to seek peace when I vehemently disagree with others.

    1   2   3   4   5   6   7   8   9   10

11. I honor God through obedience regardless of what I think.

    1   2   3   4   5   6   7   8   9   10

12. Contentment is a sign that I trust God in all things.

    1   2   3   4   5   6   7   8   9   10

13. I treat humility as the core of my spirituality, or my walk with God.

    1   2   3   4   5   6   7   8   9   10

14. I value honesty as the epitome of pleasing God.

    1   2   3   4   5   6   7   8   9   10

15. As a believer, I am dedicated to God and not the pattern of the world.

    1   2   3   4   5   6   7   8   9   10

16. I vow to God to live a life of trustworthiness.

    1   2   3   4   5   6   7   8   9   10

17. My focus is to persevere through all trials and tragedies, amid a shadow of doubt.

    1   2   3   4   5   6   7   8   9   10

18. I passionately practice living a life of sanctification for spiritual growth.

    1   2   3   4   5   6   7   8   9   10

19. I understand that confession is the start of a new life.

    1 2 3 4 5 6 7 8 9 10

20. I understand that grace is an act of God continually working on my behalf.

    1 2 3 4 5 6 7 8 9 10

21. I understand that friendship focuses on character rather than merit.

    1 2 3 4 5 6 7 8 9 10

22. I genuinely value the merit of godly wisdom regardless of my situation.

    1 2 3 4 5 6 7 8 9 10

23. I have a robust desire to be hospitable.

    1 2 3 4 5 6 7 8 9 10

24. My relationship with the Vine (Jesus) is fruitful and purposeful.

    1 2 3 4 5 6 7 8 9 10

25. I am growing spiritually and walking in the presence of God.

    1 2 3 4 5 6 7 8 9 10

26. I am to watch my tongue when in conversation with others.

    1 2 3 4 5 6 7 8 9 10

27. Compassion is an essential virtue for my Christian walk.

    1 2 3 4 5 6 7 8 9 10

28. I serve others without grumbling or complaining.

    1 2 3 4 5 6 7 8 9 10

29. Silence reminds me to listen to the Creator more during busy times.

    1 2 3 4 5 6 7 8 9 10

30. My conviction is a strong exhortation of faith.

    1 2 3 4 5 6 7 8 9 10

31. When I worship God, I view it as a passionate desire to connect to God.

    1 2 3 4 5 6 7 8 9 10

32. My discipleship needs more development.

    1   2   3   4   5   6   7   8   9   10

33. My stewardship is more credible now than two years ago.

    1   2   3   4   5   6   7   8   9   10

34. I have a deep passion for evangelism.

    1   2   3   4   5   6   7   8   9   10

35. My heart is heavy for the ministry of the mission field.

    1   2   3   4   5   6   7   8   9   10

36. I am empowered to develop a praise relationship with God.

    1   2   3   4   5   6   7   8   9   10

37. Respect reminds me to share it with others, regardless of differences.

    1   2   3   4   5   6   7   8   9   10

38. I seek to live a sacrificial life before God.

    1   2   3   4   5   6   7   8   9   10

39. I can bounce back with greater resilience.

    1   2   3   4   5   6   7   8   9   10

40. I focus on being meek when others are evasive of my accomplishments.

    1   2   3   4   5   6   7   8   9   10

Appendix 2

The Purpose Driven Disciple Life Pledge

In striving to embody the robust principles of being a purpose driven disciple, I pledge to pursue growth in character, faith, and service. My faith journey has a deeper relationship with God. With gratitude and humility, I commit myself to daily reflection and renewal, seeking wisdom through study, prayer, and genuine accountability. I vow to the Trinitarian Godhead to hold myself accountable to the teachings of Christ that guide my journey, fostering integrity within my actions, words, and relationships. I will dedicate time to serve others with compassion, passion, and generosity, recognizing that true servanthood is grounded in empathy and selflessness.

Through life's uncertainties and joys, I will remain steadfast, allowing my values to illuminate my path. As a disciple, I promise to encourage those around me, to listen deeply, and to cultivate unity and understanding wherever I am called. May this pledge be both a challenge and an inspiration—a living testimony and a commitment to transformation, stewardship, and love.

I have evaluated my spirituality to live as truthfully as possible, and the character to shape my principles to express my fundamental truths further. I yearn to grow deeper and witness wider for the glory of God. The purpose of the pledge is to commit and dedicate myself to the Holy, seeking guidance to become a more dedicated disciple and to apply the Wisdom Pearls presented in this book for edification. Each Pearl in this book has a distinct message for spiritual growth and development. Therefore, I pledge to do my best to follow the Scriptures noted for information and inspiration, as I walk by faith in ministry. I promise to focus on spiritual improvement because I am not perfect, but I seek to be a faithful disciple as I strive to live the life of a purpose driven disciple.

May you remain faithful in the name of the Father, the Son, and the Holy Ghost.

Bibliography

Barclay, William. *In the Hands of God: Inspiration from Daily Life.* Philadelphia: Westminster, 1966.
Bauer, Walter. *A Greek-English Lexicon of the New Testament and Other Early Christian Literature.* Translated and adapted by William F. Arndt and F. Wilbur Gingrich, revised by F. Wilbur Gingrich and Frederick W. Danker. 2nd ed. Chicago: University of Chicago, 1979.
Bible Hub. "842. Autarkés." https://biblehub.com/greek/842.htm.
———. "863. Aphiémi." https://biblehub.com/greek/863.htm.
———. "1342. Dikaios." https://biblehub.com/greek/1342.htm.
———. "2128. Eulogétos." https://biblehub.com/greek/2128.htm.
———. "2167. Zamar." https://biblehub.com/hebrew/2167.htm.
———. "2347. Thlipsis." https://biblehub.com/greek/2347.htm.
———. "2754. Kenodoxia." https://biblehub.com/strongs/greek/2754.htm.
———. "3135. Margarités." https://biblehub.com/greek/3135.htm.
———. "3628. Oiktirmos." https://biblehub.com/strongs/greek/3628.htm.
———. "3769. Karar." https://biblehub.com/hebrew/3769.htm.
———. "4102. Pistis." https://biblehub.com/greek/4102.htm.
———. "5218. Hupakoé." https://biblehub.com/greek/5218.htm.
———. "6960. Qavah." https://biblehub.com/hebrew/6960.htm.
———. "7133. Qorban." https://biblehub.com/hebrew/7133.htm.
———. "8416. Tehillah." https://biblehub.com/hebrew/8416.htm.
———. "Lodebar." https://biblehub.com/topical/l/lodebar.htm.
Bible Study Tools. "Barak." https://www.biblestudytools.com/lexicons/hebrew/kjv/barak.html.
Blackaby, Henry T., et al. *Experiencing God: Knowing and Doing the Will of God.* Brentwood, TN: Lifeway, 2022.
Boothe, Charles Octavius. *Plain Theology for Plain People.* Bellingham, WA: Lexham, 2017.
Bounds, E. M. *The Complete Works of E. M. Bounds on Prayer.* Grand Rapids: Baker 1990.
Butterick, George Arthur, ed. *Psalms, Proverbs.* Vol. 4 of *The Interpreter's Bible.* Nashville: Abingdon, 1983.

Chambers, Oswald. *The Love of God: An Intimate Look at the Father-Heart of God.* Grand Rapids: Our Daily Bread, 2020.

Cleveland, James. "Lord Help Me to Hold Out." Track 9 on *James Cleveland Sings with the World's Greatest Choirs 20th Anniversary Album.* Savoy Records, 1980.

Comer, John Mark. *Practicing the Way: Be with Jesus, Become like Him, Do as He Did.* WaterBrook, 2024.

Cone, James H. *God of the Oppressed.* New York: Seabury, 1975.

Cowan, Steven B., and James S. Spiegel. *The Love of Wisdom: A Christian Introduction to Philosophy.* Nashville: B&H, 2009.

Dorsey, Thomas Andrew. "Precious Lord, Take My Hand." Unichappell Music, 1938. https://hymnary.org/text/precious_lord_take_my_hand.

Earl, Riggins R., Jr. *Dark Symbols and Obscure Signs: God, Self, and Community in the Slave Mind.* Maryknoll, NY: Orbis, 2003.

Foster, Richard J. *Celebration of Discipline: The Path to Spiritual Growth.* Rev. ed. San Francisco: HarperSanFrancisco, 1988.

Gentile, Yvonne, and Debi Nixon. *The Art of Hospitality: A Practical Guide for a Ministry of Radical Welcome.* Nashville: Abingdon, 2020.

Got Questions. "What Is the Meaning of the Hebrew Word *Hesed*?" Updated January 4, 2022. https://www.gotquestions.org/meaning-of-hesed.html.

Grant, James H., Jr., and R. Kent Hughes. *1 & 2 Thessalonians: The Hope of Salvation.* Preaching the Word. Wheaton, IL: Crossway, 2011.

Grudem, Wayne. *Bible Doctrine: Essential Teachings of the Christian Faith.* Edited by Alexander Grudem. 2nd ed. Grand Rapids: Zondervan Academic, 2022.

Hayes, Charles G., and the Cosmopolitan Church of Prayer. "Everyday Is a Day of Thanksgiving." Track 8 on *I'll Never Forget.* Savoy Records, 1993.

Hull, Bill. *Building High Commitment in a Low Commitment World.* Grand Rapids: Baker, 1995.

Humphreys, Kent, and Davidene Humphreys. *Show and Then Tell: Presenting the Gospel Through Daily Encounters.* Chicago: Moody, 2000.

"I'm Gonna Live So God Can Use Me" [I Want to Live So God Can Use Me]. Hymnary. https://hymnary.org/text/im_gonna_live_so_god_can_use_me.

Käsemann, Ernst. *Commentary on Romans.* Translated and edited by Geoffrey W. Bromiley. Grand Rapids: Eerdmans, 1980.

Kierkegaard, Søren. *Works of Love.* Translated by Howard King and Edna Hong. New York: Harper Collins, 2009.

Lucado, Max. *Unshakable Hope: Building Our Lives on the Promises of God.* Nashville: Thomas Nelson, 2018.

Maples, C. C. "God's Children Have a Race to Run." Hymnary, 1944. https://hymnary.org/tune/gods_children_have_a_race_to_run_maples.

McQuilkin, J. Robertson. "The Keswick Perspective." In *Five Views on Sanctification*, by Melvin E. Dieter et al., 149–83. Grand Rapids: Academie, 1987.

Merrill, Eugene H. *Everlasting Dominion: A Theology of the Old Testament.* Nashville: B&H, 2006.

Moltmann, Jürgen. *The Crucified God: The Cross of Christ as the Foundation and Criticism of Christian Theology.* Translated by R. A. Wilson and John Bowden. New York: Harper and Row, 1974.

———. *Theology of Hope: On the Ground and the Implications of a Christian Eschatology.* Translated by James W. Leitch. New York: Harper and Row, 1975.

Mote, Edward. "My Hope Is Built on Nothing Less." Hymnary, 1834. https://hymnary.org/text/my_hope_is_built_on_nothing_less.
Mulholland, Robert M. *Invitation to a Journey: A Road Map for Spiritual Formation*. Downers Grove, IL: InterVarsity, 1993.
Murray, Andrew. *Absolute Surrender*. Start, 2017. Kindle.
———. *The Blessings of Obedience*. New Kensington, PA: Whitaker, 1984.
———. *The Essential Andrew Murray Collection*. Minneapolis: Bethany House, 2001.
———. *With Christ in the School of Prayer*. New Kensington, PA: Whitaker, 1981.
Niebuhr, Reinhold. *Human Destiny*. Vol. 2 of *The Nature and Destiny of Man: A Christian Interpretation*. New York: Scribner's Sons, 1964.
Olson, David T. *Discovering Your Leadership Style: The Power of Chemistry, Strategy and Spirituality*. Downers Grove, IL: InterVarsity, 2014.
Packer, J. I. *Knowing God*. Downers Grove, IL: InterVarsity, 1973.
Pate, Marvin C. *Romans*. Teach the Text Commentary Series. Grand Rapids: Baker, 2013.
Piper, John. *Seeing and Savoring Jesus Christ*. Rev. ed. Wheaton, IL: Crossway, 2004.
Rainer, Thom S. *Autopsy of a Deceased Church: 12 Ways to Keep Yours Alive*. Nashville: B&H, 2014.
The Rambos. "He Looked Beyond My Fault (And Saw My Need)." Lyrics by Dottie Rambo. Track D2 on *The Rambos—Silver Jubilee*. Heart Warming Records, 1979.
Richards, Lawrence. *Expository Dictionary of Bible Words*. Grand Rapids: Zondervan, 1985.
Spafford, Horatio Gates. "When Peace, Like a River." Composed by Philip Bliss. Hymnary, 1873. https://hymnary.org/text/when_peace_like_a_river_attendeth_my_way.
Spurgeon, Charles. *Daily Wisdom on Prayer: 365 Devotions from Charles Spurgeon*. Uhrichsville, OH: Barbour, 2022.
———. *God's Grace to You*. New Kensington, PA: Whitaker House, 1997.
Stanley, Charles F. *Experiencing Forgiveness: Enjoy the Peace of Giving and Receiving Grace*. Nashville: Thomas Nelson, 2019.
Stanphill, Ira P. "I Know Who Holds Tomorrow." New Spring, 1950. https://hymnary.org/text/i_dont_know_about_tomorrow.
Stedman, Ray C. *Authentic Christianity: Trading Religion & Rules for True Faith*. Grand Rapids: Our Daily Bread, 1996. Kindle.
Strong, James. *The Strongest Strong's Exhaustive Concordance of the Bible*. Large print ed. Grand Rapids: Zondervan, 2001.
Sutherland, Dave, and Kirk Nowery. *The 33 Laws of Stewardship: Principles for a Life of True Fulfilment*. Camarillo, CA: Spire Resources, 2003.
Thurman, Howard. *Jesus and the Disinherited*. Boston: Beacon, 1976.
Tillich, Paul. *The Courage to Be*. New Haven: Yale University Press, 1952.
———. *The Dynamics of Faith*. New York: Harper & Row, 1957.
Townsend, Willa A., ed. *Gospel Pearls*. Nashville: Sunday School Publishing Board, National Baptist Convention of America, 1921. https://hymnary.org/hymnal/GP1921.
Tozer, A. W. *The Crucified Life*. In *The Essential Tozer Collection*, compiled and edited by James L. Snyder, 5–210. Minneapolis: Bethany House, 2017.
———. *A Journey Into the Father's Heart*. Vol. 1 of *The Attributes of God*. Chicago: Wing Spread, 2003.

———. *The Knowledge of the Holy.* New York: HarperCollins, 1961.

Turner, Johnny. *A Biblical Theology of Christian Discipleship.* Eugene, OR: Wipf & Stock, 2021.

———. *God Is a Strong Shelter: Weathering Storms Through Reading Psalms.* Eugene, OR: Wipf & Stock, 2023.

Vine, W. E. *Vine's Expository Dictionary of Old and New Testament Words.* Tarrytown, NY: Revell, 1981.

Whitefield, Samuel. *The Gospel of Daniel 7.* Vol 1 of *Son of Man.* Grandview, MO: OneKing, 2019.

Wikipedia. "The Gate of the Year." Last edited June 13, 2024. https://en.wikipedia.org/wiki/The_Gate_of_the_Year.

Williams, Eddie. "Lord Keep Me Day by Day." Martin and Morris, 1959.

Williams, William. "Guide Me, O Thou Great Jehovah." Translated by Peter Williams. Hymnary, 1745. https://hymnary.org/text/guide_me_o_thou_great_jehovah.

Yancey, Philip. *What's So Amazing About Grace?* Grand Rapids: Zondervan, 2023.

Subject Index

Abednego, adoration of, 183
Abel and Cain, 219
abiding, in Christ, 190
Abraham, 88, 221
Abraham and Sarah, 136
abundant life, living, 194–95
accountability, stewardship and, 192–96
action in progress, commitment as, 34
actions, xxv, 203
Adam, as the first steward, 193
Adam and Eve, 66, 81, 216
administration, gift of, 193
adoration, 16, 181–86
African American tradition, 13, 184
African Americans, 37
agape love
　at the core of God's heart, 4
　extending to everyone, 8
　of the Father, 160
　focusing on God's, 5
　representing God's, 134
all your heart, loving with, 8
Amos, 53–54
Ananias and Sapphira, 82–83
anchor, perseverance as a strong, 101–5
angels, entertaining unaware, 133
anointing, 18, 172
antagonistic behavior, never falling prey to, 215
aphesis, on the dismissal or release of our sins, 21

apple of God's eye, discipleship as, 187–91
appreciating mercies, 160–61
arrogance, 66
attention, Jehovah wanting all your, 222
attitudes, of friendship, 126–27
attributes, of God, 93
autarkés, Greek word translated as "content," 69–70
authentic love, as a continuing bond, 5

bad fruit, 142, 143
Barak, summoned by Deborah, 89
barak, Hebrew for kneeling, 210–11
Barclay, William, 72
Bathsheba, David and, 89
bearing fruit. *See* fruit
beatitudes, 232
being still, 221
believers
　asking the Lord to send out workers, 200
　compassion of, 39
　compassionate conversation from, 153
　condition of weak, 229
　confession of, 113
　evangelism of, 200
　faith of, 26
　falling prey to evil, 23
　focusing on God, xxiv

believers (*cont.*)
    going beyond the ordinary, 190
    helping with missions, 202
    humility of, 74
    Jesus concerned about, 142
    lifestyle of, 80, 148
    maintaining the character of Christ, 235
    obedience of, 67
    as obedient servants, 194–95
    as peacemakers, 61
    perseverance of, 102
    persevering in spiritual excellence, xxii
    practicing servanthood humbly, 164
    in the presence of God, 185
    presenting the gospel, 198
    presenting their bodies as a sacrifice to God, 12
    recovering from setbacks, 225
    responsibility and maturity of, 238
    as spiritually minded, 149
    vigilant about the cost of discipleship, 189
Bible
    full of pearls of wisdom, xix
    on the importance of doing good, 78
    on remembering verses of, xxv
    on the value of a hidden treasure, xxii
biblical characters, who persevered, 103–4
bitterness, 154, 156
Blackaby, Henry, 203
bless, as another word for praise, 210
blessings, 50, 159–60
Bliss, Philips, 59
blood, of Jesus, 104
body of Christ. *See* the church
Bounds, E. M., 13
branches
    cannot bear fruit, 190
    depending on the vine, 142
    as essential for bearing fruit, 144
breakthrough, of worship, 184–85
the brokenhearted, 38
burden, of Moses, 225
burning bush, God called Moses from, 88

Cain and Abel, 219
calmness, patience showing, 41–45
capacity, building by thinking biblically, 149
carnal mind, as enmity against God, 149
Cave at Adullam, David in, 165
Celebration of Discipline: The Path to Spiritual Growth (Foster), 15
challenges, occurring daily, 97–98
Chambers, Oswald, 4
character, 34, 74–79, 124, 234
charis, Greek word for grace, 118
charizomai, bestowing favor unconditionally, 21
Chauvin, Derek, 38
cherished love, 8–9
chokmah, Hebrew word for wisdom, skill, and learning, 128
Christ. *See also* Jesus
    abiding in, 190
    brought all mercy with him, 42
    delivered us from darkness, 135
    improving your relationship with, 222
    requesting faithful and sincere accountability, 194
    suffered to give compassion meaning, 159–60
Christlike character. *See* character
Christ's blood, Pearl of, xxiii
the church
    gifts in, 161
    striving to keep unity, 61
    suffering because of unforgiveness, 22–23
church leadership, providing a welcoming environment, 134
circumstances, accepting as they are, 69
cleanness of sins, needed by all, 22
cloud of witnesses, 225
Comer, John Mark, 222
comforting presence, hospitality as, 133–38
commandments, most important, 7–8
commitment, 30–34, 62–63, 187
communication, prayer as a private form of, 13
community, friendship building, 124

compassion
- absent without God's love, 7
- extending fair treatment to others, 54
- forgiveness as a kind act of, 19
- mercy cries for, 37–38
- power of, 39
- as a touch of the heart, 158–62
- treating others with, 214

compassionate deliverance, divine favor and, 120

compassionate love, of God, 67

Cone, James, 38

confession, 107, 108, 112–16

confidence, trustworthiness and, 97–99

confrontations, 228, 232

consecration, 12, 17, 108, 109

contaminated lifestyle, staying away from, 83

contamination, as poisonous, 82

contentment, 69–73

conversion, love as another form of, 8

conviction, as a positive reality, 174–78

Corinthian church, sinful atmosphere, 86

corrupt communication, 152, 156

cost, of mission work, 204

courage, 98, 177

covenant, God made with Abraham, 88

COVID-19 pandemic, 37

creative agent, for God, 110

Creator. *See* God

dancing, before the Lord like David, 209

Daniel, prayer warrior, 90

David
- after God's own heart, 89
- on being still in the presence of God, 42
- danced before the Lord God, 71, 209
- plea for his pain and sorrow, 232
- reaching out to God, 208
- requesting mercy, 222
- saying "Wash me clean," 23
- as a strong leader, 165
- using *tehillah*, 211
- welcoming of Mephibosheth to eat at his table, 136

day of the Lord, will come like a "thief in the night," 228

days, cherishing each, xxiv

death, flesh directed toward, 144

Deborah, role of, 89–90

dedication, 32, 85–92, 187

defense, rock of, 148

defilement, as a profane action, 153

deliverance, availability of, 120

demonstration, of love, 6–8

despair, hope preventing, 46–50

devil. *See also* Satan
- destroying authentic friendships, 126

devotion, to one another, 216

dikaios, Greek word for "righteous," 199

dikaiosune, Greek word for "righteousness," 199

disappointments, Job did not complain, 103

discernment, of good and bad fruits, 145

disciples, 31, 35, 39, 187

discipleship, 187–91, 198

discipline
- commitment and, 32–33
- dedication and, 86, 87, 91
- gentle tongue as, 152–57

dishonest lifestyle, 51

dishonest transactions, 82–83

dishonesty, 81

disobedience, 194

disrespect, in the world, 214

disrespectfulness, 215

divine directive, to implement justice and mercy, 36

divine interventions, bringing blessings, 205

divine thoughts, initiated by the Holy Spirit, 1

doctrine
- of the perseverance of the saints, 102
- of prayer, 11

double indemnity, of Jesus and the Holy Spirit, 171

The Dynamics of Faith (Tillich), 27

SUBJECT INDEX

Earl, Riggins, Jr., 37
earthly worship, as a dress rehearsal, 184
Ecclesiastes, on valuing time and the significance of life, 129
edification, inspiring others, 156
ego, getting in the way, 156
Egyptians, harsh and ruthless toward the Israelites, 46
eirene, Greek word for "peace," 59
Elijah, 91, 172
Elisha, provided a meal to the Aramean army, 136
Elohim, xxiv, 208, 211
encouragement, gift of, 161
end times, 205, 216
endurance, 47
enemies' attacks, surviving pressures from, 228
enlightenment, spirituality and, 146–51
enslaved people, embittered by many unmerciful acts, 37
enslaved person for Christ, becoming, 166
Epaphroditus, Paul's mention of, 66
Ephesians, on salvation, 26
equality, standing up for, 55
eschatology, theology of, xx
essential fruits, 143
essentials, to guide you, xxiv–xxvi
eternal security, confirmation of, 199
eternity, 104, 105, 184
ethical life, glorifying God, 77
eulogétos, Greek word for "blessed," 159
Evangelical church, know and show method of, 204
evangelism, 8, 197–201
"Every Day Is a Day of Thanksgiving" (song), 15
evil, encountering, 227
evil lifestyle, Job avoided, 103
excellent way, sacrifice as, 218–23
expectations, of God, 220–21
Ezekiel, 110, 199

faith
 connected to resilience, 225
 first act of, 41
 history and heritage of, 224
 implementing dedication, 86
 as integral, 102
 as the most credible act of confidence, 98
 as the moving conduit for prayer, 14
 overcoming trials of painful pressure, 12
 pleasing God, 25–29, 102
 prayer of, 16, 29
 walking by, 15
faith leaders, dedicated, 87–91
faithful and fruitful living, God waiting for, 99
faithful justice, 53
false prophets, being beware of, 142
Father. *See also* God
 used the Son to initiate the mission agenda, 203
 as the vinedresser, 144
favor, expressing God's action, 118
fighting, the ongoing battle of spiritual warfare, 61–62
five-star ministry, servanthood as, 163–67
fleshly approach to God, cannot stay in the vine, 144
flourishing, need for, 147–48
Floyd, George, 38
forgiveness, 14, 19–24, 107
forgiving others, 15, 20
forty-day spiritual growth journey, xx
Foster, Richard J., 15
friendship, mattering, 123–27
fruit, relationship between the vine and the branches, 141–45
fruit of compassion, in Jesus, 125
fruit of the Spirit
 characteristics of, 233
 qualities of, xxiii, 5, 143
 spiritual prosperity of, xx

"The Gate of the Year" poem (Haskins), 147
gem for God, value of living life as, xxiv
gentle tongue, as a discipline factor, 152–57
gentleness, receiving and utilizing, 235

SUBJECT INDEX

genuine friendship, having no barriers, 125
genuine love, 4, 8
genuine relationships, lasting through tests, 127
gifts, variety of in today's church, 161
glorifying God, 139–78
God. *See also* Father
    acknowledging confession, 114
    approaching, 218
    attributes of, 36
    as the center of grace, 120–21
    comprehensiveness of, 118
    concerned about discipleship, 189–90
    connecting to, 182–83
    dedicating life to him faithfully, 220
    example of, 56
    expectations of, xxii
    faith pleasing to, 25–29
    favoring those practicing pure religion, 81–82
    following the will of, 15
    forgiving sins, 67
    gave Moses seventy elders, 225
    genuine love of, 7
    hearing the prayers of the righteous, 171
    living by the words of, 113
    longing for pure worship from his children, 181
    love of, 4, 5, 6
    made Christ Jesus to be wisdom itself, 129
    meekness pleasing, 234–35
    mercy of, 160–61
    mercy pleasing, 38–39
    monitoring fruit activity, 142
    nature of, 93
    not allowing temptation beyond what we can handle, 23
    as the object of our commitment, 32
    as the originator and giver of mercy, 36
    pleasing, xxi, 102, 166, 179–236
    praise touching, 207–12
    presence of, 21, 23, 170
    providing ways to minister to needs and issues, 159
    relationships and fellowship with, 60
    respecting, 214
    responding to sin, 23–24
    satisfying, 220–21
    sent Jesus to advocate for mercy, 38
    serving, 66–67
    significance of honoring, 93
    as sovereign, 204
    sovereignty of, 179–236
    staying attached to, 85
    strength of, 96
    trials from, 226
    trusting in, 28
    urged Micah to practice walking humbly, 39
    waiting for you to worship him, 185
    waiting on, 42–43
    walking humbly before, 75
    Wisdom Pearls glorifying, 139–78
    Wisdom Pearls honoring, 93–138
    Wisdom Pearls pleasing, 179–236
    as worthy to be praised, 216
    wrath of, 55–56, 153
God-centered life, adopting, 220
godly lifestyle, representing Christ, 77
Godly living, xxiv
God's throne of grace, approaching, 227
Goliath, David defeated, 89
good tree, cannot bear bad fruit, 142, 145
"good works," being a model of, 214
goodness, God's attribute of, 213
Gospel Pearls songbook, published in 1921, xix
grace
    faith and, 28
    of God including perseverance, 105
    included in perseverance, 102
    as sufficient, 117–22
Great Commission, 188, 189, 198
greatest commandment, 78
grudges, 22, 55
"Guide Me, O Thou Great Jehovah" church hymn, 173
guilt, 22, 115

SUBJECT INDEX

hagiasmos, Greek word for "sanctification," 107
hallel, Hebrew to give thinks, 209
hands of God, active during moments of silence, 173
harmony, living in, 54
harsh attitudes, avoiding, 98
harvest
    overflowing with unsaved souls, 200
    responding to, 190
Haskins, Minnie Louise, 147
haughty spirit, as the spirit of pride, 76–77
"He Looked Beyond My Fault" song, 159
heart, of mission activity, 203–4
heart of God, compassion from, 158–62
Hebrew words, for praise, 209, 210–11
Hebrews (book of), on living in peace, 107
helping one another, 126
hesed, on the mercy and compassion of God, 36
high exaltation, showing our praise in, 211
high-tech discussions, godly wisdom igniting, 129
holiness, 12, 76, 108, 219
Holy Scripture, as the source for prayers, 16
Holy Spirit
    anointing of after worship, 183–84
    as the change agent for accepting conviction, 175
    connecting to the leading of, 182
    conquering acts of spiritual interference, 194
    convicting individuals of personal sin and guilt, 176
    interceding in the same way as grace, 121
    keeping love alive, 9
    monitoring the seriousness of conviction, 174
    moving the hearts of individuals living in sin, 176
    praying for us, 121
    producing fruit in our lives, xxiii
    sanctification as the work of, 107, 110
    sealed by, 31
    as the source of spiritual growth, 87
    sustaining during turbulent moments, 1
    work in regeneration, 111
honest living, 51, 51–92, 83
honesty, 51, 80–84, 95–96
honor, 42, 65, 215
honoring, God, 216
hope
    faith as the catalyst of, 26
    for the hopeless, 201
    preventing despair, 46–50
    as a symbol of peace, 59
    for the unsaved, 199, 200
hopeless situations, wise words unlocking, 154
hopelessness, without love, 3, 5
hospitality, as a comforting presence, 133–38
hostile life, pushing through the rubbish of, 226
Hull, Bill, 30, 32
human nature, desiring mercy, 35
humanitarian forgiveness, in the story of Joseph and his brothers, 20
humanity, implementing God's love for, 9
humble communication, praise as, 207
a humble spirit, valuing the merit of wisdom, 130
humbleness, discipline of, 169
humility
    adopting, 232
    building character, 74–79
    showing souls at rest with God, 234
hupakoé, Greek word for "obedience," 65
huperentugchano, Greek word for "intercession," 121
hymn, Greek word for relating to the Hebrew word *hallel*, 209

"I Know Who Holds Tomorrow" hymn, embodying contentment, 72
"I Want to Live So God Can Use Me" gospel song, 99

SUBJECT INDEX 255

identity, sanctification as a genuine, 106–11
image of God, everyone created in, 216
impatience, seen in action, 43
In the Hands of God (Barclay), 72
integrity, 78, 81, 214
intercession, prayer of, 16
intimacy, listening to God building, 169–70
Isaac, 88, 221
Isaiah
    appealed to Judah to acknowledge their condition and sins, 67
    consecration connecting to Jesus' consecration, 108–9
    on the effect of righteousness will be peace, 59
    gave the Israelites hope, 42, 46
    on God's thoughts, 172
    Micah a contemporary of, 36
Israel
    Deborah focused on delivering, 89–90
    disappointed God by failing to be fruitful, 141
    under Pharaoh's servitude for 430 years, 48
Israelites
    enduring the pain of Pharaoh's camp, 37
    hopeless until Moses, 48
    witnessed God leading them, 49
"It Is Well with My Soul" hymn, 59, 103

Jabez, called upon God, 15
Jacob, commitment of, 33
James
    concerned about converted Jewish Christians, 115
    on gaining wisdom, 131
    on the importance of a strong faith, 226
    on living an honorable life, 154
    on living the right way, 81–82
    on an untamed tongue, 80, 153
    on walking humbly, 232
jealousy, of Joseph's brothers, 89
Jehovah, 148, 199. *See also* God
Jehovah Jireh, as the Lord will provide, 229
Jeremiah, 91, 169, 210
Jesus. *See also* Christ
    commitment to the Father, 204
    concerned about the unredeemed, 202–3
    demonstrated love while he was on earth, 5
    emptied Himself, 23–24
    as the epitome of hospitality, 135
    as example of leadership and servanthood, 164
    as example of true mercy, 35–36
    forgave those who crucified him, 22
    as full of grace and truth, 122
    as humble and gentle at heart, 234
    on the image of the vine and branches, 141
    interceding on our behalf, 13, 171
    on knowing truth, 81
    making the best of your relationship with, xxi
    model of the theology of confession, 114
    as our advocate, 171
    as our peace amid the dividing walls of hostility, 59
    as our Savior and King, 62
    requiring you to bear good fruit, 142
    resurrected Jairus's daughter instantaneously, 104
    as the root of sanctification, 108–9
    sacrificed vicariously, 219
    on the significance of a respectful life, 83
    teaching his disciples to pray, 12
    as the ultimate answer for inadequacies, 228
    urged mercy on a woman caught in adultery, 37
    as the vine, 144
    washed the disciples' feet, 166
    went to Zacchaeus's house and ate with sinners, 136–37
Jewish believers, 82, 115
Jim Crow Laws in the South, lack of mercy under, 39

SUBJECT INDEX

Job, 42, 43, 103, 123–24
Job (book of), filled with handling suffering, 129
John, on the sacredness of worship, 184
John's Gospel, on "The Word became flesh," 121
Joseph, 44, 89, 120, 234
Joseph and his brothers, 20, 175
Joshua, 90, 172
joyful noise, making to the Lord, 182
Jude (book of), emphasis on discipleship, 188
"judgment," justice translated as, 54
justice, 53, 53–57, 78

kalos, Greek word for "honest," 81
karar, Hebrew word for "dance," 209
Käsemann, Ernst, 220
kenodoxia, Greek word meaning empty pride, 77
Kierkegaard, Søren, on love, 7
kindness, 35–40, 124, 126, 193
King, Rodney, 124
kneeling, 210–11
know and show, example of, 204
koinonia renewal, asking God for, 22

Lamentations, on mercy, 160
lasting experience, spirituality as, 149–50
Law and the Prophets, biblical principle of, 215
law of Moses, Gospel links to the, 65
leadership, 90, 165, 193
leading, gift of, 161
liars, will not see the kingdom of God, 99
life
    of dedication, 85
    leaving the old, 114–15
    present wholly to God, 219
    pure in God's sight, 214
    shaping your, xxiv–xxv
    surrendering to God humbly, 218
    as unfulfilled, 215
    as unsustainable without obedience, 66
    without justice and mercy as empty, 38
life course, spiritual identity charting, 144
life of Jesus, making visible, 104
life pledge, of a purpose driven disciple, 243–44
lifestyles
    living balanced, 191
    the Spirit and the flesh, 144
light
    bringing hope to a hopeless situation, 101
    shining before men, 135, 136
listening to God, 168–73, 185
living faith, 46
living horizontally, 189
living sacrifice, presenting your body as, 221
living vertically, as answering to God, 189
Lodebar, town and story of, 120
"Lord, Keep Me Day By Day" gospel song, 102
"Lord Help Me to Hold Out" song, 33
lordship of Jesus, servant leadership connecting to, 165
love
    Christian character strengthened by, 78
    covering a multitude of sins, 134
    as essential for remaining obedient, 65
    inextricably bound with mercy, 160
    as key, 3–10
    needed to be efficient and effective, 238
    obedience reflecting, 64–68
loving environment, respect creating, 213–17
Lucado, Max, 96

malice, striving to avoid, 156
Mandela, Nelson, as a committed servant, 32
mark to achieve the prize of eternal life, Paul pressing toward, 104
Markan account, of forgiveness, 21
Mark's Gospel, emphasis on faith, 25–26
Martha, opened her home to Jesus, 137
Mary (Martha's sister), 137

SUBJECT INDEX

Matthew, Gospel of on compassion through testing, 7
maturity, xx, 1
McQuilkin, J. Robertson, 107
meaningful relationship, listening to God as, 172–73
meekness, 231–36, 238
memory verses, xxv
Mephibosheth, eating at David's table, 136
mercy, 35–40, 161
Merrill, Eugene H., 216
Meshach, adoration of, 183
Messiah, righteousness through sanctification, 108
Micah, 36, 221
mind
    being transformed by the renewing of your, xxv
    peace comforting, 58–63
miracles, gift of, 161–62
mission, prayer for, 206
missions, caring about the unredeemed, 202–6
Moltmann, Jürgen, 47, 114
mood, of faith, 27–28
moral goodness, wisdom as the practical side of, 130
Moses
    exemplified meekness with serenity, 234, 235
    God called and assigned, 48
    on holiness, 12
    liberator of the old covenant, 88
    stretched out his hand over the sea, 120
    wanted God to kill him, 225
Mother Teresa, as a servant of humility, 76
Mt. Sinai, God took Moses to, 88
mulligans, Satan taking, 113
Murray, Andrew, 87
music, glorifying God in worship, 184

Naomi and Ruth, dear and dedicated friends, 125
natural mind, having a heart for carnal things, 149

Nebuchadnezzar, 183
need to flourish, 147–48
negative presence, preventing spiritual nourishment, 149
negativity, describing the DNA of, 51
new creation, 200
new creature, becoming, 114
new heaven and the new earth, anticipating, 104
new life, 114, 115
Nicodemus, Jesus instructed, 113
Niebuhr, Reinhold, 119
nonbeliever, pleading for the opportunity to be saved, 113

obedience
    living by, 15
    reflecting love, 64–68
    requiring sacrifice to please God, 220
    Wisdom Pearls encouraging, xx
obedient servants, lesson of authentic accountability, 194
offense to God, unforgiveness as, 22
oiktir, Greek for "compassion" or "pity," 159
Old and New Testament servants, lived a prayer life, 14
old life, leaving, 114–15
Old Testament
    characters who provided hospitality, 136
    instances of sacrifice in, 219
    pointing to future of events leading up to the end times, 228
omnipresence and omnipotence, of God linked to worship, 182
"On Christ, the solid rock, I stand" hymn, 47
others
    respecting, 214–15
    valuing above yourselves, 76
outlook, contentment revitalizing, 69–73

Packer, J. I., 130
paliggenesia, Greek word for "regeneration," 107

SUBJECT INDEX

parable
   of the talents, 193–94
   of the vine and the branches, 142
paranoia, wise words reducing propensity for, 154
passion
   for being respectful, 215–16
   of wise words, 153–54
passionate endeavor, evangelism as, 197–201
pastoral leadership, stirring up the gift of, 75
pastors, advocate for equality, 54
pathway to God, prayer as, 11–15
patience, 41–45, 49
Paul
   on bearing fruit, 143
   on being careful how you live, xxiii
   on being content, 27–28
   being dedicated, 87
   on being free from all blame, 60
   on carnality, 86
   defending his ministry with meekness, 119
   on evilness, 27
   on facing death all day long, 226
   on the fruit of the Spirit, 233
   gave Timothy an encouraging lift, 234
   on God being with you, 61
   on God demonstrating his love for us, 6
   on God guarding your hearts, 59
   on God supplying every need, 47–48, 159
   on God's sufficiency, 67
   on grace, 120
   on helping one another, 126
   identified weak and strong in Rome, 229
   on keeping peace in your conscience, 58
   on living a life well-pleasing to God, 109
   on living as children of light, 4
   on making the best use of time, 203
   on messaging and preaching, 155
   on the new creation in Christ, 200
   on not allowing any unwholesome talk, 155
   on not being ashamed of the gospel, 197–98
   on not conforming to the pattern of this world, 86
   on not taking revenge, 55
   on offering your bodies as living sacrifices, xxiv–xxv
   on opposition and challenges, 118
   passion for evangelism, 198
   persevered, 104
   pleading for salvation, 113
   on the power of resilience, 225
   on practicing humility, 76
   on pressing toward the prize of a higher calling, 66
   on putting on the whole armor of God, 147
   on putting others above yourself, 76
   on sanctification, 109–10
   on Satan's vile action, 62
   sharing a teaching proclamation, 188
   on showing hospitality, 137
   on showing yourself to be a model of good works, 98
   on the Spirit helping us in our weakness, 33
   on stirring up the gift of God, 75
   on the touch of God's heart, 158–59
   on trust, 26, 70
   on union with Christ as a core doctrine, 110
   on valuing humility, 77
   on watching out for carnality, 149
Paul and Silas, in prison, 208
peace, 58–63, 72, 108
peacebreakers, instead of peacemakers, 62
peaceful conversation, 214
peaceful loving environment, 213
peacemakers, 59, 61
pearl, defining and explaining in the biblical context, xxiv
Pearl of great price, church as, xxiii
pearls, xxi, xxii

SUBJECT INDEX

Pearls. *See also* Wisdom Pearls
    cherishing God, xix
    God revealing the content and context of each, 237
pearly gates, focusing on, 130
peculiar love, as a stone of slyness, 4
perfection, of wise words, 153–54
perseverance, as a strong anchor, 101–5
personal devotion, as the essence of deep love for the Creator, 70
persuasiveness, of wise words, 153–54
Peter's house, hospitality at, 137
Pharaoh, Moses stood up against, 88
Philippians 2:3–4, understanding and applying, 76–77
philos love, 8
philosophy, emphasis on "the love of wisdom," 129
Piper, John, 235
pistis, as the conviction that God exists and is the Creator, 26
pneuma, for the Spirit, 144
pneumatikos, Greek word for "spirituality," 148
point of emphasis, capturing the focus of your reflection, xxv
positive actions, implementing, 154
positive mental model, trustworthiness creating, 99
positive reality, conviction as, 174–78
positive reputation, trustworthiness breeding, 95–100
power
    of contentment, 71–72
    of conviction, 177
    of faith, 28
    of forgiveness, 21
    of God, 16, 22
    of prayer, 13
    of wise words, 153–54
praise
    as the celebration of God's deliverance, 160
    as an expression of what God has done for us, 183
    touching God, 207–12
    worship and, 71
praus, Greek word for "meekness," 233
pray, without ceasing, 228
prayer
    as the antidote for life, 14, 17
    of commitment, 34
    of compassion, 162
    for confession, 116
    to conquer bitterness, 154
    for contentment, 73
    of conviction, 178
    for dedication, 92
    of discipleship, 191
    for evangelism, 201
    of faith, 29
    of forgiveness, 24
    for friendship, 127
    for fruit, 145
    for grace, 122
    as a guide from the Holy Spirit, 14
    helping believers experience the Pearl of Wisdom, 129
    of honesty, 84
    of hope, 50
    for hospitality, 138
    of humble mercy, 40
    of humility, 79
    as the immanent factor, 15
    of justice, 57
    keeping one connected to God, 13
    as the link to God to use the right words, 155
    of love, 10
    maintaining a connection with the Creator, 15
    for meekness, 236
    for mission, 206
    for obedience, 68
    as the pathway to God, 11–15
    for peace, 63
    of perseverance, 105
    of praise, 212
    prioritizing, 17
    for resilience, 229–30
    of respect, 217
    of the righteous, 228
    of sacrifice, 223
    for sanctification, 111
    of servanthood, 167
    of silence, 173

SUBJECT INDEX

prayer (*cont.*)
    for spirituality, 150–51
    for stewardship, 195–96
    that each Pearl will be used in your life, xxvi
    for the tongue, 157
    of trustworthiness, 100
    of waiting, 45
    for wisdom, 132
    of worship, 186
prayer and personal application, xxvi
prayer life, 17, 205
prayer lifters, 15
prayers, types of, 16–17
preachers, advocate for equality, 54
"Precious Lord, Take My Hand" gospel song, 120
presence of God, 147
pride, causing unforgiveness to fester, 22
prince of Egypt, Joseph appointed as, 120
procrastination habit, deleting, 99
promise, of God to Israel to deliver them, 185
prophesying, gift of, 161
prophetess, Deborah as, 89
prosperous life, living, xx
Proverbs, xix, 31, 129
Psalms, 129
pure religion, honesty as, 80–84
purification, 110–11
purpose driven disciple, life pledge, 243–44
pursuing, wisdom, 130, 132

qavah, Hebrew word for "hope," 47
qorban, Hebrew word for sacrifice, 219
quality time, xx, 168
quiet time, with God, 169, 170

rachum, describing God's consistent character, 39
rage, inciting vehement actions, 236
real love, gives sincere thoughts of righteousness, 4
rebellion, leading to a stark arrogance, 65
reciprocal process, trustworthiness as, 98
reciprocity, 6, 54
redemption, 112, 198
reflective summary, of each chapter, xxv
regeneration, 107, 110
relationship(s)
    building with others, 205
    genuine, 127
    improving with Christ, 222
    meaningful with God, 172–73
    of the vine and branches, 141–45
reliability, living a life of, 96
religion, honesty confirming pure, 80
repentance, 23, 107
resilience, 41–42, 224–30
respect, creating a loving environment, 213–17
respectful communication, edifying individuals, 155–56
resurrection, relevance of deliverance, 104
retaliation, avoiding against unmerciful acts, 38
Revelation (book of), 130, 184
revenge, not taking, 55
reverence, 65, 182
rewards, of missionary work, 205–6
right mind, being in the, 75
the righteous, 146, 147, 199
righteous living, benefits of, 198–99
righteousness, 88, 198, 232
road, to sanctification through Jesus, 108
rock, of defense, 148
Romans 12:19, applying, 54–55
running with endurance, the race that is set before us, 224
Ruth and Naomi, had a close bond, 125

sacred promise, dedication as, 85–92
sacredness of worship, 184
sacrifice, as the excellent way, 218–23
safe environment, tongue creating, 156
saints, persevering until the end, 102
salvation, 198, 199
Samuel, 65, 220
sanctification, as a genuine identity, 106–11
Sarah, 136
sarx, for sinful nature, 144

SUBJECT INDEX

Satan. *See also* devil
    attacks of, 113
    causing despair, 46
    at the center of sadistic surprises, 62
    circumventing the desire of, 142
    derailing your path of worship with God, 186
    disrupting your spiritual walk, 148–49
    interrupting hopeful moments, 48
    interrupting peace, 61
    not wanting you to experience a breakthrough, 185
satisfaction, contentment emphasizing, 72
seals, revealing the second coming of Christ, 170
Second Adam, Jesus Christ as, 121
secretion, from natural irritants creating Pearls, xxii
self, embracing with faith and hope, 228
self-awareness, fostering, 74
self-centered living, giving up, 220
self-control, exercising, 232
self-expression, praise letting go of, 211
selfish ambition, 76, 215
selfishness, avoiding, 233
self-sufficiency, 70
semnos, Greek word for "honesty," 81
serenity, meekness embracing, 231–36
servant leadership, 165–66
servanthood, as a five-star ministry, 163–67
serving
    gift of, 161
    God, 66–67
    others, 134, 166
    as the primary objective of the Savior, 164
shabach, Hebrew for exuberant praise, 210
Shadrach, adoration of, 183
shalom, Hebrew word for "peace," 59
shame, of Adam and Eve in the garden, 23
Shunammite woman, provided genuine hospitality to Elijah, 136
silence, as listening to God, 168–73

sin
    bitterness leading to further, 154
    causing an unruly tongue, 153
    confessing during prayer, 15
    God's response to, 23–24
    not allowing to influence unwise conversation, 155
    power of as no match for the mercy of God, 160
    prayer of admission of, 113
    unforgiveness of others as a serious, 22
sinful elements, experiencing, 119
situations, accepting as they are, 69
social and spiritual reciprocity, Jesus's stance on, 215
social graces, 55, 127, 214
solid foundation, trustworthiness and, 96–97
Solomon
    committed to building the temple in Jerusalem, 31–32
    comparing the tongue to the tree of life, 152
    on the integrity of the upright, 83
    on the Lord testing the heart, 227
    on the power of the tongue, 154
    Proverbs reminding believers about a committed life, 31
    on the righteous choosing friends carefully, 124
    on two as better than one, 126
    wisest man during his era, 130–31
sophia, Greek word for wisdom, 128
soul, 5, 112–16
soul fulfillment, 59
sovereignty, of God, 169, 221
Spafford, Horatio, 59
speaking, from the heart, 155
the Spirit and the flesh, as opposing principles, 144
spirit and truth, worshiping in, 183
spirit of truth, as foundational for honoring God, 98
Spirit-filled life, leaning on the Creator, 31
spiritual action plan, 150

spiritual blessings, forty-day journey for, xix
spiritual challenge, trustworthiness as, 96
spiritual compliance, meeting God's standards, 109–10
spiritual decline, as a deficit, 22
spiritual deficit life, leaving you lifeless, 220
spiritual DNA, offering a distinctive praise to God, 211
spiritual edification, 31
spiritual fervor, faith providing, 29
spiritual formation, 86–87
spiritual fruit, God's will for, 142
spiritual gifts, 1, 161–62, 193
spiritual growth
    emphasizing a unified theological premise of, 86
    evaluating your, xxv
    as a journey, xxi, 44
    prayer as the lifeline for, 13–14
    theology of, xxi
    Wisdom Pearls for, 1–50
spiritual humility, having roots in Jesus, 125
spiritual identification, getting your house together for, 110
spiritual journey, implementing, xxi–xxiv
spiritual life
    forgiveness as the road of, 19–20
    significance of, xxii–xxiv
    as useless without honesty, 81
spiritual living, contemplation of, 6
spiritual markers, Pearls as, 238
spiritual maturity, 1, 96, 221–22
spiritual person, as the opposite of carnal, 149
spiritual progress, commitment showing, 30–34
spiritual prosperity, xx, 113
spiritual resilience, God providing through faith, 225
spiritual responsibility, forgiveness as a profound, 24
spiritual sanctity, path to, 110
spiritual secretion, from the natural irritants of sinful acts, xxii
spiritual status, meditating on, 175
spiritual strength, 101, 102
spiritual walk
    characteristics of, 62–63
    engaging in, 232–33
    evaluating, xxv
    measuring your character and behavior, 232
    obedience setting the stage for, 67
    reevaluating, 175
    responsibility for monitoring, 96
    shaping and molding for a greater, 169
spiritual warfare, 61–62, 149, 172
spirituality
    elevating, xxiii
    as enlightenment, 146–51
    honesty setting the stage for, 83
    humility as a statement of genuine, 79
    living in the fragrance of high-intensity, 56
    love encouraging you to seek, 65
    possessing the attitude of, 75–76
Spurgeon, Charles, 121, 129
stages, of sacrifice, 219–20
steadfastness, to maintain peace and harmony, 235
Stephen, forgiveness by, 20–21
stewardship, accountability as, 192–96
strange love, camouflaging effect of, 4
strangers, genuine hospitality to, 133
strength
    Godly as spiritual defense, 172
    of meekness, 233
submissiveness, showing to God's will, 233
suffering, glorying in, 101
sufficiency, of grace, 117–22
sure reward, reaping, 198–99
sustainability, God providing, 139
sympathy, everyone desiring, 161

talents, parable of, 193–94
teachings, of Jesus shaping one for the abundant life, 195
tehillah, Hebrew word focusing on praising God through song, 211
tender heart, 162

tensions, showing meekness when experiencing, 234
testimony and dedication, of Jeremiah, 91
testing
   of faith, 86
   handling the outcome, 227
   times of, 147
thankful act, desiring to praise God as a, 207
thanksgiving, prayer of, 17
theology
   of eschatology, xx
   of faith, 25, 228
   of prayer, 12
   of sacrifice, 218
   of spiritual growth, xxi
   as the study of God, 126
   of worship, 182
theos, Greek word for "God," 199
thlipsis, Greek word for "tribulations," 227
Thomas, 78
thorn in the flesh, Paul's battle with, 118
Thurman, Howard, 8
thusia, Greek word for "sacrifice," 219
Tillich, Paul, 27, 98
timao, Greek word meaning valuing Christ at a price, 215
Timothy, 75, 234
Titus, on putting all evil to rest, 214
tongue
   prayer for, 157
   reflecting inward thoughts, 153
total surrender, 87
towdah, as praise, 210, 212
Tozer, A. W., 33, 36, 39
transformation, as the key to sacrifice, 221
treasure, wisdom as an insightful, 128–32
tree of life, emphasis on eternity, 153
trials, designed to strengthen and purity our faith, 226
tribulation, 227–28
Trinitarian Godhead, 124, 163, 176
true believers, as spiritually connected to God, 101

true friend, as a jewel, 127
true prayer, is praying in secret, 12
true vine, Jesus as, 142
trust
   as the answer for the spiritual journey, 44
   being passionate about personal, 97
   living a life of, 30
   living with an attitude of, 99
   violated leaving an indelible mark of a despicable reputation, 99
trusting, in the Creator as genuine faith, 28
trustworthiness, 95–100, 98
truth, justice affirming, 53–57
Tubman, Harriet, 37
twenty-four elders, worshiped God, 216

unbelievers, 143, 200
unclean lips, only God can and will purge, 109
uncompassionate individuals, 38
unforgiveness, producing bitterness and anger, 22
unfriendly encounters, experiencing, 124
unfruitful lifestyle, outcome of, 143
unity, 61, 63
unmerciful world, living in, 38
the unredeemed, missions caring about, 202–6
unreliable friends, causing ruin, 126
unsatisfied life, not experiencing the power of contentment, 72
the unsaved, hope for, 199
untruthful life, in danger with God, 99
Uriah, David and, 89
use, of wise words, 154–55

value, of Wisdom Pearls, xx
valuing, others above yourselves, 77
vengeance, leaving room for God, 56
victorious living, meeting God's standards, 195
vine, staying connected to, 142–43
voice, of God like many waters, 217
vow, making to the "Lord is your bond," 97

SUBJECT INDEX

waiting
- as the core of faith for spiritual strength, 44
- for God, 41, 42
- prayer of, 45
- refraining from being anxious during, 43
- with an urgent expectation, 47

walking
- by faith, 226
- with the Holy, 219
- with perseverance as a call of responsibility, 105
- in the Spirit, 31
- in wisdom pleasing God, 131

the weak, bearing the infirmities of, 176
weak believers, condition of, 229
weakness, meekness should not be mistaken for, 232
Whitefield, Samuel, 228
the will, to wait on God, 42–43

wisdom
- as an insightful treasure, 128–32
- as necessary to grow and implement Pearls, xxi
- in a nutshell, 155
- trust and, 97

wisdom literature, in the Bible, 129

Wisdom Pearls
- emphasize the importance of using wisdom, xx
- glorifying God, 139–78
- heavenly meaning for an earthly purpose, xxii
- of honest living, 51–92
- honoring God, 93–138
- pleasing God, 179–236
- purpose of implementing, xxi–xxii
- serving as spiritual building blocks, xx
- for spiritual growth, 1–50
- on this reading journey, xix
- value of, xx

wisdom truthful nugget, on walking with the wise, 125
wise words, faithful factors of, 153–55
woman with the issue of blood, 103–4
word of honor, no substitute for, 98–99

words
- devoid of meaning, 97
- using with restraint, 155

world, in a state of struggle, 58
worldly actions, leaving you spiritually bankrupt, 87
worldly affairs, commitment to, 32
worldly straitjacket, getting out of, 113
worldly trials, as devious and sadistic, 226

worship
- contentment and, 70–71
- showing adoration, 181–86
- silence leading to genuine, 170
- styles of, 183

worthiness, expressing God's, 183–84
wrath, leaving room for God's, 55–56

yadah, Hebrew to extol, give thanks, 209
Yahweh, as God's Hebrew name, 108, 211

zamar, as praise, 210
Zechariah, 160, 169, 173
Zephaniah, 171

Scripture Index

OLD TESTAMENT

Genesis

	175
1:27	216
2:4–25	81
2:15 NLT	193
2:16	66
3:2–10	216
3:6–7	23
3:11	66
4:4	219
4:4–5	219
12:1	88
15:6	88
18:1–15	136
22	221
22:1–19	88
32:22–32	33
37:12–13	44
37:12–36	120
37:18–20	20
37:18–36	89
37:18–37	234
37:21–36	20
42:6–8	44, 120
42:21	174, 175
45:4–7	20
47:13–27	20

Exodus

1:11–14	37, 48
1:13–14	46
3:1–5	48, 88
12:13–28	48
12:40	37
12:40–41	48
13:21	49
14:11	49
14:13–14 NKJV	49
14:14	172
14:21–29	120
20:16	81
32:11	88

Leviticus

19:2	12
19:11	81
19:18	55
26:9 NASB	213

Numbers

11:14–16	225
12	235
12:3 ESV	234
30:2 NLT	95

Deuteronomy

4:31	39
6:5	192
6:9	147
32:35	55
32:35a	56

Joshua

1:1–5	90
1:9	172
1:9 ESV	90
10:12–13	90
22:5	66
22:5 ESV	64

Judges

4:4–10	89
4:6	89

1 Samuel

12:24 ESV	66
15:22	220
15:22 NLT	65
16:11	165
17:34–35	165
17:50 RSV	89
22:1–2	165

2 Samuel

6:14	209
6:14–22	71
9	136
9:4–5	120
11:2–15	89
17:27	120

1 Kings

3:4–5	131
6	31
8:61	30
19:12–13	172

2 Kings

4:8–10	136
6:22	136

1 Chronicles

4:10	15
15:29	71

2 Chronicles

7:14	74, 75

Job

	129
1:1	103
1:1–21	103
1:21	103
6:14	123
6:24 ESV	170
13:3	42
14:14	42
19:25	43
42:10–17	103

Psalms

	129
5:1–3 ESV	232
18:2 ESV	148
18:3	208
19:14 ESV	222
22:3	211
22:8	211
22:19	211
22:23–28	211
33:1	211
33:18	5
37:7 NLT	41
37:30–31	129
37:39–40	129
42:1–2	182
46:1	41
46:10	210, 221
46:10 ESV	168
51:1 ESV	112
51:1–2	89
51:2	23
51:17	219
59:9–15	228
61:1	169
63:1–4	207
63–64	208
66:20	211

73:1–2 ESV	230
78:70–72	165
89:5	208
92:12	147
92:12–15	146
98:4	210
100:2 ESV	182
100:4	210
103:20	208
106:3	54
107:1 KJV	81
113:3 KJV	209
116:5	214
118:24 ESV	17
119:105 NLT	xxi
121:1–13	60
145:1–20	209
145:4	210
145:18	xx
150:2	209
150:6	208
212:1–2 RSV	78

Proverbs

	129
3	31
3:5–6	28, 129, 228
3:5–7	131
3:5–8	30
3:13–20	xix
4:5–9	xix
4:12–14	xxiv
8:11–13	xix
11	198, 199
11:3	83
11:18	199
12:26	124
13:20	125
15:4	152
15:29	171
16:3	32
16:16	128
17:3 NLT	227
17:9	124
17:27	155
18:21	154
18:24	126
21:15	53

22:1 NASB	99
28:13	113

Ecclesiastes

	129
3:7b NASB	170
4:9–10 ESV	126

Isaiah

1:18–20	67
6:1–5	108
6:5	108
6:6	109
25:1	181, 208, 209
32:17 ESV	59
40:31	46, 46–47, 47
41:10 NLT	98
43:1–30	185
55:8–9 RSV	172
60:1 ESV	177
61	38
61:1–2	78

Jeremiah

1:4–7	91
1:16–17	91
8:18–22	91
18:1–4	169
20:7–9	91
20:9	91
33:11 NKJV	210

Lamentations

3:22–23 ESV	160

Ezekiel

37:28	110
38:1–3	199
38:23	199

Daniel

3:16–17	183
7:25	228
9:3–4	90

Amos

5:24	53
6:8	75

Micah

5:4	202
6:1–16	160
6:8	35, 37, 39, 221

Habakkuk

2:20	169

Zephaniah

1:7	171
2:3	231

Zechariah

2:10–13	169
2:13 NLT	168
7:9–10	160

NEW TESTAMENT

Matthew

	7
5:3–11	xix
5:5 ESV	232
5:7	161
5:9	58, 59
5:9 NLT	61
5:16 ESV	136
5:16 NKJV	135
5:33	97, 100
5:44–45	8, 77
6:14	21
6:14–15	19
6:15–16	20
7:12	215
7:15–20	142
8:14–15	137
8:32 NLT	177
9:35–38	164
9:37–38	200
9:37–38 ESV	190
9:38	200
11:28	189
11:29 NLT	234
13:44	xxii
13:45–46	xxii, xxiii, 117
15:11	153
20:29–34	161
24:14	205
25:21 RSV	194
25:22	194
25:23 RSV	194
25:24–25	194
25:26 RSV	194
26:6–10	137
26:39	17
28:18–20	198
28:18–20 ESV	187

Mark

	25
2:1–17	21
6:56	203
9:35 NLT	165
10:45	164
11:22–25	11
11:24	11
11:24 ESV	16
12:28–31	8, 78

Luke

4:16	38
4:18–19	38
4:19–19	78
7:42–43	21
8:15	81
8:42–27	103
11:1	12
12:8	114
18:10–14	77
19:1–10	137
23:24	22

John

1:14	121
1–14	164
3:3	113
3:4	113
3:16 NLT	3

4:24 ESV	170, 183
4:24 NLT	70
8:1–9	37
8:32 KJV	81
13:12–14	163
14:6	78, 83, 188
14:15 NLT	64
14:16	171
14:20–23	200
14:27	63
15	141
15:1 RSV	144
15:1–12	125
15:4 NKJV	190
15:5	141
15:7 KJV	194
15:8	141, 189
15:16	142
16:7–11	175
16:8 NKJV	176
17	109
17:18	204
17:19 RSV	108

Acts

1:8 ESV	202
4	82
5	82
5:1–11	82
7:54—8:2	21
16:25	208
16:25–26	208
17:29	233
18:1	118
18:4	118
18:8	118
18:11	118
28:16–30	119

Romans

	229
1:5	65
1:11 NLT	87
1:16	198
1:16–17	197
1:17	199
3:23 KJV	233
4:7	23
5:3–5	101
5:5	233
5:8–9	6
6:10	148
7:21	27
7:21 KJV	234
8:3–4	xx
8:6–7 KJV	149
8:26	33, 173
8:26 NLT	121
8:26–27	71
8:26–28	171
8:34	171
8:35	228
8:36–37	226
10:9–10	112, 113
10:17 ESV	26
11:21–22	23
12:1	221
12:1–2	xxv, 12
12:1–2 KJV	218
12:1a	87
12:6	161
12:6–7	164
12:6–8	161
12:8 NLT	193
12:10	216
12:13	134
12:13 ESV	137
12:16	76
12:19	20, 54–55
14:1—15:13	229
14:13–23	176
15:1	176

1 Corinthians

1:3–4	211
1:8–9 NLT	60
1:30 NLT	129
2:4	155
2:14–15	149
5:17 ESV	200
10:13	23
12:8	130
15:58	85, 225
15:58 ESV	86
16:13	177

2 Corinthians

1:3–4 ESV	158
2:7	21
2:10	21
4:8–11 ESV	104
5:17	114
10:1–6	119
11:14–15 NKJV	62
12:7b	118
12:9	117, 227

Galatians

1:4 NLT	107
5:16	xx
5:22–23	xx, 5
5:22–23 NLT	xxiii
5:23–23	143
5:25	xx
6:10	134

Ephesians

1:3–11	114
1:3–14	xix
1:7	203
1:13	31
1:17	27
2:8–9	26, 28
2:8–9 NLT	120
2:14–22	59
3:20 KJV	159, 190
3:20–21 NKJV	25
4:29	155
4:31	154
4:32	21
5:1–2	56
5:2	221
5:8	4
5:15–16 ESV	xxi
5:15–17 NLT	xxiii
5:16	xx
5:16 ESV	203
5:26–27	110
6:10–11	147
6:16	226
15:29 KJV	152

Philippians

2:3–4	77
2:4–5 RSV	75
2:5 RSV	137
2:25–29	66
3:13–14	190
3:14	66
3:14 KJV	104
4:3	215
4:4–7	66
4:6–7	58
4:7	59
4:9	61
4:10–13 KJV	69
4:11	69
4:11–12	69
4:11–13 ESV	28
4:12–13	71
4:15–16	67
4:19	xix, 144, 166, 204
4:19 ESV	48
4:19 NLT	67

Colossians

1:10	143
1:28–29 ESV	188
2:9	233
2:13	21
3:9–10	95
3:13	21
3:13 RSV	20
4:5–6	128

1 Thessalonians

	109
4:11	214
5:2 ESV	228
5:5	55
5:11	126
5:22–24	109
5:23	106
5:23 ESV	109

2 Thessalonians

1:4 ESV	231

1 Timothy

2:1	16
2:1 ESV	16
6:11 ESV	234

2 Timothy

1:6 KJV	75
2:15	118
2:15 RSV	149
3:16	96

Titus

2:7	98
2:7 ESV	214
2:7–8	214
2:7–8 ESV	213

Hebrews

	224
4	227
4:12	174, 175
4:15–16	227
7:15	171
7:25	71
9:15	171
10:4–10	218
10:30	55
11:1 ESV	27
11:6	26, 102, 225
11:6 NLT	25
12:1	xxiv, 219
12:1–3	226
12:1–3 ESV	224
12:2	26, 87
12:2 NKJV	47
12:14	12, 107
13:2	135
13:2 ESV	133

James

	232
1:1	115
1:2	226
1:2 ESV	226
1:2–4 ESV	86
1:2–8	226
1:5	131

1:17 ESV	192
1:26–27	80
3:7–12	153
3:13 NLT	154
4:10	77, 232
4:10 NASB	74
5:16	13, 228

1 Peter

2:2	149, 188
3:9	55
3:10	154
3:12	171
3:13–18	78
4:8	7
4:9–10 ESV	134
4:10	192, 193
5:7 RSV	206

2 Peter

1:3–4	xix
3:18	xxii, 33, 87, 117

1 John

1:9	106
2 ESV	171
3:17	7
4:9	233
4:20	9
4:21	9

Jude

1:1–4	188

Revelation

	170, 184
4:10–11	184
4:10–11 ESV	216
4:11 NKJV	184
5–8	170
8:1	169, 170
21:1–4	104
21:8 KJV	99
21:21	xxi
21:21 ESV	130
22:2	153

www.ingramcontent.com/pod-product-compliance
Lightning Source LLC
Chambersburg PA
CBHW051630230426
43669CB00013B/2245

"At the age of ninety-seven, I am indeed honored to serve as an endorser of the book, *The Purpose Driven Disciple*. I thank God for Johnny Turner's deep thoughts and composition of daily devotions for Christian growth. I find it insightful for these times; it is simply magnificent!"

—**Rudolph McKissick Sr.**, Pastor Emeritus, Bethel Institutional Baptist Church, Jacksonville, Forida

"Dr. Johnny Turner has written a masterpiece for spiritual growth and Christian development. This book is loaded with 'pearls' for living the abundant life, the quiet life, and a quality life. Dr. Turner is one of the most faithful Christian writers in this century. His commitment to biblical principles, Christian ethics, and church growth is a testament to his love for learning. He is answering the call to discipleship according to the apostle Paul's appeal, 'For the perfecting of the saints, for the work of the ministry, for the edifying of the body of Christ' (Ephesians 4:12)."

—**R.B. Holmes**, Pastor, Bethel Missionary Baptist Church, Tallahassee, Florida

"*The Purpose Driven Disciple: Implementing Wisdom Pearls for Spiritual Growth* is a challenge to those of us who profess Christ. Through self-reflection, Dr. Turner has the reader assess her/his commitment of relationship with God. By employing the language of 'pearls,' the person on this forty-day journey of self-discovery is repeatedly exposed to the value and purity of God's work and its relevance for today's world and the ways in which Christians are continually called to grow, leaving behind milk for meat."

—**Linda Hickmon Evans**, Pastor, St. Luke Tabernacle, Rochester, New York

"In the life of a Christian, being a mature disciple is a goal we all should desire to attain. *The Purpose Driven Disciple: Implementing Wisdom Pearls for Spiritual Growth* is an instrument that can be used to assist in reaching such a goal. Dr. Turner has profoundly introduced wisdom pearls that are to be treasured in our quest for spiritual growth and personal advancement. As you dive into the richness of God's word and this book through forty days of reflection and revelation, may you find a peace that passes all understanding and grow in ways that may have been unimaginable."

—**Thurmond N. Tillman**, Pastor, First African Baptist Church, Franklin Square, Savannah, Georgia

"It gives me a great pleasure to recognize one of the greatest minds of our time, Pastor Johnny Turner. His book, *The Purpose Driven Disciple*, is a must read. Each chapter is crafted in a way to allow everyone who is a true disciple to glean from these pearls to live a purpose driven life. Let the reading of this book propel you to be the disciple you are destined to be."

—**Carl Johnson**, President, Florida General Baptist Convention